Additional Praise for *Marriage and Sexuality in Early Christianity*

"Having studied this book's earlier incarnation for twenty-five years, my undergraduate students have always profited from Hunter's readable translations and his clear, well-crafted introduction. With this new edition, Hunter has not only included a greater scope of primary texts but also augmented the introduction, appended brief introductions to each primary text, and attended to recent scholarly discussion. The result is a compendium that still belongs in the student's backpack, yet should now appear on every patristic scholar's bookshelf."
W. Trent Foley, Davidson College

"This volume, edited and compiled by one of the field's foremost experts on ancient Christian marriage, provides an essential resource for students seeking to understand the social and theological climate of early Christianity. The selection of texts reflects an excellent and carefully contextualized survey of Christian views on marriage from both East and West, spanning a wide range of genres. From them, marriage emerges not only as a topic of vital importance and frequent contention in its own right but as a fulcrum for some of the era's most pressing theological controversies."
Maria Doerfler, Yale University

D1546278

Marriage and Sexuality in Early Christianity

Marriage and Sexuality in Early Christianity

DAVID G. HUNTER, VOLUME EDITOR

FORTRESS PRESS
MINNEAPOLIS

MARRIAGE AND SEXUALITY IN EARLY CHRISTIANITY

Cover image: Mosaic depicting the wedding of Moses and Zipporah, with Jethro acting as pronubus, Sta. Maria Maggiore, Rome, 5th century. Photo: Josef Wilpert, *Die römischen Mosaiken und Malereien der kirchlichen Bauten vom IV. bis XIII. Jahrhundert* (Freiburg im Breisgau: Herder, 1916), Vol. 3, 17.
Cover design: Laurie Ingram

Print ISBN: 978-1-5064-4593-9
eBook ISBN: 978-1-5064-4600-4

The paper used in this publication meets the minimum requirements of American National Standard for Information Sciences — Permanence of Paper for Printed Library Materials, ANSI Z329.48-1984.

Manufactured in the U.S.A.

To my parents

Evangeline Fell Hunter
and
Richard Benedict Hunter

In memoriam
Carol M. Cottrill, MD (1937–2017)

Contents

Series Foreword

In his book *The Spirit of Early Christian Thought*, Robert Louis Wilken reminds us that "Christianity is more than a set of devotional practices and a moral code: it is also a way of thinking about God, about human beings, about the world and history."[1] From its earliest times, Wilken notes, Christianity has been inescapably ritualistic, uncompromisingly moral, and unapologetically intellectual.

Christianity is deeply rooted in history and continues to be been nourished by the past. The ground of its being and the basis of its existence is the life of a historic person, Jesus of Nazareth, whom Christians identify as God's unique, historical act of self-communication. Jesus presented himself within the context of the history of the people of Israel, and the earliest disciples understood him to be the culmination of that history, ushering in a new chapter in God's ongoing engagement with the world.

The crucial period of the first few centuries of Christianity is known as the patristic era or the time of the church fathers. Beginning after the books of the New Testament were written and continuing until the dawn of the Middle Ages (ca. 100–700 CE), this period encompasses a large and diverse company of thinkers and personalities. Some came from Greece and Asia Minor, others from Palestine and Egypt, and

---

1. Robert Louis Wilken, *The Spirit of Early Christian Thought: Seeking the Face of God* (New Haven: Yale University Press, 2003), xiii.

still others from Spain, Italy, North Africa, Syria, and present-day Iraq. Some wrote in Greek, others in Latin, and others in Syriac, Coptic, Armenian, and other languages.

This is the period during which options of belief and practice were accepted or rejected. Christian teachers and thinkers forged the language to express Christian belief clearly and precisely; they oversaw the life of the Christian people in worship and communal structure; and they clarified and applied the worshiping community's moral norms.

Every generation of Christians that has reconsidered the adequacy of its practice and witness and has reflected seriously on what Christians confess and teach has come to recognize the church fathers as a precious inheritance and source for instruction and illumination. After the New Testament, no body of Christian literature has laid greater claim on Christians as a whole.

The purpose of this series is to invite readers "to return to the sources," to discover firsthand the riches of the common Christian tradition and to gain a deeper understanding of the faith and practices of early Christianity. When we recognize how Christian faith and practices developed through time, we also appreciate how Christianity still reflects the events, thought, and social conditions of this earlier history.

Ad Fontes: Sources of Early Christian Thought makes foundational texts accessible through modern, readable English translations and brief introductions that lay out the context of these documents. Each volume brings together the best recent scholarship on the topic and gives voice to varying points of view to illustrate the diversity of early Christian thought. Entire writings or sections of writings are provided to allow the reader to see the context and flow of the argument.

Together, these texts not only chronicle how Christian faith and practice came to adopt its basic shape but also summon contemporary readers to consider how the events, insights, and social conditions of the early church continue to inform Christianity in the twenty-first century.

George Kalantzis
Series Editor

Preface

In 1992 Fortress Press published a different version of this book under the title *Marriage in the Early Church*, in its series Sources of Early Christian Thought. In the twenty-five years since the publication of that book, a great deal of research has appeared in the field of early Christian studies, especially on celibacy and asceticism, matters directly relevant to the present work. Inspired by the pioneering research of scholars such as Peter Brown,[1] Elizabeth Clark,[2] and Philip Rousseau,[3] a new generation of researchers has devoted enormous energy to exploring many features of the ascetic and monastic movements in late antiquity. New perspectives have developed, new theories have been applied, and new texts have been brought to light. This focus on asceticism, together with other developments in cultural studies and social history, in turn has stimulated intense interest in children, family, marriage, and sexuality in the late Roman and early Christian worlds.

1. The foundational text is *The Body and Society: Men, Women, and Sexual Renunciation in Early Christianity* (New York: Columbia University Press, 1988).

2. Among her many studies, see especially *Jerome, Chrysostom, and Friends: Essay and Translations* (New York: Edwin Mellen, 1982); *Ascetic Piety and Women's Faith: Essays on Late Ancient Christianity* (New York: Edwin Mellen, 1986); *Reading Renunciation: Asceticism and Scripture in Early Christianity* (Princeton: Princeton University Press, 1999).

3. In addition to his books on Basil of Caesarea and Pachomius, see especially *Ascetics, Authority, and the Church in the Age of Jerome and Cassian*, 2nd ed. (Notre Dame: University of Notre Dame Press, 2010).

I have not been able to give attention to all of these developments here, although several have had a direct impact on this new edition and must be mentioned. First and foremost is the discovery and publication by François Dolbeau of a new collection of Augustine's sermons. One of these sermons was devoted to the subject of marriage, and, as I have argued elsewhere, it presents us with important evidence of the development of Augustine's thought on marriage.[4] It seemed appropriate, therefore, to include it in the present volume as an example of how Augustine addressed the actual lives of married Christians in his own congregation.

Several other sources, which did not appear in the earlier edition, have been added. Among these is a selection from Tertullian's radical treatise *On Monogamy*, and one from Jerome's equally eccentric book *Against Jovinian*. Tertullian's text shows the culmination of his development toward accepting the positions of the "New Prophecy," otherwise known as Montanism, as is evident in his complete rejection of second marriages. Jerome's polemic against Jovinian made extensive use of Tertullian's book and provoked negative reactions from many quarters. Augustine's extensive discussions of marriage took shape in the aftermath of this controversy and must be understood as a reaction against Jerome's views.

Another addition to the present volume is an excerpt from the *Commentary on the Pauline Epistles* by the fourth-century Roman writer whom modern scholars have named "Ambrosiaster" ("pseudo-Ambrose"). Recent decades have seen something of a renaissance of interest in this mysterious figure, whose exegetical work exerted great influence in late antiquity and the Middle Ages. Scholars such as Marie-Pierre Bussières, Stephen Cooper, Sophie Lunn-Rockliffe, and Theodore de Bruyn, have done much to make Ambrosiaster better known in the Anglophone world, and I have learned much from my collaborations with them. My own studies of

---

4. "Augustine, Sermon 354A: Its Place in His Thought on Marriage and Sexuality," *Augustinian Studies* 33, no. 1 (2002): 39–60.

Ambrosiaster have led me to believe that he was a significant voice of moderation in the "ascetic debates" that roiled the city of Rome and the West in the late fourth century, and this is sufficient reason to include him in this new edition.

It is worth noting, perhaps, some of the topics that will *not* be covered in this new edition. Although "sexuality" has been added to the title, I have not been able to give attention to the question of Christian views of same-sex relationships, although the issue appears tangentially in the excerpts from Clement of Alexandria and Lactantius.[5] Nor have I taken account of the burgeoning literature on the family in the early Christian and Roman worlds, or in the extensive discussion of gender that has emerged in recent decades. My focus has remained on the texts that give evidence of early Christian views of marriage and sex within marriage.

I have also made numerous modifications to the volume's original introduction, incorporating footnotes, which the earlier edition lacked, and updating the scholarship. In one significant case, I have noted that current scholarly opinion has raised serious doubts about the date and unity of the collection known as the "Council of Elvira." It can no longer be used to illustrate the practice of the Spanish church in the early fourth century; its canons appear to date from a variety of times and places. I have revised all of the translations from the earlier edition and, in several instances, corrected errors or omissions.

Last but not least, I wish to acknowledge the invaluable assistance I have received from several quarters. Felipe Vogel, a graduate student in Classics at the University of Kentucky, reviewed all of the translations in the earlier edition and made numerous suggestions for improvement. Professor W. Trent Foley of Davidson College, North Carolina, offered moral support when he learned this volume was in preparation and suggested some additions based on his use of the earlier edition in his own teaching. Professors Mark Ellison of Brigham

---

5. Studies by Eva Cantarella, David M. Halperin, and Bernadette J. Brooten provide a helpful starting point on this topic.

Young University and Professor Robin Jensen of the University of Notre Dame assisted me in acquiring the image used on the front cover. I also wish to express my thanks to Professor George Kalantzis of Wheaton College, who invited me to produce this new edition, and to my editors at Fortress Press, Scott Tunseth, who was patient with my numerous questions and delays, and Layne Johnson, who facilitated a smooth production. And, finally, my appreciation to Mr. Daniel Persigehl, graduate student at the University of Kentucky, who assisted in the preparation of the indexes.

PART I

Introduction

The purpose of this anthology is to introduce the reader to the wide range of texts that reflect early Christian thought and practice on the subject of marriage. Documents from the second to the sixth century are presented in chronological order to provide a sense of the dynamic development that has characterized Christianity in this area, as in so many others. Various genres are represented: the sermon, letter, theological treatise, legal document, novel, liturgical blessing, and marriage poem. This diversity of form reveals something of the diversity of outlook among the various texts.

Early Christian thought on marriage and sexuality has had an enormous influence on the development of Christian ethics and, indeed, on the marital ethos of the Western world more generally. But these ancient traditions were themselves shaped by a variety of historical factors, both intrinsic and extrinsic to Christianity itself. The issues confronting Christians varied considerably between the first and sixth centuries. Changing circumstances required new responses in every aspect of Christian life, and marriage was no exception.

This introduction discusses some of the more important factors that shaped the early Christian documents presented in this anthology, beginning with the New Testament. The modern reader is invited into a world of discourse that is sometimes quite familiar and at other times quite alien to contemporary sensibilities. The voices of the early Christian writers will speak directly to some Christians today; others will be repulsed by the anti-sexual or anti-female bias in some of the texts. Both reactions are legitimate, for the early Christians bequeathed to posterity a legacy that is profoundly ambiguous. These traditions, for better or for worse, have shaped the identity of the church itself and, therefore, the attitudes of many Christians today.

1.

The New Testament Evidence

1.1 JESUS AND THE GOSPELS

The world into which Christianity first emerged was profoundly ambivalent on the question of marriage. While the earliest Christians inherited from Judaism a rich tradition of reflection on marriage, other currents of thought, such as apocalyptic, tended to run counter to that tradition. Jesus himself, almost certainly, was unmarried. His proclamation of the imminent coming of God's kingdom seemed to require a degree of commitment so radical as to eclipse all other, "worldly" loyalties: "Whoever comes to me and does not hate father and mother, wife and children, yes, and even life itself, cannot be my disciple."[1] Sharing the apocalyptic perspective of many Jews of his day, Jesus, as recorded in the Synoptic tradition, regarded the life of the resurrection as an angelic life, "where they neither marry nor are given in marriage."[2]

Among the Synoptic stories, however, one passage sheds a somewhat different light on Jesus's teaching, one that would

---

1. Luke 14:26; cf. Matt 10:37; Mark 10:29.
2. Mark 12:25; cf. Matt 22:30; Luke 20:35.

have considerable impact on the development of early Christian thought. All three Synoptic Gospels report a discussion with Pharisees regarding the permissibility of divorce. In Mark's version, Jesus responds to the statement that the Mosaic law allowed a man to divorce his wife: "Because of your hardness of heart [Moses] wrote this commandment for you. But from the beginning of creation, *God made them male and female.*[3] *For this reason a man shall leave his father and mother and be joined to his wife, and the two shall become one flesh.*[4] So, they are no longer two, but one flesh. Therefore what God has joined together, let no one separate."[5]

Jesus's teaching on the indissolubility of marriage seems to have been closely linked to his eschatological preaching. Those entering the kingdom of God were expected to manifest the holiness and perfection that was characteristic of God's original creation, and this included monogamous unions. Like the Jewish sectarians at Qumran, who took a similar position on the question of divorce, Jesus also may have wished his followers to imitate the holiness of the temple priests, who were forbidden to marry divorced women.[6]

An important departure from the version of Mark is found in the Gospel of Matthew. After citing the saying of Jesus in almost the same words as Mark and Luke 16:18, Matthew placed this significant exception on the lips of Jesus: "And I say to you, whoever divorces his wife, except for sexual immorality [*porneia*], and marries another commits adultery."[7] This important qualification, "except for sexual immorality," may have been added by the evangelist to make Jesus's teaching conform more closely to that of the Mosaic law. Because

3. Gen 1:27.
4. Gen 2:24.
5. Mark 10:5–9.
6. Cf. Lev 21:7. On the apocalyptic character of Jesus's message about marriage and its parallels in Judaism, see E. P. Sanders, *Jesus and Judaism* (Philadelphia: Fortress, 1985), 230, 257–59.
7. Matt 19:9; cf. 5:32. The precise semantic range of the Greek word *porneia* is disputed. For a recent discussion, see Jennifer Glancy, "The Sexual Use of Slaves: A Response to Kyle Harper on Jewish and Christian *porneia*," *Journal of Biblical Literature* 134 (2015): 215–29.

of this exception in Matthew's Gospel, some early Christians allowed not only divorce but also remarriage if one of the spouses committed adultery.[8] The basic bias against divorce, however, remained even in Matthew's version, along with the citation of the Genesis creation narratives.

Early Christians, from the apostle Paul onward, looked back on these traditions about Jesus whenever they needed guidance on questions of marital morality. They found two primary lessons in these traditions. On the one hand, the texts affirmed that the normal state of marriage is indissoluble: except in the case of adultery, remarriage after divorce is forbidden. On the other hand, the passage shows Jesus citing the original intention of God the Creator to "make them male and female" and to unite man and woman "in one flesh." The first lesson—on indissolubility—became a teaching that helped to define Christian identity in a world where marital stability was not always cherished. The second lesson—on the original place of marriage in God's creative plan—became a valuable resource for Christians confronted with a denial of the goodness of marriage.

1.2 THE APOSTLE PAUL

The apostle Paul's extensive discussion of marriage in chapter 7 of his First Letter to the Corinthians exercised an equal influence on early Christian views of marriage. Writing in response to questions sent to him from this predominantly gentile Christian community, Paul faced a group of ascetics who seemed to take pride in their spiritual gifts (*charismata*) and spiritual knowledge (*gnōsis*). Christians at Corinth were questioning the value, and even the permissibility, of marriage. Their slogan was: "It is good for a man not to touch a woman."[9] Paul carefully distanced himself from the views of such ascetics. He insisted that sexual relations between

8. See, e.g., the selection from Ambrosiaster translated in part 2, chapter 8.
9. 1 Cor 7:1.

spouses were allowed;[10] furthermore, husband and wife were bound by a reciprocal duty to render to each other their due: "The wife does not have authority over her own body, but the husband does; likewise the husband does not have authority over his own body, but the wife does."[11] Abstention from sex should occur only by mutual consent for the sake of prayer, and only for a limited time.[12]

Paul proceeded to argue, citing the teaching of Jesus, that Christian spouses ought not to divorce or remarry: "To the married I give charge, not I but the Lord, that the wife should not separate from her husband (but if she does, let her remain single or else be reconciled to her husband), and that the husband should not divorce his wife."[13] Even a marriage with a non-Christian spouse was to be preserved, for the non-Christian is made holy in the Christian spouse.[14] Paul's general rule was that Christians should remain in the state in which God first called them.[15] He taught that the unmarried and widows would do better to remain unmarried, although they were free to marry if they wished, "for it is better to marry than to be on fire."[16]

Toward the end of chapter 7 Paul revealed the reason for his ambivalent view of Christian marriage: "I mean, brothers and sisters, the appointed time has grown short; from now on, let even those who have wives be as though they had none. . . . For the present form of this world is passing away."[17] Like Jesus, Paul viewed the lives and duties of married Christians through the lens of the expectation of the imminent end of

---

10. 1 Cor 7:2–3.

11. 1 Cor 7:4.

12. Cf. 1 Cor 7:5.

13. Cf. 1 Cor 7:10–11. It is noteworthy that Paul did not explicitly forbid remarriage by the man, as he did in the case of the woman. This omission led some early Christians to allow remarriage in the case of a man who divorced his wife because of her adultery. This view, which may have been the dominant tradition prior to the late fourth century, was eventually challenged by Augustine, who argued for absolute indissolubility for both spouses, even in the case of adultery.

14. Cf. 1 Cor 7:14.

15. Cf. 1 Cor 7:17–28.

16. 1 Cor 7:9; cf. 7:28.

17. 1 Cor 7:29–31.

time. Although he strongly resisted the attempts of the ascetic Christians at Corinth to impose a requirement of celibacy on the community, he maintained that, because of the imminent end of this age, the burdens and distractions of the married life were best foregone.[18]

Like the accounts of Jesus's teachings in the gospels, the writings of Paul were eventually adopted into the developing canon of scripture. But when subsequent generations of Christians read the teachings of Jesus or Paul, they generally did so in a context no longer troubled by the impending end of time. Shorn of their apocalyptic significance, Paul's views took on a rather different significance: many of the earliest Christians came to regard marriage itself as inferior to celibacy and saw Paul's recommendation of celibacy as advice for all times, not merely for the interim before the "end times." But, again like that of Jesus, Paul's clear acceptance of marriage, at least as an alternative to fornication, provided early Christians with a powerful rejoinder to those who would forbid marriage altogether.

1.3 LATER NEW TESTAMENT WRITINGS

Most of the later New Testament writings continued Paul's resistance to the demands of ascetic Christians for sexual renunciation. They also developed further his desire to preserve the established structures of society, marriage among them. Written in an age less anxious about the end of time and more concerned to present a good appearance to non-Christian society, documents from the later years of the first century tended to construct a bridge between the teachings of Jesus and Paul, on the one side, and the structures and values of Greco-Roman society, on the other. The household codes found in several New Testament writings provide a good example of the early Christian adaptation to a changed environment: the traditional roles and structures of the

18. 1 Cor 7:28, 31, 38, 40.

Roman household were now regarded as normative for the church.[19]

Among these codes is a passage in the Letter to the Ephesians, in which the author (probably not the apostle Paul) treated the union of husband and wife by analogy with the union of Christ and the church.[20] Not only did human marriage provide the author with an image for the marriage of Christ and the church, but the reverse was also the case: the union of Christ and the church became a paradigm for the mutual love and respect that should subsist between husband and wife. Quoting the same Genesis text cited by Jesus, "A man will leave his father and mother and be joined to his wife, and the two will become one flesh,"[21] the author of the Letter to the Ephesians took the passage to refer both to the union of Christ and the church and to human marriage.

With very few exceptions, most of the later documents of the New Testament followed the same basic trajectory of thought. Marriage was regarded as the work of a good Creator, and any attempt to forbid marriage was repudiated.[22] The Pastoral Epistles went so far as to make marriage, along with the successful management of a household, a prerequisite for appointment to the position of overseer or bishop (*episkopos*) in the Christian community.[23] This close identification of church leadership with the households of married Christians is significant. Both structures were considered useful in combating alternative varieties of Christianity that were emerging at the time. Threatened by the radical ascetic tendencies of some Christian groups in the second century, the author of the Pastoral Epistles insisted on the close association between the order of the church and the order of the Greco-Roman household.

19. For example, Col 3:18—4:1; 1 Pet 2:17—3:9; 1 Tim 2:8—15; 6:1—10; and Titus 2:1—10.
20. Cf. Eph 5:21—33.
21. Gen 2:24.
22. Cf. 1 Tim 4:1—5.
23. Cf. 1 Tim 3:1—5; Titus 1:6.

2.

The Greco-Roman Environment

2.1 MARRIAGE AS A LEGAL INSTITUTION

Marriage in the Roman world was something quite different from what it has come to be in the modern West. Although it was a state with serious legal implications, marriage itself was a private act that took place between free persons (slaves could not contract legal marriages until the third century CE). No formal contract was required, except when the transfer of a dowry was involved; nor was it necessary for a ceremony to be held, although ceremonies of betrothal and marriage were certainly performed. Marriage itself was a matter of intention: if two persons lived together intending to be husband and wife, legally they were regarded as married. Not even consummation of the marriage was required for its legal validity.

The legitimacy of marriage was important to the Romans, especially in the upper classes, for a variety of reasons. The family name could be passed down only to children born in a legal marriage; only the legitimate children could inherit from their father's estate. For a man to marry in order to receive his wife's dowry was considered a respectable way of acquiring wealth. Concubinage was also widely practiced and was socially acceptable for similar reasons. If a man and woman were of unequal social status, they would live in concubinage, without the benefits and duties of marriage. If a man did not wish the children from his second marriage to inherit along with children from the first marriage, he might also choose to live in concubinage. Such unions were often lifelong and monogamous; Augustine of Hippo's long-term relationship with the mother of his son, Adeodatus, was probably intended to be a form of concubinage.

Around the beginning of the Christian era, the emperor Augustus issued a series of laws that attempted to encourage legitimate marriage and procreation: the *lex Iulia de maritandis ordinibus* (18 BCE), the *lex Iulia de adulteriis* (18 BCE), and the *lex Papia-Poppaea* (9 BCE). These laws imposed financial penalties on men between the ages of twenty-five and sixty, if they did not marry, and on women between the ages of twenty and fifty, if they did not marry. Widows were required to be remarried within two to three years; divorcees within eighteen months. Inheritance restrictions were also imposed on married couples that were childless. By contrast, privileges were bestowed on both men and women who produced three children, the *ius trium liberorum*: men were given priority in receiving government appointments and women were freed from the requirement of a guardian (*tutor*). These laws, which were not well received by the Roman aristocracy, who felt their impact the most, were intended to limit concubinage, reinforce the institution of legitimate marriage, and encourage the bearing of legitimate children. In the early fourth century, the emperor Constantine retracted the penalties on those who remained celibate or childless.

Prior to Augustus, divorce was as easy to contract as marriage. Divorce appears to have been quite frequent, especially among the upper classes, where alliances based on political and financial considerations were common. Either the husband or the wife could dissolve the marriage, unilaterally or by mutual consent. All that was required was separation with the intention of divorce; it was not even necessary to notify the former spouse. Along with his legislation on marriage, the emperor Augustus introduced stricter procedures for initiating divorce. It was now necessary that a notification of divorce be issued in the presence of seven witnesses to be fully valid.

The Augustan legislation also entailed the criminalization of adultery, which was defined as sexual relations between a married woman and a man other than her husband. Penalties included relegation to an island and confiscation of a portion of the property of the guilty woman and her lover. As Judith Evans Grubbs has observed: "This was the first time sexual offenses had been punished as public crimes; in the Republic, chastisement of adulterous wives had been the role of the *paterfamilias* and the family council, not the state. Husbands were required to divorce adulterous wives or risk being prosecuted themselves for *lenocinium* (pimping)."[1] Christians, in general, agreed with these principles, although some (e.g., Hermas and Augustine) believed that it was important for a repentant spouse to be received back after committing adultery, at least after a first offense.

2.2 MORAL AND PHILOSOPHICAL IDEALS

The ideals preached by the moralists and philosophers of the Greco-Roman era had a great impact on the development of Christian perspectives on marriage. Marriage in ancient cultures, as a rule, was closely linked to the aim of producing children, and the Romans were no exception. Procreation was regarded as a civic duty, and all citizens of marriageable age were expected to contribute. Some scholars have noted shifting emphases in the rhetoric of Roman philosophers and moralists on the subject of marriage around the time of the rise of Christianity. What was once a mainly civic institution, it has been argued, became internalized as a private, moral code. "In the first century BC a man was supposed to think of himself as a citizen who had fulfilled all his civic duties. A

1. Judith Evans Grubbs, *Women and Law in the Roman Empire: A Sourcebook on Marriage, Divorce, and Widowhood* (London: Routledge, 2002), 84.

century later he was supposed to consider himself a good husband; as such he was officially required to respect his wife."[2]

The result of this new morality, which was supported by the widespread influence of Stoic philosophy, was an emphasis on marriage as a friendship (*philia*, *amicitia*) between spouses; stress was placed on the importance of harmony (*homonoia*, *concordia*) as an indispensable condition for an ideal, philosophical marriage. Both the Latin writer Seneca and the Greek author Plutarch propagated this ideal: the former in his *Moral Epistles* and in a treatise *On Matrimony* (extant only in fragments cited by Jerome, *Against Jovinian*), the latter in his famous *Conjugal Precepts*.

Musonius Rufus, a Stoic philosopher who taught at Rome in the first century CE and who was read with great appreciation by several early Christian writers, offers a clear illustration of this philosophical discourse on marriage. In marriage, Musonius writes, husband and wife come together for the purpose of making a life in common and to procreate children: "They should regard all things as common between them, and nothing peculiar or private to one or the other, not even their bodies." Children alone, however, do not constitute a marriage: "But in marriage there must be above all perfect companionship (*symbiōsis*) and mutual affection (*kēdemonia*) of husband and wife, both in health and sickness and under all conditions, since it was with desire for this as well as for having children that both entered upon marriage."[3]

This ethic of conjugal morality was also accompanied by a new circumspection regarding the dangers of unrestrained sexuality. The philosopher Michel Foucault has called this phenomenon "the care of the self," and it included the careful regulation of the body and its impulses, especially for aristocratic males. Prescriptions for marriage became more stringent. Extramarital sexual activity in men was condemned,

2. Paul Veyne, "The Roman Empire" in *A History of Private Life*, vol. 1: *From Pagan Rome to Byzantium*, trans. Arthur Goldhammer (Cambridge, MA: Harvard University Press, 1987), 36.

3. Musonius, *Reliquiae*, frag. 13A, in Cora E. Lutz, ed., "Musonius Rufus: The Roman Socrates," *Yale Classical Studies* 10 (1947): 89.

as well as in women; homosexual relations were no longer viewed with the same tolerant attitude as in ancient Greece; sexual relations in marriage were viewed as legitimate only for the purpose of procreation. Again, Musonius Rufus provides a helpful illustration. Sexual intercourse, he wrote, "is justified only when it occurs in marriage and is indulged in for the purpose of begetting children, since that is lawful, but unjust and unlawful when it is mere pleasure-seeking, even in marriage."[4] Christians were soon to find much to admire in this Greco-Roman philosophical discourse.

2.3 CHRISTIAN RESPONSES: THE GREEK APOLOGISTS

While these marital ideals of the Greco-Roman philosophers took shape independently of Christian influence, they became an important bridge between the early Christians and the surrounding culture. Since the beginning of the second century, when Christianity first came to the attention of the Roman authorities as a sect distinct from Judaism, Christians had been subject to suspicion and sporadic persecution. The legal grounds for persecution involved the charge of "impiety" or "atheism," which was frequently coupled with the accusation that Christians were guilty of "contempt for the human race."[5] What lay behind this charge was not only the early Christian rejection of Roman religion but also the disruption to the Roman household that conversion to Christianity could cause.

In the second century, a variety of Christians began to write in response to these accusations. Known as "apologists," these authors attempted to show that Christian beliefs and practices were not criminal, and that Christians had positive intellectual and moral benefits to offer to the Roman Empire. This apologetic strategy nearly always entailed the argument that the morality of Christians in marriage was exemplary.

4. Frag. 12 (Lutz, 87).
5. Tacitus, *Annales* 15.44.

For example, both Aristides (pre–138 CE) and Justin (ca. 155 CE) noted that adultery and fornication were contrary to Christian principles.[6] Both Justin and Athenagoras (ca. 176 CE) pointed out that Christians married only for the sake of procreation, and both added their strong disapproval of divorce and remarriage. Athenagoras went so far as to suggest that remarriage after the death of a spouse was merely "adultery in disguise."[7]

These second-century apologists were clearly influenced by Greco-Roman philosophical traditions on marriage. The apologists' portrait of the monogamous Christian couple, devoted solely to the task of procreation, was a calculated argument, designed to demonstrate the compatibility of Christianity with the high ideals of Greco-Roman philosophical culture. The apologists claimed that among the Christians it was possible to achieve the standards of virtue to which the philosophers only aspired. One prominent apologist, whose writings have been included in this anthology, was Clement of Alexandria, who was active in the late second century. Borrowing directly from the works of Musonius and Plutarch, Clement articulated a Christian theology of marriage that was in harmony with the prevailing philosophical ideals, especially those of the Stoic tradition.

6. Aristides, *Apology* 15; Justin, *1 Apology* 15.
7. Justin, *1 Apology* 29; Athenagoras, *Plea for Christians* 33.

3.

The Second and Third Centuries

3.1 DIVORCE AND REMARRIAGE

The Christian literature that appeared immediately after the New Testament, that is, early in the second century, generally did not give sustained attention to marriage. Documents such as the *First Epistle of Clement to the Corinthians* (ca. 96 CE) and the letters of Ignatius, bishop of Antioch (ca. 110 CE), made only passing reference to marriage. Both texts mentioned that celibate Christians might be tempted to be arrogant, and both writers affirmed the goodness of marriage.[1] Both texts were also concerned to maintain (or impose) the power of the clergy: Ignatius did so by insisting that men and women who marry be united with the approval of the bishop.

The first sustained discussions of marriage in the second century focused on the issue of remarriage after the death or divorce of a spouse. The earliest treatment is found in the curious work known as the *Shepherd*, composed at Rome by Hermas, sometime in the first half of the second century. Hermas's discussion of marriage occurs in the section of the work known as the "Mandates," a portion of which is the first

---

1. *Clement* 33.4–8; 38.2; Ignatius, *Polycarp* 5.1–2.

document in this anthology. An angel has appeared to Hermas in the guise of a shepherd to offer teaching on the moral duties of the Christian. The fourth Mandate contains his most explicit teaching on marriage, as well as his decree on repentance. If a husband finds that his wife is committing adultery, he must separate from her and must not remarry. The same rule applies to the woman who finds her husband in adultery. Reconciliation of the spouses may take place, Hermas allowed, but, like repentance in the church, it can happen only once.[2] Hermas' prohibition of remarriage seems to be intended mostly to make possible reconciliation with the adulterous spouse.

The question of remarriage after the death of a spouse also concerned a number of Christian writers in the second and third centuries. Hermas raised the question of remarriage after the death of a spouse after discussing divorce. The angel informed him that second marriages were not forbidden, but that a person would acquire greater merit with God if he or she remained single.[3] But it was Tertullian, more than any other writer in the first three centuries, who devoted sustained attention to the question of remarriage. Tertullian is an unusually rich and complex writer because his thought underwent significant development, especially on the issue of remarriage. He composed three treatises on the subject: *To His Wife*, *An Exhortation to Chastity*, and *On Monogamy*. In the first work, written between the years 200 and 206, Tertullian advised his wife against remarriage after his death, although he admitted that remarriage was no sin. Then he proceeded to discuss the question of remarriage with a non-Christian spouse, a phenomenon that he thoroughly deplored, although it seems to have been widespread.

By the time he wrote his second treatise, *An Exhortation to Chastity* (208–210), Tertullian had begun to move away from his earlier position. He did not totally forbid remarriage, but his attitude had hardened and his language was more intran-

---

2. *Shepherd*, Mandate 4.29.
3. *Shepherd*, Mandate 4.32.

sigent. To remarry, he argued, was to oppose God's positive will; since God prefers single marriage, it is a sin (*delictum*) to remarry. By the time of the third treatise, *On Monogamy* (ca. 217), Tertullian had rejected the possibility of remarriage altogether. He proclaimed that all second marriages were equivalent to adultery, and he rejected as "Psychics" (i.e., "sensualists") those Christian leaders who permitted remarriage.

Tertullian's development on the question of remarriage is to be attributed to his progressive adherence to the "New Prophecy," a charismatic movement that had originated in Asia Minor in the middle of the second century. The original prophets, Montanus and his associates Priscilla and Maximilla, proclaimed that a new age of the Paraclete or Holy Spirit had begun. They prophesied that a literal resurrection of the flesh and a thousand-year reign of the saints were imminent. The Montanists also held rigorous positions regarding marriage and martyrdom, encouraging the latter and discouraging the former. Their uncompromising morality appealed to the mentality of Tertullian, who became the most famous convert to the "New Prophecy." Selections from all three of Tertullian's treatises on marriage are included below.

3.2 CHRISTIAN RADICALS: MARCION AND THE "ENCRATITES"

At the same time as the Greek apologists were defending Christianity to the non-Christian world, another battle was being waged on a different front. The second century saw a proliferation of diverse sects or parties within Christianity, some of which insisted that complete sexual renunciation was required of church members. As early as Paul's First Letter to the Corinthians, it is clear that some groups of Christians favored celibacy and wished to impose it on others. Early in the second century, the Pastoral Epistles had warned against "hypocritical liars" who forbade Christians to marry and ordered them to abstain from certain foods.[4] Such early ascetics may have held views similar to those of the Christians attacked by Ignatius of Antioch for their denial of the full humanity of Jesus ("docetism").

By the middle of the second century, a number of sects had emerged, each with its own distinctive teachings. These groups have often been generically labeled as "Gnostic," although the usefulness and accuracy of that label has been strongly questioned by recent scholars.[5] But teachers such as Valentinus and Marcion, despite their differences, shared some similar perspectives: a belief that the being who created the material world (sometimes called the "Demiurge" or "Craftsman") was not the true God or heavenly Father, but rather some kind of hostile or incompetent figure; a conviction that salvation, understood as escape from this material world, was effected by a savior, the Christ, who did not partake fully of human, physical nature; and a belief that human sexual activity (as a prominent aspect of physical existence) was something to be transcended or repudiated.

There were some groups that did not embrace all of these beliefs, but that rejected marriage on other grounds. Tatian, a former pupil of the apologist Justin, stood at the head of a long line of Christians who came to be called "Encratites" (the "Chaste Ones," from the Greek word *enkrateia,* meaning "chastity" or "self-control"). Christians with these views interpreted the stories about Adam and Eve in the opening chapters of Genesis as an account of the fall of humanity from a pristine, Spirit-filled existence into the sinful, mortal condition now characterized by human sexuality. Only by rejecting marital intercourse and procreation could people be restored to their original, spiritual condition intended by God the Creator. In this view of salvation, the end becomes like

---

4. Cf. 1 Tim 4:1–3.
5. For a good recent account, see David Brakke, *The Gnostics: Myth, Ritual, and Diversity in Early Christianity* (Cambridge, MA: Harvard University Press, 2011).

the beginning: by renouncing sex, Christians can be restored to the life of paradise before the fall.[6]

Encratite Christianity found a potent form of expression in various stories about the missionary journeys of the first apostles, known as the "apocryphal acts" of the apostles, which began to appear around the middle of the second century. Works such as the Greek *Acts of Paul and Thecla* and the Syriac *Acts of Thomas* portrayed the apostles as missionaries not only of Christ but also of sexual renunciation. The *Acts of Paul and Thecla*, for example, described the apostle entering the house of a Christian, Onesiphorus, and beginning to preach "the word of God concerning continence [*enkrateia*] and the resurrection."[7] A virgin named Thecla, hearing Paul's voice, decided to repudiate her fiancé and to follow Paul as a missionary. Such stories of ascetic renunciation became extremely popular in Christian circles, not merely among the so-called "heretical" sects. A selection from the *Acts of Thomas* is included below to give the reader a taste of this radical rejection of marriage that captivated many minds in the early Christian world.

3.3 HERESIOLOGY AND THE EMERGENCE OF "PROTO-ORTHODOXY"

The rejection of marriage by the different ascetical groups did not go unchallenged by others in the Christian church. By the end of the second century, a number of Christian writers began to produce extensive literary compositions in response to the views of Valentinus, Marcion, and the other dissidents. Heresiologists (that is, anti-heretical writers) such as Bishop Irenaeus of Lyons (ca. 180) and Tertullian made a point of defending marriage, especially against the views of Marcion and Tatian. Appealing to the Creator's original command-

---

6. For a good introduction to Tatian's theology, see Emily J. Hunt, *Christianity in the Second Century: The Case of Tatian* (London: Routledge, 2003).

7. *Acts of Paul and Thecla* 5.

ment that Adam and Eve should "increase and multiply," the anti-heretical writers argued that marriage and procreation were part of God's original intention for the human race and that sexual relations were not a result or symptom of the sin of Adam and Eve.[8]

Another popular strategy adopted by the early Christian heresiologists was to compose lists of heretics that conjured up connections among them that could not have existed in reality. Irenaeus, for example, suggested that Tatian may have drawn some of his ideas from Valentinus, Marcion, and Saturninus, and referred to Tatian as the "connecting point of all the heretics."[9] The point of this heresiological fiction was to connect Tatian and the so-called "Encratites" with even more devious heretics in order to suggest a kind of guilt by association. It was the mirror image of Irenaeus's defense of his own "orthodoxy," as he traced his teaching authority back to the original apostles through the succession of bishops ("apostolic succession").

The fullest and most articulate defense of marriage and response to the radicals came from Clement of Alexandria, author of the third chapter of texts in this anthology. Clement represents a fusing of both the apologetic and the anti-heretical traditions of the second century. Like the earlier apologists, Clement was concerned to show the compatibility of Christianity with the best of Greek culture and philosophy. In his treatise the *Instructor*, he portrays Christ, the divine *Logos*, in the role of an educator, fashioning the morals of the youth according to a scriptural *paideia*. At the same time, Clement laced his discourse with constant references to classical literature; he especially shows the influence of Stoicism and Middle Platonism, and on several occasions he echoed Musonius Rufus verbatim.

But Clement was also an anti-heretical writer, and in his *Miscellanies*, book 3, he responded directly to a series of views that he regarded as "heresy." While Clement referred in pass-

---

8. Irenaeus, *Against Heresies* 1.28.1; 4.11.1; Tertullian, *Against Marcion* 1.29.1–9.
9. Irenaeus, *Against Heresies* 1.28.1; 3.23.8.

ing to the schools of Valentinus and Marcion, his real target was the group of thinkers associated with Tatian, namely the Encratites. The reason for this focus may have been the fact that the views of Tatian were much closer to those of the mainstream or "proto-orthodox" church. Clement responded in detail to specific arguments of Tatian, including his exegesis of biblical texts, such as Paul's discussion of marriage in 1 Corinthians 7. He also attacked another Encratite thinker, Julius Cassian, whose writings are no longer preserved. Clement's response to the radical encratism of Tatian and Julius Cassian was the most extensive and most positive discussion of marriage in the first three centuries.

By the end of the third century, it appears that a kind of détente had emerged between those Christians who favored sexual renunciation and those who advocated marriage. Within the mainstream of the Christian tradition, a moderate attitude toward marriage seems to have prevailed: the superiority of celibacy was asserted, but the permissibility of marriage was also upheld. Typical of this view are the next two texts in this anthology, the *Symposium of the Ten Virgins* of Methodius of Olympus and the *Divine Institutes* of the Christian rhetorician Lactantius. Both authors accepted the view that celibacy was a higher way of life, but both also recognized the validity of marriage. Taking his cue from Irenaeus and Clement, Methodius regarded sex and procreation as part of God's plan for the human race, although he held that the coming of Christ had inaugurated a new era in which the practice of virginity was preferable for all Christians. Lactantius, likewise, insisted that sexual desire (*libido*) had been instilled in human beings by God for the purpose of procreation, but it was an urge that had to be carefully managed to avoid excess and distortion.

4.

The Post-Constantinian Church

4.1 FROM THE DESERT TO THE CITY: JOHN CHRYSOSTOM

The rise of the emperor Constantine in the early fourth century and the gradual Christianization of the Roman Empire during the subsequent decades caused a shift of focus in early Christian thought and practice regarding marriage. On the one hand, the influx of new converts into the church forced Christian pastors to confront congregations that now had a wider array of values and commitments, not all of which were readily compatible with earlier Christian ideals. As a result, pastors and preachers had to pay greater attention to the problems of living the Christian life "in the world," including the problems of Christian marriage.

On the other hand, toward the end of the third century a new phenomenon had emerged within the Christian movement: the flight of Christians from the towns and villages into deserted places, whether the sands of Egypt, the mountains of Syria and Palestine, or the caves of Cappadocia. The appearance of "solitaries" or "monks" (from the Greek *monachoi*) captured the imagination of many in the Roman world, especially through literary texts such as the *Life of Antony* by

Athanasius, the fourth-century bishop of Alexandria. Communities of male and female ascetics soon appeared, and under the able leadership of monks, such as Pachomius in Egypt, monasteries flourished throughout the east.[1] The rise and widespread popularity of monasticism gave further impulse to the traditions of asceticism and sexual restraint that were already deeply imbedded in Christianity, and by the end of the fourth century the Christian monk or ascetic, whether male or female, had replaced the earlier martyrs as the model of the ideal Christian.

The result of this new development was not only the appearance of a vast corpus of writings dealing with asceticism (lives, sayings, and rules of monks) but also rather strident debates among Christians regarding how most properly to live the Christian life. It was in the context of these new challenges and conflicts that pastors and preachers, such as Augustine and John Chrysostom, made the first attempts at a true theology of Christian marriage. John Chrysostom is an especially informative case, because his career included an attempt to live as a solitary in a mountain retreat near Antioch, then a return to the life of a pastor and preacher in the city, and eventually appointment to the highest ecclesial rank in the imperial capital, Constantinople.

Chrysostom had developed an early enthusiasm for the ascetic life and attempted to live as a hermit in a monastic enclave on Mount Silpios, which overlooked Antioch. After several years, for reasons of ill health, he returned to the city and assumed pastoral duties, first as a deacon and later as a presbyter (386 CE). In his earliest writings Chrysostom had been a strong advocate for the monastic life. For example, in his three-book treatise *Against the Opponents of the Monastic Life*, he had argued that parents should allow their sons to leave the city and enter monasteries in order to receive proper moral training. But there is also evidence that Chrysostom

---

1. A distinguished English edition of texts from the Pachomian communities has been published in three volumes by Armand Veilleux, *Pachomian Koinonia: The Lives, Rules, and Other Writings of Saint Pachomius and His Disciples* (Kalamazoo, MI: Cistercian, 1980).

had begun to entertain some doubts about the monastic life, or at least that he did not view it uncritically. In one of his earliest works, a two-book treatise, *On Compunction*, addressed to the monks Demetrius and Stelechius, he criticized monks for not accepting a ministry in the church and for being excessively concerned about their own "peace and quiet" (*anapausis*).[2] He also praised King David and the apostle Paul for embracing an active life in the world and yet preserving interior virtue.[3]

As Chrysostom engaged more deeply in the pastoral life, he eventually came to regard the active life of the bishop and preacher as a more valuable contribution to the Christian community than the asceticism of the monk, who lived only for himself. In his famous book *On the Priesthood*, Chrysostom explicitly contrasted the monastic life unfavorably with the life of the pastor who devoted himself to the welfare of the community.[4] Over time he also revised his earlier view of monasteries as the ideal location for moral formation. In his book *On Vain Glory and the Right Way to Bring Up Children*, Chrysostom explicitly stated that he no longer expected Christians to abandon marriage and civic life in order to pursue a moral education.[5] Now it was the responsibility of parents and pastors to foster the moral development of young people while remaining in the city, and *On Vain Glory* provided precise guidelines to parents on how to raise virtuous children. Chrysostom's own extensive preaching on marriage, a sample of which is given below, should also be viewed in this light, that is, as an effort to bring the desert into the city, so to speak, by incorporating certain monastic principles into the marriages of Christians.

---

2. *On Compunction* 1.6.
3. *On Compunction* 2.2–3.
4. *On the Priesthood* 6.5–9.
5. *On Vain Glory* 19.

4.2 WESTERN CONTROVERSIES:
FROM JOVINIAN TO AUGUSTINE

At the very time when John Chrysostom was forging his ascetic ideal of Christian married life, Christians were becoming embroiled in a series of debates that were forever to shape Western attitudes toward sexuality and marriage. During the later 380s in Rome, a monk named Jovinian began to teach that married Christians and their celibate brothers and sisters did not essentially differ in sanctity. "Virgins, widows, and married women, once they have been washed in Christ, are of the same merit, as long as they do not differ in other works," Jovinian maintained.[6] Baptism is the great equalizer, according to Jovinian, and there is one reward in the kingdom of heaven for all who have preserved their baptismal commitment. "Be not proud," Jovinian warned the Christian virgin, "you and your married sisters are members of the same church."[7] Jovinian seems to have been concerned about the problem of ascetic elitism in the church, as well as the spread of heretical views of sex and marriage.[8]

Jovinian's teaching found a receptive audience among many Christians at Rome. His message would have appealed to those newly converted Roman aristocrats who saw no essential contradiction between their new faith and their commitment to traditional aristocratic values, including marriage and childbearing. But Jovinian's popularity went further than that. His most bitter opponent, the ascetic Jerome, said that there were even clerics and monks at Rome who led lives of sexual abstinence, but who nonetheless supported Jovinian's view on the equal merits of virgins, widows, and married Christians.[9]

Jovinian's claims about the essential equality of married and

6. Cited in Jerome, *Against Jovinian* 1.3.

7. Cited in Jerome, *Against Jovinian* 1.5.

8. For a study of the controversy, see David G. Hunter, *Marriage, Celibacy, and Heresy in Ancient Christianity: The Jovinianist Controversy* (Oxford: Oxford University Press, 2007).

9. Jerome, Letter 49.2 to Pammachius.

celibate Christians clearly had touched a sensitive nerve in Western Christianity. His supporters no doubt felt that his views were a healthy corrective to an overzealous asceticism that, at times, seemed to border on the heretical rejection of marriage. Others, however, especially the leaders of the ascetic movement such as Ambrose and Jerome, regarded Jovinian's views as a frontal assault on asceticism itself and a significant departure from Christian tradition. In the early 390s Jovinian and his followers were condemned by synods of clergy at Rome and at Milan, led respectively by the bishops Siricius and Ambrose.

At this point (393 CE) the noted ascetic and biblical scholar Jerome entered the fray and wrote a scathing attack on Jovinian from his monastic retreat in Bethlehem. Jerome's *Against Jovinian* immediately provoked outrage at Rome because of its overt hostility toward marriage. Jerome had been forced to leave Rome in the spring of 385 CE, and *Against Jovinian* may have been an attempt to reestablish his literary authority there. If so, he badly miscalculated. Over the next two decades, other Western writers on marriage tended to distance themselves both from the teachings of Jovinian and from the views espoused by Jerome.

The next four sets of texts in this anthology all emerged from the environment of the Jovinianist controversy. The first of these is an excerpt from the *Commentary on the First Letter to the Corinthians* by an anonymous biblical commentator at Rome, now called "Ambrosiaster." This mysterious author was active in Rome during the period of Jerome's sojourn there (382–385 CE), and it seems likely that he may have been among the Roman clerics (dubbed by Jerome "the senate of the Pharisees") who objected to Jerome's presence there and were ultimately responsible for his expulsion from the city in the spring of 385 CE. Ambrosiaster's discussion of 1 Corinthians 7 gives us a glimpse of what a moderate member of the clergy thought about the issues of marriage, divorce, and remarriage on the eve of the Jovinianist controversy.

Also included here is an excerpt from Jerome's treatise *Against Jovinian*. Jerome's response to Jovinian, as noted above, was extremely hostile and provoked a very negative response when it was sent to Rome. Borrowing liberally (but without acknowledgement) from the Montanist writings of Tertullian and from treatises of Origen, Jerome had treated marriage with barely veiled contempt. Citing Paul's discussion of marriage in 1 Corinthian 7:1, Jerome argued that, since Paul had said, *It is good for a man not to touch a woman*, then it was bad to touch one. Jerome consistently presented marriage as simply a lesser evil than fornication, not something truly good in itself. Jerome even compared the (married) apostle Peter unfavorably to the (supposedly celibate) apostle John. Although tradition held that Peter had died a martyr's death, whereas John had lived to a ripe old age, to Jerome this was simply evidence that "virginity does not die and not even the blood of martyrdom washes away the defilement of marriage."[10]

Comments like these deeply disturbed many Western Christians. Jerome's Roman friend Domnio told him about a monk at Rome who had rejected the views of both Jovinian and Jerome. This may have been Pelagius, who mentioned Jovinian several times in his extant writings, including his *Letter to the Matron Celantia*, excerpted below. Another explicit critic of Jerome's teachings on marriage was Rufinus of Aquileia, who had once been a close friend of Jerome, but who later parted company with him over the issue of Origen's writings. In his *Apology against Jerome*, Rufinus cited verbatim from Jerome's treatise *Against Jovinian* as evidence of the latter's "Manichaean" tendencies. According to Rufinus, Jerome's work "had been read by a great many people, and almost everyone was offended by them."[11] Rufinus pointed to Jerome's statement about the blood of Peter's martyrdom not wiping away the "defilement" of his marriage as an egregious example of Jerome's abuse of marriage.

10. *Against Jovinian* 1.26.
11. *Apology against Jerome* 2.42.

Of all the opponents of Jovinian and Jerome, Augustine of Hippo was the one who offered the most sophisticated and the most influential response to the controversy. A decade after Jovinian's condemnation, Augustine tells us, the views of Jovinian continued to be circulated surreptitiously by people who claimed that Jovinian could be refuted only by condemning marriage. Augustine wrote his book *The Good of Marriage* to demonstrate that it was possible to maintain the superiority of celibacy (against Jovinian) and yet to uphold the genuine goodness of marriage (against Jerome and other extremists). As Robert A. Markus once observed, "Augustine's rehabilitation of the married state is a thinly veiled answer to Jerome's denigration of it: his covert work Against Jerome."[12] In this book Augustine laid the foundation for what eventually became classic Christian teaching on the three "goods" of marriage: offspring (*proles*), fidelity (*fides*), and the sacramental bond (*sacramentum*).

Beginning with the affirmation that human nature is itself a "social reality," Augustine located the primary good of marriage (procreation) squarely within this larger social purpose: "Therefore, the first natural union of human society is the husband and wife," and the bonding of society, which results from and requires the procreation of children, is the "one honorable fruit" of sexual intercourse.[13] But Augustine also insisted that procreation was not the only good of marriage. There is also the duty of mutual fidelity (*fides*) that each spouse owes to the other, especially in the matter of sexual intercourse. Augustine had no sympathy with any unilateral rejection of sexual relations. If a married couple engaged in sex not in order to have children but simply out of sexual desire, such intercourse, while regrettable, was still permissible, he insisted. Augustine argued that such acts fell under the "concession" granted by the apostle Paul in 1 Corinthians 7:5–6.

12. Robert A. Markus, *The End of Ancient Christianity* (Cambridge, MA: Cambridge University Press, 1990), 45.
13. *The Good of Marriage* I.1.

Against Jerome, as well as in opposition to more radical ascetics, Augustine maintained that marriage is truly good, not merely the lesser of two evils: "Marriage and fornication . . . are not two evils, one of which is worse, but marriage and continence are two goods, one of which is better."[14] Against the Manichaeans, who rejected procreation and criticized the sexual mores of the Old Testament patriarchs, Augustine argued that procreation was once an act of piety since it contributed to the formation of the people of Israel that gave rise to the Savior.[15] But against Jovinian, who had appealed to the married saints of the Old Testament as examples of the excellence of the married state, Augustine argued that married persons today could not be compared to those in the past. The change in time between the old dispensation and the new had caused the desire for children, which was once something "spiritual," to become "carnal."[16]

Compared to the views of many earlier and contemporary Christians, Augustine's perspectives on marriage appear generally well-balanced. Lurking beneath the surface, however, was a problem that was soon to be exploited by a new set of opponents, the supporters of Pelagius. In the opening pages of *The Good of Marriage*, Augustine had raised, but did not answer, an important question: would the first human beings have reproduced in a sexual manner if they had not sinned? He provided a range of possibilities for how God might have arranged for reproduction before the fall,[17] but declined to offer a definitive answer. Augustine soon returned to the question in his *Literal Commentary on Genesis*, which he composed gradually over the next decade (405–415 CE). There he concluded that God had originally created human beings to procreate in a physical, sexual manner. But unlike sexual relations in the present, sexual intercourse in paradise (which had never actually occurred) would have been conducted in

14. *The Good of Marriage* VIII.8.
15. Cf. *The Good of Marriage* XV.17.
16. *The Good of Marriage* XVII.19.
17. These options included asexual reproduction, as well as God spontaneously creating each new person from scratch.

an entirely rational manner as a result of a decision of the will. It would not have been driven by the irrational impulses that now characterize human sexual desire.

In one sense, Augustine's development in the *Literal Commentary on Genesis* was a step forward. Unlike many earlier Christians, Augustine grounded sex and procreation in the original (pre-lapsarian) order of creation. It was part of God's original intention for the human race, not merely a concession to the mortality occasioned by the first sin, as many other Christians had taught. But there was also a downside to this development: once Augustine had placed the body and sex back into paradise, he began to describe the impact of sin on the body and sexuality as well. Augustine came to believe that the sin of Adam and Eve had introduced into the human race not only mortality but also disordered desires and movements of the body, which he called the "concupiscence of the flesh." Although the "original sin" of Adam and Eve had been an act of pride and arrogant self-assertion and did not involve sexual relations, the impact of this sin was felt very directly in the human body and affected its sexual functioning. While Augustine still saw sex and procreation as good creations, he began to teach that these created goods were now experienced in a vitiated way as a symptom of original sin, and this vitiated nature was passed on to all of the descendants of Adam and Eve who are born of sexual intercourse.[18]

Augustine's views on the nature of sexual desire, original sin, and its transmission via human generation met with strong criticism, first from those with the most ascetic leanings. Initially, the opposition focused on Augustine's understanding of the weakness of the human will apart from grace and the necessity of divine intervention for salvation. At Rome, for example, the monk Pelagius is said to have been shocked to hear the prayer in Augustine's *Confessions*: "You command continence; grant what you command, and com-

---

18. Augustine first developed these ideas in his *Literal Commentary on Genesis* IX.10.17 and IX.31.41–32.42.

mand what you will."[19] Such words, to the perfectionist Pelagius, sounded like passivity and an abdication of human responsibility in the face of moral evil. From the year 412 onward, Augustine had to defend his views against Pelagius and those like him who wished to maintain the basic integrity of human nature, and the freedom of the human will, even after the fall.

In the later phases of the Pelagian controversy (post-418 CE), Augustine met his sharpest and most relentless critic, Julian, bishop of Eclanum in southern Italy. Julian regarded Augustine's positions on original sin and human sexuality as a survival of his Manichaean past. Sexual desire, Julian argued, was a creation of God; it was an innocent and necessary drive, required for the propagation of the human race. In Julian's view, the sexual desires of Adam and Eve before the fall did not differ essentially from what human beings now experience. Augustine's teaching on the transmission of sin and guilt by means of sexual intercourse and his position on the corruption of the sexual urge appeared to Julian as nothing other than a denial of the goodness of creation. During the final years of his life, Augustine was embroiled in a relentless exchange of letters and treatises in answer to the criticisms of Julian.

Among the most succinct accounts of Augustine's responses to Julian is a letter written to Atticus, patriarch of Constantinople, included in chapter 15 below. In this letter, Augustine attempted to meet Julian's criticisms by distinguishing between the "concupiscence of marriage" (*concupiscentia nuptiarum*) and the "concupiscence of the flesh" (*concupiscentia carnis*), a distinction not usually found in his writings.[20] The former is the rational desire for children, under the control of the human will, that characterized the state of Adam and Eve before the fall and that still constitutes one of the goods of marriage today. The concupiscence of the flesh, "which we feel at work in stormy, disordered desires

19. *Confessions* 10.29.40.
20. Letter 6*.5.

against our will," is the result of the fall, whose impact is still felt even in "the hearts of the faithful and the saints."[21] Whatever sexual desire Adam and Eve may have experienced in paradise, Augustine argued, "it certainly would not have been the great and hateful burden that people now experience it to be, as they struggle against it with the chastity of marriage, widowhood, or virginity."[22] Neither Julian nor Augustine managed to convert the other. Augustine's debate with Julian of Eclanum was finally cut short by Augustine's death in 430 CE, as his final work against Julian lay uncompleted.

4.3 THE "CHRISTIANIZATION" OF MARRIAGE: POEMS, LAWS, AND LITURGIES

The careers of John Chrysostom and Augustine both illustrate, though in rather different ways, the challenges that faced Christian pastors in "Christianizing" the marital mores of their congregations, and represent the first tentative steps toward a Christian theology of marriage. The remaining texts in this book present somewhat different perspectives on marriage than those offered by the theological treatises and sermons. On the one hand, there are liturgical or paraliturgical sources, such as the marriage poem or *epithalamium*, composed by Bishop Paulinus of Nola on the occasion of the wedding of Julian, future bishop of Eclanum, and his wife, Titia. We also possess several nuptial blessings from the Western sacramentaries, which date from the sixth and later centuries. Liturgical evidence of Christian marriage practice is extremely scarce prior to this time; the earliest evidence is found in the writings of Ambrosiaster from the later fourth century. The absence of explicit witnesses to Christian blessings or ceremonies before the fourth century suggests that the actual ritualizing of Christian marriages occurred very gradually and that marriage customs remained largely "unChristianized" for a long time.

21. Letter 6*.7.
22. Letter 6*.7.

The sources of ecclesiastical legislation that began to appear in the post-Constantinian era show us bishops engaging in the difficult task of imposing Christian regulations on congregations that were often not willing to accept them. Two sets of texts are included as chapter 17 in this anthology: a collection of canons attributed to the Spanish council of Elvira, which met sometime in the early fourth century, and selections from the *Canonical Epistles* of Basil, bishop of Caesarea in Cappadocia. Both documents show the wide range of issues that bishops had to deal with: from adultery and fornication, to incest and intermarriage with non-Christians, to divorce and remarriage. The presence of these detailed regulations indicates that the process of "Christianizing" marital morality took place in a very slow and piecemeal fashion. While Christian preachers and teachers had long envisioned Christian marriage in profound theological terms—indeed, as an image of Christ and the church—the reality often fell short of this ideal.

PART II

Texts and Translations

5.

Hermas

Little is known about Hermas, the author of the intriguing prophetic text known as the *Shepherd*. Numbered among the Apostolic Fathers—the generation of Christian writers who succeeded the original apostles—the work of Hermas is usually dated to the early decades of the second century. Internal evidence of the text indicates that he belonged to one of the Christian congregations at Rome and was once a slave. One source claims that his brother, Pius, was bishop in Rome, but that claim cannot be verified. The *Shepherd* circulated widely in the ancient world and was occasionally cited as Scripture.[1]

The *Shepherd* consists of a series of revelations, first delivered by a woman who represents the church, then by an angel of repentance. The book is arranged into five Visions, twelve Mandates, and ten Parables. Hermas was deeply concerned with the problem of inequalities of wealth in the church of Rome, as well as with the issue of sins committed after baptism and the possibility of penance. He presents the view that it is possible to receive ecclesiastical penance only once after baptism. He accepts the possibility of remarriage after the death of a spouse, but suggests that if a person

1. A full-scale commentary on the *Shepherd* can be found in Carolyn Osiek, *Shepherd of Hermas: A Commentary*, Hermeneia (Minneapolis: Fortress, 1999).

remains single, "he gains for himself more extraordinary honor and great glory with the Lord."

THE *SHEPHERD*, MANDATE 4

(29.1) "I command you," he said, "to guard your chastity (*hagneia*). Do not allow the desire for another woman to enter your heart, nor any thought of fornication, or any similar vice. For to do this is to commit a great sin. If you always remember your own wife, you will never sin. (2) But if this desire enters your heart, you will sin, and if any similar wicked desire should enter, you will commit sin. For this desire is a great sin for the servant of God. If anyone commits this wicked deed, he brings about his own death. (3) See to it, then, that you avoid this desire. For where holiness dwells, in the heart of the righteous man, there lawlessness should not enter."

(4) I said to him: "Lord, permit me to ask you a few questions."

"Speak," he said.

"Lord," I said, "if a man has a wife who believes in the Lord and he catches her in adultery, does the man sin if he continues to live with her?"

(5) "As long as the man is unaware," he said, "he does not sin. But if he discovers her sin and the woman does not repent, but rather persists in her adultery, the man shares the guilt of her sin and participates in her adultery, if he continues to live with her."

(6) "What, then," I said, "will the man do, Lord, if the woman persists in this passion?"

"He must divorce her," he said, "and the man must live by himself. But if, after divorcing her, he should marry another woman, he himself commits adultery."[2]

(7) "And if, Lord," I said, "the woman repents after she has been dismissed and wishes to return to her husband, shall he not take her back?"

2. Cf. Mark 10:11.

(8) "Yes," he said, "if the man does not take her back, he sins and brings great sin upon himself, for it is necessary to welcome back the sinner who has repented. But this must not occur more than once, because the servants of God have permission for only one repentance. Therefore, for the sake of repentance the man must not marry. This course of action applies to the woman as well as to the man.

(9) "Adultery occurs," he said, "not only when a person defiles his flesh but also when he acts as the pagans do.[3] So then, if a person persists in such practices and does not repent, you shall separate from him and not live with him, or else you participate in his sin. (10) That is why you were instructed to live alone, whether you are male or female, so that repentance might be possible in these cases.

(11) "I do not intend," he said, "to provide an excuse for this kind of behavior to happen, but only that the one who has sinned might sin no more. For the first sin, there is one who is able to provide healing, since he is the one who has the power to do all things."

(30.1) I continued to question him: "Since the Lord has judged me worthy for you to dwell with me always, bear with me as I speak a little more, for I have no understanding and my heart has been hardened by my former deeds.[4] Grant me understanding, for I am very foolish and completely devoid of knowledge."

(2) Answering me he said: "I have authority over repentance (*metanoia*), and to all who repent I give understanding. Or do you not think that repentance itself is understanding? To repent is great understanding. For the sinner understands that he has done evil in the sight of the Lord, and the deed that he has done enters into his heart. When he repents, he no longer does evil, but rather puts all his effort into doing good,

---

3. It is unclear what sort of practices of the "pagans" or "Gentiles" (*ethnē*) Hermas has in mind. He may be thinking of those biblical texts that identify idolatry as a type of fornication. See, e.g., Jer 3:8–11.

4. In Visions 5.25.2 the shepherd appeared to Hermas and said: "I was sent by the most holy angel to live with you the rest of the days of your life."

humbling and tormenting his soul because he has sinned. You see, then, that repentance is great understanding."

(3) "It is for this reason, Lord," I said, "that I am asking you all these detailed questions. First, because I am a sinner, I wish to know what I must do in order to live, for my sins are many and varied."

(4) "You shall live," he said, "if you keep my commandments and walk in them, and whoever hears and keeps these commandments shall live for God."

(31.1). "Lord," I said, "I will ask another question."

"Speak," he said.

"I have heard," I said, "from certain teachers that there is no repentance other than the one given when we went down into the water and received forgiveness of our past sins."

(2) He said to me: "You have heard correctly, for that is the way it is. For the person who has received forgiveness of sins ought to sin no longer, but rather he should remain in purity. (3) But since you are making a precise inquiry, I will also explain this to you, without giving an excuse to those who will believe in the Lord in the future or to those who now believe in the Lord. For those who now believe or those who will believe do not have repentance from sins, but they have the forgiveness of their former sins. (4) It is for those who were called before these days, therefore, that the Lord established repentance. For the Lord knows hearts and, knowing all things in advance, he knew the weakness of human beings and the cunning of the devil, who was to cause evil for the servants of God and to act against them with malice. (5) Being merciful, therefore, the Lord showed mercy to his creation and established this repentance, and the authority over this repentance has been given to me. (6) But I say to you, if, after this great and solemn calling, anyone should be seduced by the devil and commit a sin, he has one repentance. But if he sins and repents repeatedly, [repentance] will be useless for such a person, for only with great difficulty will he live."

(7) I said to him: "Lord, I have been restored to life after

hearing these precise answers of yours. For I know that if I no longer add to my sins, I will be saved."

"You will be saved," he said, "and so will all who do these things."

(32.1) Again I asked him: "Lord, since you bore with me once, please explain something else."

"Speak," he said.

"If a wife," I said, "or a husband should die, and the surviving spouse should marry, does the one who marries sin?"

(2) "He does not sin," he said, "but if he remains single, he gains for himself more extraordinary honor and great glory with the Lord. But if he marries, he does not sin. (3) Therefore, preserve your chastity and holiness and you will live for God. From now on, from the day on which you were entrusted to me, observe all that I have said and will say, and I will dwell in your house. (4) For your former transgressions there will be forgiveness, if you keep my commandments. There will be forgiveness for all, if they keep my commandments and walk in this purity."

6.

Tertullian

The first great Christian writer of the North African church, Tertullian of Carthage, flourished during the final years of the second century and early decades of the third. His writings span a large number of genres: from anti-heretical treatises, to apologies, to moral and ascetical writings. Tertullian was a strict moralist, and his rigor was reinforced by his gradual adherence to the prophetic, apocalyptic movement known as the New Prophecy, also known as the Cataphrygian or Montanist sect. Led by the Phrygian prophets Montanus, Priscilla, and Maximilla, the Montanists proclaimed that a new era had dawned upon the church, evidenced by a new outpouring of the Holy Spirit, also known as the Paraclete.

Under the influence of the New Prophecy, Tertullian came to believe that the Paraclete had revealed new moral prescriptions for Christians, surpassing the strictness required by Jesus and the apostles. Tertullian's writings on marriage and remarriage provide clear evidence of his graduate adoption of Montanist principles. In his early letter *To His Wife* (ca. 200–206 CE), Tertullian attempted to discourage her from remarrying after his death, although he did not take an absolute stance against remarriage. He insisted, however, that only marriage to a fellow Christian was permissible. His second essay, *An Exhortation to Chastity* (ca. 208–210), took a firmer position, although he still did not overtly forbid remarriage. By the time he composed his final book on the subject, *On Monogamy* (ca. 217 CE), Tertullian had concluded that remarriage was absolutely forbidden to Christians under orders of the Paraclete, a move that marked his full embrace of the New Prophecy.

TO HIS WIFE

(1.1) I thought it appropriate, my beloved fellow servant in the Lord, to give some thought even now to the manner in which you should live after my departure from this world, if I am called before you. I trust your faithfulness to follow what I have provided. For we spend enough time in worldly affairs and we secure our mutual interests even to the point of drawing up wills. Why should we not give even greater thought to our posterity, when it comes to divine and heavenly business? Ought we not to bequeath in advance, as it were, a legacy of advice and an account of what will be allotted out of our immortal goods and from our heavenly inheritance? May God grant that you are able to receive intact the advice I have bequeathed. To him be honor, glory, splendor, majesty, and power, now and forever.

I enjoin you, therefore, to exercise all the continence in your power and to renounce marriage after my death. You will confer no benefit on me by this action, other than the good you do for yourself. In any case, there is no promise of a restoration of marriage on the day of resurrection for Christians who have departed this life, for at that time they will be transformed into a state of angelic holiness. Therefore, there is no cause for that anxiety which comes from carnal jealousy.

Even that woman, who is portrayed as having successively married seven brothers, will offend none of her many spouses on the day of resurrection; nor will any of them be waiting to accuse her.[1] Our Lord's response silenced this objection of the

1. Cf. Mark 12:18–23.

Sadducees. Do not think that I have counseled you to remain a widow in order to reserve to myself the integrity of your body because I am afraid that someday I might suffer hardship. On that day we will not resume any disgraceful pleasures. God does not promise such frivolous, filthy things to those who are his own. But now we must consider whether my advice is valuable to you or to any other women who belong to God.

(2) Of course, we do not reject the union of man and woman. It has been blessed by God to be the seedbed of the human race; it was devised to fill up the earth and to set the world in order. Thus it was permitted, but only once. For Adam was the one husband of Eve, and Eve his one wife; one woman, one rib. It is true that our ancient forebears, the patriarchs, were allowed not only to marry but also to practice polygamy; they even had concubines. Now although the church existed in a figurative way in the synagogue, we can give the simple interpretation that it was necessary in the past to establish practices that later would be either abrogated or modified. The law was meant to be added, for it was necessary that it should first become clear that the law needed to be fulfilled; in a similar manner, the Word of God had to succeed to the law, introducing spiritual circumcision. Thus the general license of former times provided grounds for the subsequent emendations by which the Lord through his gospel, and the apostle in these last days, either eliminated excesses or regulated disorders.

(3) But I have not set forth these remarks about the liberty granted to the old and the rigor imposed on posterity in order to argue that Christ came to dissolve marriage or to abolish sexual relations, as though from now on marriage is to be outlawed. Let them beware who, among their other perversities, teach the separation of the *two in one flesh*,[2] rejecting him who first derived the woman from the man and then reunited in the marriage compact the two bodies that were taken from the harmonious union of the same material substance.

---

2. Gen 2:24; Matt 19:5–6.

In sum, nowhere do we read that marriage is forbidden, since it is something good. But we have learned from the apostle what is better than this good, when he allowed marriage but preferred abstinence;[3] the former because of the danger of temptation, the latter because of the end of time. If we examine the reasons given for each position, it is easy to see that the power to marry was granted to us out of necessity. But what necessity allows, it also depreciates. Scripture says: *It is better to marry than to burn.*[4] What sort of good is it, I ask, that is commended only by comparison with an evil, so that the reason why marriage is better is because burning is worse? How much better it is neither to marry nor to burn!

For example, in times of persecution it is better to flee from town to town,[5] as we are permitted, than to be arrested and to commit apostasy under torture. But far more blessed are those who have the courage to render the blessed testimony of martyrdom. I can say this: what is merely permitted is not good. Why? Suppose that I facing the necessity of death. If I pass the test, then death is a good. But if I am afraid . . . that which is merely permitted is suspect because of the very reason why it is permitted. No one merely permits what is better, since a true good is indubitable and simply evident as such.

Nothing should be sought merely because it is not forbidden; in fact, in a certain way such things are forbidden, since others are preferable to them. To prefer higher things is, in effect, to reject the lower. A thing is not really good simply because it is not bad; nor is something not bad simply because it does no harm. Something that is good in the true sense of the word achieves its excellence not only because it does no harm but also because it does some good. Therefore, you ought to prefer that which does some good over that which merely does no harm.

Every competition is a struggle for first place; second place has its consolation, but not the victory prize. But if we listen

3. 1 Cor 7:1–2, 26.
4. 1 Cor 7:9.
5. Cf. Matt 10:23.

to the apostle, *forgetting what lies behind and straining forward to what lies ahead,*[6] *let us eagerly desire the better prizes.*[7] Therefore, although the apostle does not lay any restraint upon us,[8] he does show what is beneficial when he says: *The unmarried woman is concerned about the things of the Lord, how to be holy in body and spirit, but the married woman is anxious about how to please her husband.*[9] Now whenever he permits marriage, he does so in a manner that shows he prefers us to follow his own example. Happy the person who proves to be like Paul!

***

(2.1) I have just finished discussing as best I could, my dearest fellow servant in the Lord, what course of action a holy woman must take when, for whatever reason, her marriage has come to an end. Let us turn now to a second line of advice, in response to human frailty. The occasion is the behavior of certain women who, when given the chance to practice continence because of divorce or the death of a spouse, not only rejected the opportunity for such a good but in remarrying did not even wish to remember the rule that they should *above all marry in the Lord.*[10]

I am embarrassed that I, who recently exhorted you to remain the wife of one man and a widow, may now cause you to fall from the heights merely by mentioning remarriage. Now if you reason correctly, you will certainly realize that you should observe the course of action that confers the greater advantage. But because it is especially difficult and not without its demands, I have abated my proposal somewhat. I would have had no reason to bring the matter to your attention at all, if I did not have an even more serious concern regarding these women.

For inasmuch as the continence of the flesh that makes possible the state of widowhood is nobler, so much more excus-

---

6. Phil 3:13.
7. 1 Cor 12:31.
8. Cf. 1 Cor 7:35.
9. 1 Cor 7:34.
10. 1 Cor 7:39.

able is the failure to sustain it. It is easy to grant pardon in matters that are difficult. But as far as marriage in the Lord is easily within our power, it is so much more blameworthy not to fulfill what you can.

Moreover, the apostle merely advises widows and unmarried persons to remain as they are, when he says: *I desire all to follow my example.*[11] But regarding marriage in the Lord, when he adds *only in the Lord,*[12] he is no longer merely giving advice, but an explicit command. Thus if we disobey in matters of this type, we run a great risk. For one can ignore a suggestion with impunity, but never a command; the former is a piece of advice, but the latter is decreed by authority and imposes an obligation. To disobey in the former case is a form of freedom; in the latter case, it is rebellion.

***

(3) Since this is the case, it is clear that believers who marry pagans are guilty of fornication and should be excluded from all communication with the Christian fellowship, in accordance with the letter of the apostle who writes: *You should not even take food with someone like this.*[13] Will we present our marriage certificates before the tribunal of the Lord on the last day and claim that a marriage that he explicitly forbade was properly contracted? Is it not adultery that is prohibited? Is it not fornication? Does not union with an outsider violate the temple of God? Does it not mingle the members of Christ with the members of an adulteress?[14] As I see it, we do not belong to ourselves, but we have been purchased at a great price.[15] Purchased? At what price? By the blood of God! When we injure our own bodies, we directly injure him.

What did that man mean when he said that to marry an outsider was a sin, but only a very slight one? Leaving aside the fact that harm is being done to the body of one

11. 1 Cor 7:7.
12. 1 Cor 7:39.
13. 1 Cor 5:11.
14. Cf. 1 Cor 6:15.
15. Cf. 1 Cor 6:19–20.

who belongs to the Lord, in other respects any voluntary sin against the Lord is a great one. To the extent that one had the power to avoid it, to that extent one bears the guilt of obstinacy.

Let us now recall the other dangers or wounds to the faith that, as I have said, were foreseen by the apostle and that do damage not only to the body but even more so to the spirit. For who would doubt that involvement with an unbeliever diminishes one's faith day by day? *Bad company corrupts good morals.*[16] How much more will a common life and constant contact do so!

Every Christian woman must obey God. But how can she serve two masters, the Lord and her husband, especially when the husband is a pagan? If she obeys a pagan, her conduct will be pagan: beauty, ornaments, worldly elegance, and more shameful allurements. Even the private acts of marriage will be tainted. Such is not the case among the saints who conduct the duties of sex modestly and moderately out of respect for its necessity, as if in the sight of God.

(4) But let her consider how she discharges her duties to her husband, since she certainly cannot fulfill the teachings of the Lord, since she has at her side a servant of the devil, who will act as an agent of his lord to obstruct the duties and pursuits of believers. If she must attend a prayer service (*statio*), the husband decides that they should go to the baths that day; if a fast must be observed, the husband orders a banquet for that very day; if it is necessary for her to go out, household business is never more pressing.

Who would allow his wife to run around the streets to the houses of strangers and even to the poorest hovels in order to visit the faithful? Who would willingly let his wife be taken from his side for nightly meetings, if it be necessary? Who, then, would tolerate without some anxiety her spending the entire night at the paschal solemnities? Who would have no suspicions about letting her attend the Lord's Supper, when it has such a bad reputation? Who would endure her creeping

16. 1 Cor 15:33.

into prison to kiss the chains of the martyrs? Or even to greet any of the brothers with a kiss? Or to wash the feet of the saints? To desire this? Even to think about it? If a Christian travelling on a journey should arrive, what hospitality will he find in the house of a stranger? If anyone needs assistance, the granary and pantry are closed.

***

(8) What words can describe the happiness of that marriage that the church unites, the offering strengthens, the blessing seals, the angels proclaim, and the Father declares valid? For even on earth children do not rightly and lawfully wed without their fathers' consent. What a bond is this: two believers who share one hope, one desire, one discipline, the same service! The two are brother and sister, fellow servants. There is no distinction of spirit or flesh, but truly they are *two in one flesh.*[17] Where there is *one flesh,* there is also one spirit. Together they pray, together they prostrate themselves, together they fast, teaching each other, exhorting each other, supporting each other.

Side by side in the church of God and at the banquet of God, side by side in difficulties, in times of persecution, and in times of consolation. Neither hides anything from the other, neither shuns the other, neither is a burden to the other. They freely visit the sick and sustain the needy. They give alms without anxiety, attend the sacrifice without scruple, perform their daily duties unobstructed. They do not have to hide the sign of the cross, or be afraid of greeting their fellow Christians, or give blessings in silence. They sing psalms and hymns to one another and strive to outdo each other in chanting to their Lord. Seeing and hearing this, Christ rejoices. He gives them his peace. Where there are two, he also is present;[18] and where he is, there is no evil.

17. Gen 2:24; Mark 10:8.
18. Cf. Matt 18:20.

AN EXHORTATION TO CHASTITY

(5) The very origin of the human race supports the law that prescribes a single marriage. It attests that what God established in the beginning ought to be observed by future generations. For when he had formed the man and foreseen that he would need a companion, he took one of the man's ribs and made one woman from it. Both the Craftsman and the matter were capable of creating more. Adam had several ribs, and God's hands were tireless, and yet God created no more wives. Therefore, the man of God, Adam, and the woman of God, Eve, by observing a single marriage, established a rule for the people of God based on the authority of their own origin and on the primordial will of God.

In short, he said: *They will be two in one flesh,*[19] not three, not four. In that case they would not be *one flesh* or *two in one flesh.* They will be such only when the union and fusion into one happens only once. But if they marry a second time, or more frequently, there will cease to be *one flesh,* and they will no longer be *two in one flesh,* but rather *one flesh* in many. But when the apostle interprets the text *They will be two in one flesh*[20] by applying it to Christ and the church, that is, as a reference to the spiritual marriage of the church and Christ (for Christ is one and his church is one), we ought to realize that the law of one marriage has been repeated for us with an even greater emphasis. It is founded both on the creation of the human race and on the sacrament of Christ. In both cases we derive our origin from a single marriage: physically in Adam, spiritually in Christ. From these two nativities we receive the one law of monogamy. In either case, to deviate from monogamy is to degenerate. Plurality of marriage started with a man who was cursed: Lamech was the first to marry two wives, thereby making three in *one flesh.*[21]

(6) "But," you say, "the patriarchs had intercourse not only

19. Gen 2:24.
20. Eph 5:31.
21. Cf. Gen 4:19.

with several wives, but even with concubines." Will this, then, allow us to marry countless times? Certainly it will, if there are still types of some future sacrament, which your marriages prefigure, or if even now there is a place for that saying: *Increase and multiply*,[22] that is, if it has not yet been superseded by another saying, such as: *The time is short, and those who have wives should live as though they had none.*[23] For by enjoining continence and restricting intercourse, the seedbed of the human race, he abolished that *Increase and multiply*.[24]

In my view, both pronouncements and arrangements were the work of one and the same God. In the beginning he gave full rein to marriage in order to provide a seedbed for the human race, until the world should be filled up, until there should be grounds for a new way of life. But now, in these last days, he has suppressed the seedbed and revoked his previous indulgence. It is not unreasonable that there should be concessions in the beginning and restrictions at the end. Beginnings are always lax, endings constrained. A person plants a forest and allows it to grow, so that at the proper time he may cut it down. The forest stands for the old dispensation, which is being pruned by the new gospel, in which *the ax is laid to the root of the tree.*[25] In a similar manner, *An eye for an eye and a tooth for a tooth*[26] became the old law, when *Do not return evil for evil*[27] became the new. I think that even in the case of human institutions and laws, the later ones prevail over the earlier ones.

ON MONOGAMY

(1) We know one marriage, just as we know one God. The

---

22. Gen 1:28.
23. 1 Cor 7:29.
24. Gen 1:28.
25. Matt 3:10.
26. Exod 21:24; Matt 5:38.
27. Matt 5:39.

law of marriage conveys greater honor, when it is accompanied by modesty. But the Psychics, who do not receive the Spirit, are not pleased by things that are of the Spirit.[28] Thus, while they are not pleased by spiritual things, they are pleased by carnal things, as these are contrary to the Spirit. *The flesh lusts against the Spirit*, he says, *and the Spirit against the flesh.*[29] What does the flesh lust after, except more flesh? That is why in the beginning the flesh was made alien to the Spirit: *My Spirit*, he says, *will not remain in these people forever, because they are flesh.*[30]

(2) And so they reject the discipline of monogamy as a heresy, and they are forced to deny the Paraclete for no reason other than that they think he has introduced a novel discipline, and one that is most harsh to them. So now our first task must be to examine whether it is possible for the Paraclete to have taught anything that can be considered either an innovation against catholic tradition, or an onerous addition to the *light burden*[31] of the Lord. But the Lord has pronounced on both of these matters. For he said: *I still have many things to say to you, but you are not able to bear them now. When the Holy Spirit comes, he will lead you into all truth.*[32] Obviously, he has asserted clearly enough that the Spirit will teach things that can be considered innovations, since they were not issued previously, and to some degree burdensome, since that is why they were not issued previously.

"Therefore," you object, "according to this line of argument, anything novel or onerous can be attributed to the Paraclete, even if it comes from an opposing spirit." No, not at all! For the opposing spirit is apparent in the divergence of his preaching: by first corrupting the rule of faith, and then by corrupting the order of discipline, since what is first in order

---

28. Tertullian used the term "Psychics" (*psychici*) to refer his Christian opponents. He derived the term from 1 Cor 2:14–15, where Paul drew a distinction between the "psychic person" (*psychikos anthrōpos*) and the "spiritual" one (*pneumatikos*).

29. Gal 5:17.

30. Gen 6:3.

31. Matt 11:30.

32. John 16:12–13.

must be the first thing corrupted; that is, the faith, which is prior to discipline. One must first become a heretic in one's view of God, and then in one's view of what God has instituted. But the Paraclete has many things to teach, which the Lord postponed for him in accordance with a predetermined plan. First, he will give testimony[33] that Christ himself is as we believe him to be, along with the entire order that God has created; and the Paraclete will glorify him,[34] and will remind us of him. And thus, having been recognized by the foundational rule, he will reveal many things that pertain to the disciplines; the integrity of his preaching will guarantee the authenticity of these disciplines, even though they are novel (since they are only now being revealed), and even though they are onerous (since they are not being followed now). Nevertheless, he is no different from Christ, who said that he also had many other things, which would be taught by the Paraclete, things no less burdensome to people today than those things which people back then could not bear.

***

(4) Now let mention of the Paraclete be put aside, as he is an authority of our own. Let us roll out the tools of the ancient Scriptures. This is what we are proving: that the discipline of monogamy is neither novel nor alien; indeed, it is ancient and the property of the Christians, so that you should think of the Paraclete as one who is restoring, rather than establishing, the discipline.

In so far as it pertains to antiquity, what pattern can be brought forth which is more ancient than the origins of the human race? God formed one woman for the man, after removing one of his ribs,[35] even though he had many. And as a preface to his work, he said: *It is not good for the man be alone; let us make him a helpmate.*[36] God would have said, "helpmates," if he had intended for him to have several wives.

---

33. Cf. John 15:26.
34. Cf. John 16:13–14.
35. Cf. Gen 2:21.
36. Gen 2:18.

And he added a law for the future, since this is an utterance of prophecy: *And they will be two in one flesh.*[37] Not three, not several; otherwise, there would no longer be two, if there were several. This law remained firm, and the union of marriage in the founders of the human race was preserved until the end, not because there were no other women, but because there were none so that the origins of the race might not be defiled by second marriage. Otherwise, if God had wanted to, it could have been that way; certainly Adam could have taken one of his many daughters,[38] having another Eve who was no less of his bones and flesh, if this could have been done in an upright manner.

But when the first crime was committed, which was homicide in the form of fratricide,[39] there was no crime so fitting to follow in second place as second marriage. For it makes no difference whether someone has two wives in succession or two at the same time. The number is the same, whether they are separate or together. Although God's ordinance suffered violence once through Lamech,[40] it stood firm thereafter until the end of that race. A second Lamech did not arise to marry two women. Scripture denies what it does not explicitly state. Other iniquities brought forth the flood. They were avenged once, whatever they were; they were not avenged seventy-seven fold,[41] which is the penalty for second marriages.

But the recreation of the second human race is distinguished by monogamy as its mother. Once again *two in one flesh* begin to *increase and multiply*:[42] Noah and his wife and their sons in single marriages.[43] Even among the animals one can see monogamy, so that not even beasts were born of adultery. *Of all the beasts,* he said, *of all flesh you shall take two into the ark, so that they may live with you. They shall be*

---

37. Gen 2:24.
38. Cf. Gen 5:4.
39. Cf. Gen 4:1–16.
40. Cf. Gen 4:18–19.
41. Cf. Gen 4:24.
42. Gen 1:28; 9:1.
43. Cf. Gen 7:7.

male and female. Of the birds according to their kind, and of all the creeping things according to their kind; two of each shall go in to you, male and female.[44] On the same pattern God also ordered groups of seven to be gathered into pairs, both male and female.[45] What more should I say? Even the unclean birds were not allowed to enter with two females.

***

(8) Now, having turned to the law that is properly ours, that is, the gospel, what sort of examples do we find when we come to the texts? Behold, right away, on the threshold, as it were, two high priestesses of Christian sanctity come to meet us, Monogamy and Continence, the one chastely present in the priest Zacharias,[46] the other present virginally in John the forerunner; the one appeasing God, the other proclaiming Christ; the one proclaiming the perfect priest, the other revealing *something more than a prophet*,[47] namely the one who not only proclaimed and pointed personally to Christ but even baptized him. For who was more worthy to initiate the body of the Lord than the one whose flesh was like the flesh that conceived and bore him? And, indeed, a virgin labored and gave birth to Christ, she who was to marry only once after the birth, so that both titles of sanctity might be approved in the origin of Christ, through a mother who was both a virgin and married only once.[48]

And when the infant was presented in the temple, who took him in his hands? Who was the first to recognize him in the Spirit? *A man just and wise*,[49] and certainly no digamist, or else Christ would have been proclaimed more worthily a short while later by the elderly woman, who was both a

44. Gen 6:19–20.
45. Cf. Gen 7:1–3.
46. Cf. Luke 1:5–6.
47. Matt 11:9; Luke 7:26.
48. Tertullian held that after the virginal conception of Jesus, Mary and Joseph had a normal married life and produced the "brothers and sisters" of Jesus mentioned in the Gospels. His argument that Mary was the model of both the virginal and the married lives was later taken up by Jerome's opponent Helvidius.
49. Luke 2:25.

widow and once-married.[50] In her dedication to the temple she revealed in herself what sort of people ought to belong to the spiritual temple, that is, the church. These were the kinds of witnesses the Lord had when he was an infant; they were no different when he was an adult. I find that Peter alone was married, because he had a mother-in-law.[51] I presume he was married only once, because the church, which was built upon him,[52] was to appoint every level of its hierarchy from among the once-married. As for the rest, since I do not find that they were married, I will take it that they must have been either eunuchs or continent.

For even if among the Greeks, women and wives are referred to by the same word[53] out of ease of linguistic usage (for there is a proper term for "wife"), we will not for that reason interpret Paul as if he demonstrated that the apostles had wives. For if he were discussing marriage (as he did in the following passage, where the apostle could have mentioned an example), with reason he would have seemed to say: "Do we not have the right to be accompanied by wives, just as the rest of the apostles and Cephas?"[54] But then he adds words that indicate his abstinence from the provision of supplies, saying: *Do we not have the right to our food and drink?*[55] This shows that the apostles did not take wives with them—for they who did not have wives did have the right to eat and drink—but simply women who ministered to them according to the same practice as those women who accompanied the Lord.[56]

But if Christ rebukes the scribes and Pharisees, who were sitting on the chair of Moses and were not doing what they taught,[57] how would he have appointed to his own chair

---

50. Cf. Luke 2:25–38. Tertullian refers to the stories about the reception of the infant Jesus in the temple by Simeon and the prophetess Anna.

51. Cf. Matt 8:14–15.

52. Cf. Matt 16:18.

53. Tertullian refers to the Greek word *gynē*. Much of the following argument was adopted by Jerome in *Against Jovinian*; see below.

54. Cf. 1 Cor 9:5.

55. 1 Cor 9:4.

56. Cf. Luke 8:2.

57. Cf. Matt 23:2.

someone who would have remembered to preach sanctity of the flesh, but not to follow it, which he insisted that they should both teach and practice? He taught this first by his own example, then by other arguments: when he says that the kingdom of heaven belongs to children;[58] when he makes their companions those who are children after marriage;[59] when he calls people to the simplicity of the dove,[60] a bird that is not only gentle but also chaste, for one male knows only one female; when he denies that the Samaritan woman has a husband, to show that she had many adulterous husbands;[61] when at the revelation of his glory, of all the saints and prophets, he chose Moses and Elijah to be with him,[62] the one a monogamist, the other a eunuch (for Elijah was no different from John, who came in the power and spirit of Elijah);[63] lastly, when he who was *a glutton and a winebibber, who associates with tax-collectors and sinners*[64] at meals and banquets—when he attended only one wedding feast, although there were many others to attend. He did not wish to attend these festivities more times than he wanted them to be celebrated.

58. Cf. Matt 19:13–14.
59. Cf. Matt 18:3.
60. Cf. Matt 10:16.
61. Cf. John 4:16–18.
62. Cf. Matt 17:3.
63. Cf. Luke 1:17; Matt 17:12.
64. Cf. Matt 11:19; Mark 2:16; Luke 7:34.

7.

Clement of Alexandria

Clement's writings date from the final years of the second century, when he was a teacher and head of the school of catechumens in Alexandria. His major work is a three-part treatise, intended to lead the reader in three distinct stages from a state of ignorance to one of enlightened "knowledge" (*gnōsis*). The first volume of his trilogy, the *Exhortation to the Greeks* (in Greek, *Protreptikos*), is a traditional apology aimed at converting the reader from paganism to Christian belief. The second volume, the *Instructor* (*Paedagōgos*), portrays Christ in the role of a tutor, instructing new converts in the moral requirements of the Christian life. The final volume, the *Miscellanies* (*Strōmata*), offers the Christian the final stage of teaching, the higher truths and principles of Christianity that Clement calls *gnōsis*.

Clement's teaching on marriage is found mainly in the *Instructor* and the *Miscellanies*. In the former work, Clement develops the view, found previously in Stoic philosophers, such as Musonius Rufus, and the Greek apologists, that sexual relations exist only for procreation. He rejects marital intercourse during pregnancy or the menstrual period because it involves the illegitimate wasting of seed. Like contemporary medical writers (e.g., Galen), Clement seems to have regarded the loss of semen during ejaculation as a drain of the body's vital energy.[1]

Despite this rather limited account of the purpose of human sexuality, Clement insists that marriage and procreation are an intrinsic and positive part of God's plan for the human race. He frequently cites Genesis 1:28 (*Increase and multiply*) and regards human procreation as an act of co-creation with God.[2] Echoing Musonius Rufus, Clement also maintains that marriage serves a civic function: "By all means, then, we must marry, both for the sake of our country and for the succession of children and for the completion of the world. . . . For if people do not marry and produce children, they contribute to the scarcity of human beings and destroy both the cities and the world that is composed of them."[3]

The bulk of Clement's discussion of marriage is found in the third book of his *Miscellanies*, which was devoted to refuting the heretical rejection of marriage by "Encratites" and other extremists. His theological starting point is the doctrine of creation. Those who reject marriage, he argues, "blaspheme both the creation and the holy Creator, the almighty and only God."[4] Those who claim to be rejecting marriage because they are already living the resurrected life ought logically to stop eating and drinking as well, Clement maintains, since these bodily functions will also be obsolete in the next life.[5]

Appealing to the married saints of the Old Testament and to the married apostles of the New Testament, Clement argues that there is no incompatibility between the practice of a self-controlled marriage and a life of service in the church. Both celibacy and marriage offer distinctive forms of service (*leitourgia*) and ministry (*diakōnia*) to the Lord. Indeed, Clement is even capable of regarding marriage as, in some respects, superior to celibacy. The celibate who is concerned

1. *Instructor* 2.94.
2. *Instructor* 2.10.83.
3. *Miscellanies* 2.23.140–41.
4. *Miscellanies* 3.6.45.
5. *Miscellanies* 3.6.47.

only for his salvation is "in most respects untried." By contrast, the married man who must devote himself to the administration of a household is a more faithful reflection of God's own providential care.[6]

THE *INSTRUCTOR*, BOOK 2

(10.83) Our next task is to discuss the proper time for sexual intercourse, which is solely for married persons. The intention of those who marry is to produce children, and the ultimate aim is to produce good children. In a similar manner the farmer sows seed with the aim of producing food, intending ultimately to harvest the fruit. But far superior is the farmer who sows in living soil. The one farms with the aim of producing temporary sustenance; the other does so to provide for the continuance of the entire universe. The one plants solely for himself; the other does so for God, since God himself said, *Multiply*,[7] and we must obey. In this way the human being becomes the image of God, by cooperating in the creation of another human being.

***

(90) We must think of young men as our sons and regard other men's wives as our daughters. It is of the utmost importance to exercise restraint when it comes to the pleasures of the stomach and maintain complete mastery over the region below the stomach. If, as the Stoics say, the wise man is forbidden even to lift his finger in an irrational manner, how much more must those who pursue wisdom exercise control over the sexual organs. For it seems to me that the genitals are called the "private parts"[8] because they must be treated with greater privacy or modesty than other members of the body.

Nature treats legitimate marriages as it does eating and drinking: it allows us to desire to produce children to the

---

6. *Miscellanies* 7.12.70.
7. Gen 1:28.
8. Literally "the shameful parts."

extent that it is appropriate, useful, and dignified. But those who indulge in excess violate the laws of nature and harm themselves in illegitimate unions. Above all, it is never right to have intercourse with young boys as if they were girls. That is why the philosopher, following Moses's lead, said: "Do not sow seed on rocks and stones because it will never take root and achieve the fruitfulness that is its nature."[9]

(91) The Logos has proclaimed this loudly and clearly through Moses: *Do not lie with a male as with a female, for it is an abomination.*[10] Besides these things, when the noble Plato recommended that "you shall abstain from every female field that is not your own,"[11] he derived this not from himself but from his reading of the biblical injunction: *You must not lie with your neighbor's wife and defile yourself with her.*[12] "There should be no sowing of sterile, bastard seed with concubines."[13] Do not sow "where you do not wish the seed to grow."[14] "Do not touch anyone except your own wedded wife."[15] Only with a wife are you permitted to enjoy physical pleasure for the purpose of producing descendants, for only these things are in accordance with reason. We who have a share in the divine work of creation must not scatter seed randomly, nor should we act disrespectfully or sow unproductive seed.

(92) That is why Moses himself even prohibited men from having intercourse with their own wives, if they happened to be experiencing their monthly periods.[16] For it is completely contrary to reason to defile with the impurities of the body the most fertile part of the seed, which is destined to become a human being. We must not allow it to be washed away in the filthy, impure flow of matter, for it is a seed capable of proper birth that is thus torn away from the furrows of the womb.

9. Plato, *Laws* 8.838E.
10. Lev 18:22.
11. Plato, *Laws* 8.839A.
12. Lev 18:20.
13. Plato, *Laws* 8.841D.
14. Plato, *Laws* 8.839A.
15. Plato, *Laws* 8.841D.
16. Cf. Lev 18:19.

Furthermore, Moses left no example of any ancient Hebrew who had intercourse with a pregnant wife. For mere pleasure, even when pursued in marriage, is illicit, improper, and irrational. On the contrary, Moses ordered men to abstain from their wives until they were delivered. In fact, the uterus, which is situated below the bladder and above that part of the intestine called the rectum, extends its neck between the two into the bladder. The opening through which the seed penetrates is closed when the uterus is full. But when the uterus is emptied of the fetus, it is free again; after bearing its fruit, it can then receive the sperm. We are not ashamed to mention the organs of generation for the benefit of our hearers since God was not ashamed to create them.

(93) When the uterus has conceived a thirst for childbearing, it receives the sperm and rejects any blameworthy intercourse. But after the seed has been sown, it closes its opening to completely eliminate licentiousness. Previously the body's desires were taken up with loving embraces, but now they are redirected and occupied with the development of the child within; in this way they cooperate with the Creator. It is not right to disturb nature when it is at work by engaging in acts of excessively wanton conduct.

Wanton conduct has many names and takes many forms. When it concerns itself with sexual pleasure in a disordered way, it is called "vulgarity," since it is something common, impure, something obsessed with coition, and vulgar, as the name itself suggests. As these disorders increase, a great crowd of other diseases flows from them: love of luxury, love of wine, love of women, and every sort of prodigality and love of pleasure, over which lust holds sway. Countless passions related to these multiply endlessly and ultimately produce a dissolute character.

Scripture says: *Whips are prepared for the dissolute, and chastisements for the shoulders of the unchaste.*[17] By shoulders of the unchaste it means both the strength of dissolute conduct and its vigorous endurance. That is why Scripture says: *Keep vain*

---

17. Prov 19:29.

hopes far from your servant, and turn away from me improper desires; do not let the impulses of the stomach or of the sexual organs overtake me.[18] We must, therefore, keep away from the great wickedness of these treacherous vices. For it is not only the Pera of Crates[19] but also our own city that "no foolish parasite may enter, nor debauched glutton who delights in the buttocks, nor deceitful prostitute."[20] Nor, for that matter, may anyone who is such a beast of pleasure. So, then, we must sow good behavior throughout the whole of our lives.

(94) In general, then, this is the question to be investigated: whether we should marry or completely abstain from marriage. In my work *On Continence* (*Peri Enkrateias*) I have already treated the subject. Now if we have to ask whether we may marry at all, how can we allow ourselves to make use of intercourse on every occasion, as if it were a necessity like food? It is clear that the nerves are stretched like threads and break under the tension of intercourse. Moreover, sexual relations spread a mist over the senses and drain the body of energy. This is obvious in the case of irrational animals and in persons undergoing physical training. Among athletes it is those who abstain from sex who defeat their opponents in the contests; as far as animals are concerned, they are easily captured when they are caught in and all but dragged away from the act of rutting, for all their strength and energy is completely drained.

The sophist of Abdera[21] called sexual intercourse a "minor epilepsy" and considered it an incurable disease. Is it not accompanied by weakness following the great loss of seed? "For a human being is born of a human being and torn away from him."[22] See how much harm is done: a whole person is torn out with the ejaculation that occurs during intercourse.

18. Sir 23:5–6.

19. The word *pera* means a beggar's wallet, which was commonly carried by Cynic philosophers. It refers here to the ideal Cynic city, as described by Crates.

20. The quotation derives from a fragment of Crates that describes the ideal city of Pera.

21. Clement refers to Protagoras, whom Plato considered a founder of the Sophist school.

22. Democritus, frag. 32.

This is now bone of my bone and flesh of my flesh,[23] Scripture says. By spilling his seed a man loses as much substance as one sees in a body, for what has been expelled is the beginning of a birth. Moreover, the shaking of the body's material substance disturbs and upsets the harmony of the whole body.

(95) Wise, then, was the person who, when asked his opinion of the pleasures of love, replied: "Silence, man; I am very glad to have fled from them as from a fierce and raging tyrant."[24] Nevertheless, marriage should be accepted and given its proper place. Our Lord wanted humanity to multiply,[25] but he did not say that people should engage in licentious behavior, nor did he intend for them to give themselves over to pleasure as if they were born for rutting. Rather, let the Pedagogue put us to shame with the words of Ezekiel: *Put away your fornications.*[26] Even irrational animals have a proper time for sowing seed.

But to have intercourse without intending children is to violate nature, which we must take as our teacher. We should observe the wise precepts that her pedagogy has established concerning the proper time, by which I mean old age and childhood. You will lead them to marry, but not at any time at all: the young are not permitted to marry, the old are no longer permitted to do so. So marriage is the desire (*orexis*) for procreation,[27] but it is not the random, illicit, and irrational scattering of seed.

(96) Our entire life will be spent observing the laws of nature, if we control our desires from the start and if we do not kill off with devious instruments the human creature that has been conceived according to divine providence. For

23. Gen 2:23.
24. Plato, *Republic* 1.329C.
25. Gen 1:28.
26. Ezek 43:9.
27. When Clement indicates "desire" in what he considers a positive and rational sense, he uses the Greek word *orexis*; when he speaks of "desire" in a negative sense, he uses the word *epithumia* or "lust." See my discussion in "The Language of Desire: Clement of Alexandria's Transformation of Ascetic Discourse," in *Discursive Strategies, Ascetic Piety, and the Interpretation of Religious Literature,* ed. Vincent Wimbush, Semeia 57 (Atlanta: Scholars, 1992), 95–111.

women who, in order to conceal their incontinence, make use of death-dealing drugs that completely expel the mortal creature abort not only the embryo but also human kindness.

But those who are permitted to marry have need of the Pedagogue, so that they might not fulfill the mystic rites of nature during the day, nor have intercourse after coming home from church or from the marketplace or early in the morning like a rooster, for these are the proper times for prayer and reading and the other deeds done during the day. But the evening is the proper time to take one's rest, after dinner and after giving thanks for the benefits one has enjoyed.

(97) Nature does not always provide the opportunity to consummate marital intercourse, and the union becomes the more desirable the more it is delayed. But one must not become intemperate at night under the pretext of the cover of darkness; rather, one should preserve modesty in the soul, as if it were the light of reason. We will be no different from Penelope at her loom,[28] if during the day we weave the teachings of self-restraint, but at night undo them when we go to bed. For if we must practice self-control, as certainly we must, we ought to manifest it even more with our own wives by avoiding indecent embraces, and we should show at home the same trustworthy proof of chastity that we display toward our neighbors.

It is absolutely impossible for a man to be considered dignified by his wife if he does not show any sign of dignity in these same sharp pleasures. The good feeling that admittedly accompanies intercourse blossoms only for a short time and grows old along with the body. But sometimes it happens that it grows old even before the body, and desire is extinguished; this occurs when marital chastity has been violated by pleasure taken with prostitutes. The hearts of lovers have wings, and charms are quenched by a change of mind. Love frequently changes into hate whenever satiety perceives condemnation.

---

28. Cf. Homer, *Odyssey* 2.104–5; Plato, *Phaedo* 84A.

MISCELLANIES, BOOK 2

(23.137) Since marriage seems to fall under the rubric of pleasure and desire, we must speak about this. Marriage is the first legal union of man and woman for the procreation of legitimate children. That is why Menander the comic poet writes: "For the bearing of legitimate offspring, I give to you my daughter."[29] We ask if we ought to marry, which is one of those matters that is considered relative to the condition one is in. For it is necessary that a specific person marry, and this person must be in a specific condition, and he must marry a specific person, and she must be in a specific condition. For it is not necessary that everyone should marry, nor at all times, but there is a time when it is appropriate, and a person with whom it is appropriate, and a time up to which it is appropriate to marry. It is not suitable for just anyone to marry just anyone else at any time, nor in some utterly random way. But a person must be in a certain condition, and he must marry an appropriate person at an appropriate time for the sake of children. The partner should be similar in all respects, and she should not be compelled by force to submit to the man who loves her.

(138) That is why Abraham said, while looking upon his wife as his sister: *She is my sister by my father, but not by my mother, and she became my wife,*[30] to teach that children of the same mothers should not marry.

Let us make a brief review of history. Plato ranks marriage among the external goods that provide for the immortality of our species and pass down, as it were, a torch of perpetuity to our children's children.[31] Democritus repudiates marriage and childbearing because they produce many troubles and distractions from more necessary tasks.[32] Epicurus agrees with him, as do those who locate the good in pleasure and in

29. Menander, frag. 720.
30. Gen 20:12.
31. Plato, *Laws* 6.773, 776.
32. Democritus, frag. 179N.

tranquility or even in freedom from pain.[33] According to the Stoics, marriage and childbearing are matters of indifference, but according to the Peripatetics a good. In short, these men, by putting their teachings into words, became enslaved to pleasures: some with concubines, others with mistresses, and most with young men. That wise quaternion in the garden together with his mistress honored pleasure by his deeds.[34]

(139) So, then, they will not escape the curse of yoking an ass with an ox, if they command others to do that which they regard as unsuitable for themselves, and vice versa. Scripture showed this briefly when it said: *Do not do to another what you hate.*[35] But those who approve of marriage say, "Nature has made us well adapted for marriage, as is evident from the arrangement of our bodies into male and female." They constantly cry out: *Increase and multiply.*[36]

Now even though this is the case, they should still consider it shameful if the human person, created by God, should show less restraint than the irrational beasts who do not mate with many partners indiscriminately, but with one of the same species, as do pigeons, ringdoves, and turtledoves, and animals such as these. Furthermore, they say, the childless man falls short of his natural perfection when he does not provide his own successor to take his place. For the perfect man is the one who has produced from himself his like, or rather, who sees that he has produced his like, when the begotten one attains the same nature as the one who begot him.

(140) By all means, then, we must marry, both for the sake of our country and for the succession of children and for the completion of the world, in so far as it pertains to us. The poets also pity a marriage that is "half-complete" and childless, but they consider happy one that is "blossoming." Physi-

33. Epicurus, frag. 526.
34. The reference is to Epicurus, whose school met in a garden. The quaternion (*tetraktus*), the sum of the first four numbers, was a Pythagorean concept of perfection: 4+3+2+1=10. Clement may also be alluding to the Epicurean *tetrapharmakos*, the four foundational principles of Epicurean ethics. Clement is speaking ironically about the moral "perfection" of the Epicureans.
35. Tob 4:15; cf. Acts 15:29.
36. Gen 1:28.

cal illnesses also reveal how necessary marriage is. The loving care of a wife and the depth of her faithfulness exceed the endurance of all other relatives and friends. Just as she surpasses them in sympathy, she prefers to be always at his side, and truly she is, as Scripture says, *a necessary help*.[37]

(141) That is why the comic poet Menander, after disparaging marriage, but also considering its benefits, responded to the one who said, "I am ill-disposed to the thing," with these words: "For you take it in the wrong manner." Then he added, "You see all the difficulties and troubles in marriage, but you do not regard its advantages," and so on.[38]

Now marriage is a help, especially to those who are advanced in years, when it provides a caring spouse and produces children by her to nourish one's old age. "Children are a man's glory after his death, just as corks hold up the net, saving the fishing lines from the deep," according to the tragic poet Sophocles.[39] Lawmakers do not entrust the highest offices to unmarried men. For example, a Spartan lawmaker established a penalty not only for failure to marry but also for unlawful marriages, late marriages, and the single life. The noble Plato orders the unmarried man to pay into the public treasury the cost of a wife's maintenance and to give to the magistrates the appropriate expenses.[40] For if people do not marry and produce children, they contribute to the scarcity of human beings and destroy both the cities and the world that is composed of them.

(142) What a great impiety it is to destroy divine generation! Indeed, it is unmanly and weak to avoid living with a wife and children. When the loss of something is an evil, its possession is a good in every way; and this pertains to everything else. But the loss of children is the greatest of evils, they say. Therefore, the possession of children is a good, and if this is good, then so is marriage. "Without a father," they say,

---

37. Gen 2:18.
38. Menander, *The Misogynist*, frag. 325.1–4.
39. The reference is to Aeschylus, *Choephori* 505–7, not Sophocles.
40. Cf. Plato, *Laws* 6.774.

"there can be no child; without a mother, no conception of a child."[41]

(143) Marriage makes a father, just as a husband makes a mother. That is why Homer offers the greatest prayer for "a husband and a house," but adds the qualification "with good harmony."[42] The marriage of some people is an agreement to indulge in pleasure, but the marriage of philosophers leads to a harmony that is in accordance with reason. In such a marriage wives are ordered to adorn themselves not in outward appearance but in character; husbands are commanded not to use their wives like mistresses, with the aim of indulging bodily wantonness, but rather to preserve marriage as a help for their whole life and as an occasion for the highest form of self-restraint.

As I see it, far more honorable than the seeds of wheat and barley that are sown at the proper season is the human being who is sown, for whose sake all things grow and for whom sober farmers sow those seeds. Therefore, every foul and defiling practice must be purged from marriage, so that the couplings of irrational beasts may not be thrown in our face as being more in accord with nature than human intercourse. Some animals, following a commonly accepted limit, cease copulating as soon as the proper time commands them, leaving creation to providence.

(144) The writers of tragedy have described how Polyxena, even though she had been murdered, took great care to fall with grace and dignity even as she died, "concealing from the eyes of men what ought to have been concealed."[43] To that woman marriage was a misfortune. To fall under the sway of the passions, then, and to yield to them is the ultimate slavery; similarly, to keep the passions under control is the only true freedom. The divine Scripture, therefore, says that those who have violated the commandments are sold to strangers,

---

41. Menander, frag. 1085.
42. Homer, *Odyssey* 6.181.
43. Euripides, *Hecuba* 568–70.

that is, to sins that are alien to nature, until they turn around and repent.[44]

(145) We must, then, keep marriage pure and free of all defilement, as if it were a sacred offering, as we rise from our sleep with the Lord and go to sleep with thanksgiving and prayer, "both when we lay down to sleep and when the holy light comes."[45] Let us bear witness to the Lord with the whole of our lives, preserving piety in our soul and exercising control over the body. It truly pleases God when we extend good conduct from our lips to our actions, for shameful speech leads to shamefulness, and both end up in shameful behavior. Scripture recommends marriage and does not allow release from the union; this is evident from the precept: *You shall not put away your wife, except because of fornication.*[46] It is regarded as adultery if either of the separated partners marries, while the other is alive. (146) If a wife does not adorn and decorate herself beyond what is proper, she will not be subject to slanderous accusations. She should devote herself to constant prayer and avoid leaving the house too often; she should shut herself away as much as possible from the gaze of all but her relatives; she should consider the care of the household as more profitable than worthless chatter. *He who marries a woman who has been put away by another commits adultery*, he says; *and if a man puts away his wife, he makes her an adulteress*,[47] that is, he forces her to commit adultery. Moreover, not only does the man who puts away his wife become guilty of adultery, but also the man who receives her, since he provides the woman with the opportunity to sin. For if he did not receive her, she would return to her husband.

(147) What, then, is the law? In order to restrain the flow of the passions, it commands that a woman who has committed adultery and been convicted of this should be put to death.[48] If she is the daughter of a priest, it commands that she

44. Cf. Judg 2:14.
45. Hesiod, *Works and Days* 339.
46. Matt 5:32.
47. Matt 5:32; 19:19.
48. Cf. Lev 20:10; Deut 22:22.

be burned in the fire.[49] The adulterer is also stoned, but not in the same place, so that they may not share even a common death.

The law is not at variance with the gospel, but agrees with it. How could it be otherwise, when one Lord is the master of both? She who commits adultery lives in sin; she is dead to the commandments. But she who has repented, having been born again, as it were, through the change in her life, experiences a rebirth of life. The old adulteress has died, she who has been regenerated by repentance has entered into life. The Spirit testifies to these words through Ezekiel: *I do not desire the death of the sinner, but that he should repent.*[50] Now they are stoned to death, since through their hardness of heart they have died to the law in which they did not believe. In the case of the priest's daughter, the punishment is increased, since *from the one who has been given much, much more will be required.*[51]

MISCELLANIES, BOOK 3

(6.45) To those who blaspheme both the creation and the holy Creator, the almighty and only God, through their supposedly sacred continence, and who teach that marriage and childbearing should be rejected and that one should not bring other unfortunate people into the world or provide further fodder for death, this is what I have to say. First, from the apostle John: *And now many antichrists have come; this is how we know it is the final hour. They went out from us, but they did not belong to us. For if they had belonged to us, they would have remained with us.*[52] They must be refuted because they distort the very evidence that they present to make their case. For example, when Salome asked the Lord, "How long will death reign?" she did not mean that life was evil or that creation

49. Lev 21:9.
50. Ezek 33:11.
51. Luke 12:48.
52. 1 John 2:18–19.

was corrupt. And when the Lord responded, "As long as you women bear children," he was merely teaching what is the natural course of things, for death always follows birth.[53]

(46) The purpose of the law is to lead us away from luxury and all disorderly behavior; its ultimate end is to conduct us from unrighteousness to righteousness, so that we choose to be self-controlled in marriage, childbearing, and way of life. The Lord came *not to destroy the law, but to fulfill it.*[54] To *fulfill* does not mean that it was defective, but rather that the prophecies in the law have now been fulfilled by Christ's coming. For before the law the elements of good conduct were proclaimed by the Logos to those who lived righteously. Most people know nothing of continence and live for the body, not for the spirit. But the body without the spirit is *earth and ashes.*[55] Now the Lord condemns adultery even in thought.[56] What does this mean? Is it not possible to live chastely even in marriage and not to try to dissolve *what God has joined together?*[57] This is the teaching of those who divide the union, because of whom the name is blasphemed. Since they say that intercourse is impure, although they themselves derive their existence from intercourse, does it not follow that they are impure? But I think that even the seed of those who have been made holy is holy.

(47) It is proper that not only our spirit be made holy, but also our behavior, our way of life, and our body. What did Paul mean when he said that *the wife is sanctified by her husband and the husband by his wife?*[58] What did the Lord mean when he said to those who asked him whether it was lawful to put away one's wife, as Moses commanded: *Moses wrote this because of your hardness of heart. But have you not read that God said to the first man "You shall be two in one flesh"? Therefore,*

53. Clement is citing from the *Gospel according to the Egyptians*, a text that circulated widely in the second and third centuries.
54. Matt 5:17.
55. Gen 18:27.
56. Cf. Matt 5:28.
57. Matt 19:6.
58. 1 Cor 7:14.

whoever puts away his wife, except because of adultery, makes her an adulteress?[59] *But after the resurrection,* he says, *they will neither marry nor be given in marriage.*[60] Furthermore, concerning the stomach and its food, it is written: *Food is for the stomach and the stomach for food, but God will destroy them both.*[61] This is to refute those who wished to live like wild pigs and goats, to prevent them from eating and mating without restraint.

(48) If, as they say, they already participate in the resurrection and for this reason reject marriage, they should also stop eating and drinking. For the apostle says that in the resurrection both the stomach and food will be destroyed. Why then do they hunger and thirst and endure the sufferings of the flesh and all the rest, when the person who through Christ attains the anticipated final resurrection will not have to endure such things? Even those who worship idols abstain from food as well as from sex. *But the kingdom of God, he says, is not a matter of eating and drinking.*[62] In fact, even the astrologers are careful to abstain from wine and meat and sex, all the while worshipping angels and demons. Just as humility is meekness, not the abuse of the body, so, too, is chastity (*enkrateia*) a virtue of the soul, which is hidden, not visible.[63]

(49) Some openly declare that marriage is fornication and teach that it was introduced by the devil. They boast that they are imitating the Lord himself who neither married nor possessed anything in the world, and they claim to understand the gospel better than anyone else. To them Scripture says: *God resists the proud, but gives grace to the humble.*[64] Moreover, they do not know the reason why the Lord did not marry. First, he had his own bride, the church; second, he was no ordinary man who had need of a helpmate after the flesh.[65]

---

59. Matt 19:3–9.
60. Matt 22:30.
61. 1 Cor 6:13.
62. Rom 14:17.

63. Against those who insist on *enkrateia* in the sense of total abstinence, Clement argues that it is possible to exercise "restraint" (*enkrateia*) even in acts of sexual intercourse.

64. Jas 4:6; 1 Pet 5:5.
65. Cf. Gen 2:18.

Nor did he need to beget children, since he lives eternally and was born the only Son of God. The Lord himself says: *What God has joined together, man must not separate.*[66] And again: *As it was in the days of Noah, they were marrying and giving in marriage, building and planting, and as it was in the days of Lot, so will be the coming of the Son of Man.*[67] To show that he is not speaking to the Gentiles, he adds: *When the Son of Man comes, will he find faith upon the earth?*[68] And again: *Woe to those who are pregnant and nursing in those days,*[69] although this has to be interpreted allegorically. The reason he did not determine *the times that the Father has established in his own power*[70] was so that the world might continue from generation to generation.

***

(52) Did not the righteous people in ancient times partake of created things with thanksgiving? Some of them married and produced children in a self-controlled manner. Elijah, for example, was fed bread and meat by the ravens.[71] The prophet Samuel gave Saul a piece of the thigh to eat, of which he himself had already eaten.[72] But these people, who say that they are superior to the ancients in conduct and way of life, cannot even be compared to them in their actual deeds. *The one who does not eat, then, should not despise the one who eats, and the one who eats should not judge the one who does not eat. For God has accepted him.*[73] Furthermore, the Lord said this about himself: *John came neither eating nor drinking, and they say "he has a demon." The Son of Man has come eating and drinking, and they say "See what a glutton and a drunkard he is, a friend to tax collec-*

---

66. Matt 19:6.
67. Matt 24:37–39.
68. Luke 18:8.
69. Matt 24:19.
70. Acts 1:7.
71. Cf. 1 Kgs 17:6.
72. Cf. 1 Sam 9:24.
73. Rom 14:3.

tors and a sinner."[74] Do they also reject the apostles? For Peter and Philip produced children, and Philip gave his daughters in marriage.

(53) Even Paul did not hesitate in one letter to address his *yokefellow*,[75] whom he did not take around with him because it would have been an inconvenience to his ministry. That is why he says in one letter: *Do we not have the right to take with us a wife who is a sister, as the other apostles do?*[76] These apostles, in order to devote themselves to preaching without distraction, as befitted their ministry, took their wives with them, not as married women but as sisters, to be their fellow ministers to women in the households. Through these women the teaching of the Lord penetrated even into the women's quarters without any scandal. We also know the kind of regulations that were given regarding women deacons by the noble Paul in his second letter to Timothy.[77]

Furthermore, Paul himself proclaims that the kingdom of God is not a matter of food and drink, nor does it consist in abstinence from wine and meat, but it is a matter of righteousness and peace and joy in the Holy Spirit.[78] Who among them goes around wearing a sheepskin and a leather belt like Elijah?[79] Which one goes about naked except for a sack and with bare feet like Isaiah?[80] Or clothed only in a linen loincloth like Jeremiah?[81] Who among them will imitate the gnostic mode of life of John?[82] In fact, the blessed prophets lived in the very same manner and gave thanks to the Creator.

---

74. Matt 11:18–19.

75. Phil 4:3. Paul's use of the term *yokefellow* (*syzygos*) was very unusual. It probably referred to a "companion" in his missionary journeys who is currently in Philippi and not, as Clement suggests, Paul's wife.

76. 1 Cor 9:5.

77. The reference is actually to 1 Tim 3:11.

78. Rom 14:17.

79. Cf. 2 Kgs 1:8.

80. Cf. Isa 20:2.

81. Cf. Jer 13:1.

82. The reference is to John the Baptist's ascetic mode of life in imitation of the biblical prophets; cf. Matt 3:4.

***

(7.57) The human ideal of self-control (*enkrateia*), I mean the one found among the Greek philosophers, consists in struggling against lust (*epithumia*), and in not yielding to it so as to manifest its deeds. But among us self-control means not to experience lust at all. Our aim is not merely to be self-controlled while still experiencing lust in the heart, but rather to be self-controlled even over lust itself. But this kind of self-control is attained only by the grace of God. That is why he said: *Ask and it will be given to you.*[83] Moses received this grace, even though he was clothed in the needy body, so that for forty days he felt neither thirst nor hunger.[84]

Just as it is better to be healthy than to be sick and to talk about health, so to be light is better than merely to talk about light, and the true self-control is better than that which is taught by the philosophers. For where there is no light, there is darkness. Where lust is still rooted, residing alone as it were, even if it is quiet in respect to bodily activity, it still unites itself in the memory with the object it desires, although the object is not present.

(58) In general, then, let this be our position regarding marriage, food, and other matters: to do nothing out of lust, but to wish only for those things that are necessary. For we are children not of lust, but of the will.[85] The married man must exercise self-control in procreation, so that he does not feel lust for his wife, whom he must love, while he produces children by a holy and chaste will. For we have learned not to *have concern for the flesh to fulfill its lusts,*[86] but to behave *decently as in the day,* that is, in Christ and in the path that the Lord has illumined, *walking not in orgies and drunkenness, not in immorality and debauchery, not in dissension and jealousy.*[87]

(59) Furthermore, one should not look at self-control merely in regard to one form of it, that is, sexual relations, but

83. Matt 7:7.
84. Cf. Exod 24:18.
85. Cf. John 1:13.
86. Rom 13:14.
87. Rom 13:13.

also in regard to the other things that our souls lustfully crave when they are not content with the necessities and yearn for luxury. It is self-control to despise money, delicacy, property, to have little regard for outward appearance, to control the tongue, and to master wicked thoughts. Once certain angels lost their self-control and were seized by desire so that they fell from heaven down to earth. Valentinus in a letter to Agathopus says: "Having undergone all things, Jesus was self-controlled. He was exercising his divine nature: he ate and drank in a unique manner, without evacuating his food. He had such power of self-control that the food within him did not undergo corruption, since he himself did not have to undergo corruption."[88]

But we embrace the self-control that comes from the love of the Lord and from a desire for the good in itself, as we sanctify the temple of the Spirit. For it is good to make oneself *a eunuch for the kingdom of heaven*[89] in respect to all lust, and to *purify the conscience from dead works for the worship of the living God.*[90]

***

(12.79) But if *by agreement* sexual relations are suspended *for a time for the purpose of prayer,*[91] this teaches self-control. But he adds the words *by agreement* to prevent anyone from dissolving the marriage, and the words *for a time,* so that the married man who is compelled to practice self-control does not fall into sin; for if he abstains from intercourse with his own wife, he may conceive a desire for another woman. On these grounds the apostle also said that if a man thinks that he is not behaving properly by raising his daughter as a virgin, he does well to give her in marriage.[92]

88. Valentinus (ca. 100–165) was a prominent teacher from Alexandria, who established a Christian school in Rome. His teaching was the source of much of what modern scholars have called Gnosticism.

89. Matt 19:12.

90. Heb 9:14.

91. Cf. 1 Cor 7:5.

92. Cf. 1 Cor 7:36.

Whether one chooses to be celibate or to marry for the sake of procreation, one must remain unyielding to what is inferior. If a person can endure such a life, he will acquire for himself greater merit with God, since he practices self-control in a manner that is both pure and rational. But if he has gone too far in choosing the rule for the greater glory, he may fall short of his hope. Just like celibacy, marriage has its own distinctive services and ministries for the Lord; I refer to the care of one's children and wife. The special characteristic of the marital union, it seems, is that it gives the person who is committed to a perfect marriage the opportunity to show concern for everything that pertains to the household he shares with his wife. That is why the apostle says that bishops must be appointed who have learned how to supervise the whole church by supervising their own households.[93] So, then, let each one complete his ministry by the work to which he was called,[94] so that he may be free in Christ and may receive the proper reward for his ministry.[95]

93. Cf. 1 Tim 3:4–5.
94. Cf. 1 Cor 7:24.
95. Cf. 1 Cor 7:22.

8.

Acts of Thomas

The next text in this anthology is an excerpt from the *Acts of Thomas*, a work originally composed in Syriac (ca. 220) and subsequently translated into Greek, Latin, Ethiopic, and Armenian. The *Acts of Thomas* seems to have originated within ascetical circles in Syria, but it was quickly adopted by other groups, such as the Manichaeans and the followers of Priscillian, as well as by more orthodox Christians.

The genre of the *Acts* is that of the Hellenistic-oriental novel or romance. The hero of the narrative, the apostle Judas Thomas, appears in the *Acts* as a twin brother of Jesus, like him both in appearance and in his capacity for revelation and redemption. In the first part of the *Acts* the apostle sings a wedding hymn of the marriage of a maiden of light with the heavenly Bridegroom. Certain features of the hymn are reminiscent of what might be considered "gnostic" mythology. Later the apostle is called upon to pronounce a blessing over a newly married couple. As a result of his prayer, and after an apparition from the Lord Jesus, they announce their intention to reject sexual relations and to live in complete continence. The *Acts of Thomas* is an example of the radical asceticism that seems to have characterized much of early Syrian Christianity.

ACTS OF THOMAS, ACT 1

(1) At that time all of us apostles were in Jerusalem: Simon, who was called Peter, and Andrew his brother; James, the son of Zebedee, and his brother John; Philip and Bartholomew; Thomas and Matthew the tax-collector; James, the son of Alphaeus, and Simon the Canaanean; and Judas, the son of James. And we divided the regions of the entire world, so that each of us might go to the region that fell to him and to the nation to which the Lord sent him. According to lot, India fell to Judas Thomas, who was also called Didymus (or "Twin"). But he did not want to go, saying that he was unable to travel because of the weakness of his flesh: "How can I, a Hebrew man, travel among the Indians to proclaim the truth?" And while he was discussing the matter and talking in this way, the Savior appeared to him during the night and said to him: "Do not be afraid, Thomas. Go to India and proclaim the word there. For my grace is with you." But Thomas would not obey and said: "Send me wherever you wish, as long as it is somewhere else, because I am not going to the Indians."

(2) And as he was saying this and becoming angry, it happened that a certain merchant from India was passing by, whose name was Abbanes. He had been sent by the king Gundaphoros with orders to purchase a carpenter and bring him back to him. Now the Lord, having seen him walking in the marketplace at midday, said to him: "Do you want to buy a carpenter?" And Abbanes replied: "Yes." And the Lord said to him: "I have a slave who is a carpenter and I would like to sell him." And after saying this, he pointed out Thomas to him from a distance and agreed with him on a price of three pounds of uncoined silver. Then he wrote a bill of sale, saying: "I, Jesus, the son of Joseph the carpenter, declare that I have sold my slave, who is called Judas, to you, Abbanes, a merchant of Gundaphoros, king of the Indians." When the sale was complete, the Savior took Judas, who is also Thomas, and led him to the merchant Abbanes. When

Abbanes saw him, he said to him: "Is this man your master?" And the apostle answered him, saying: "Yes, he is my Lord." Then Abbanes replied: "But I have bought you from him." And the apostle was silent.

(3) Early the next morning, after praying and entreating the Lord, the apostle said: "I will go wherever you want, Lord Jesus. Your will be done!" Then he went to Abbanes the merchant, carrying nothing with him but the price of his sale. For the Lord had given it to him, saying: "Let your price be with you, along with my grace, wherever you go." The apostle found Abbanes carrying his baggage on to the ship and, therefore, he began to carry it with him. After they boarded the ship and sat down, Abbanes questioned the apostle, saying: "What sort of work do you know?" And he replied: "In wood [I can make] ploughs, yokes, and balances, as well as ships, oars for ships, masts, and pulleys; in stone, pillars, temples, and royal palaces." And the merchant Abbanes said to him: "We have need of such a workman." And so, they began to set sail. They had a favorable wind and sailed quickly until they reached Andrapolis, a royal city.

(4) Leaving the ship the apostle Thomas and the merchant Abbanes went into the city. Behold, the noise of flutes and water-organs and trumpets sounded around them. The apostle asked: "What festival is happening in this city?" Those who were there said to him: "The gods have also led you to make merry in this city. For the king has an only daughter and now he is giving her in marriage to a husband. The festival you have seen today is the rejoicing and assembly for the wedding. The king has sent messengers everywhere to announce that all should come to the wedding, rich and poor, slave and free, foreigners and citizens. If anyone refuses and does not attend the wedding, he will have to answer to the king."

When Abbanes heard this, he said to the apostle: "We too should go, so as not to offend the king, especially since we are foreigners." And the apostle said: "Let us go." They found lodging in an inn and, after resting for a little while, they went to the wedding. When the apostle saw everyone reclining, he also lay down in their midst. Everyone looked at him because he was a stranger and from a foreign land. But Abbanes the merchant, since he was a master, reclined in another place.

(5) While the others ate and drank, the apostle tasted nothing. Therefore, those who were nearby said to him: "Why have you come here, neither eating nor drinking?" He answered them in these words: "I have come here for something better than food or drink, that I may fulfill the will of the king. For the messengers announce the king's message, and whoever does not listen to the messengers will be liable to the king's judgment."

So then, after they had eaten and drunk, and after the crowns and ointments had been brought out, each person took some ointment. Some anointed their eyes, others their beards, and others different parts of their bodies. But the apostle anointed the top of his head and smeared a little on his nose, and dropped some into his ears, and placed some on his teeth, and carefully spread some around his heart. He took the crown that was brought to him, which was woven out of myrtle and other flowers, and placed it on his head. Then he took a branch of a reed and held it in his hands. There was a flute girl who had a flute in her hands, and she went around to all of them and played. When she came to the place where the apostle was, she stood in front of him for a long while, playing over his head. This flute girl was a Hebrew by birth.

(6) As the apostle remained looking at the ground, one of the wine pourers reached out his hand and struck him. The apostle lifted his eyes, looked at the one who struck him, and said: "My God will forgive you this injustice in the age to come, but in this world he will reveal his wonders, and we shall now see this hand that has struck me dragged away by dogs." Having said this he began to sing and chant this song:

The maiden is the daughter of light,
Upon her stands and in her rests the proud glory of kings.
Delightful is the sight of her,

She shines with radiant beauty.
Her garments are like the flowers of spring,
And from them flows a sweet fragrance.
On the crown of her head the king is seated,
And he feeds with his ambrosia those who are seated around
    him.
Truth is established upon her head,
And with her feet she radiates joy.
Her mouth is open and it well becomes her,
Thirty and two are the number who sing her praises.
Her tongue is like the curtain on the door,
Which waves to those who enter.
Her neck lies like the steps that the first craftsman constructed,
And her two hands make signs and signals.
They announce the dance of the blessed Aeons,
And her fingers reveal the gates of the city.
Her chamber is full of light.
It breathes forth the fragrance of balsam and of every spice.
It gives out the sweet scent of myrrh and silphium.[1]
Within are strewn branches of myrtle and all kinds of sweet-
    smelling flowers,
And the doorposts are adorned with reeds.
(7) Surrounding her are the groomsmen, whose number is
    seven.
She herself has chosen them.
There are eight bridesmaids,
Who form a chorus before her.
Twelve is the number of those who serve her,
Who are her followers.
They gaze upon the Bridegroom,
So that through this vision they may be enlightened.
Forever they will be with him in that eternal joy,
And they will be present at that wedding feast,
Where the great ones will gather,
And where the eternal ones will be counted worthy to rejoice
    forever.
They shall put on royal robes and wear bright raiment.
In joy and exultation they both shall be,
And they shall glorify the Father of all.

---

1. The word used here, *phyllon*, could refer to a generic leaf, but more likely refers
to the leaf-like fruit of silphium, a plant used in antiquity as seasoning and medicine.

His proud light they have received,
Those who have been enlightened in the vision of their Master.
His ambrosial food they have received,
Which will never run out.
They have drunk of his wine,
Which gives them neither thirst nor desire.
And they have glorified and praised, with the living Spirit,
The Father of Truth and the Mother of Wisdom.

(8) When the apostle had finished this song, all who were present there gazed at him, but he kept silent. They also saw that his appearance was changed, but they did not understand what he had said, since he was a Hebrew and what he said was spoken in Hebrew. Only the flute girl heard it all, since she was a Hebrew by birth. Moving away from him, she played for the others, but for much of the time she gazed at him, for she loved him very much as a man of her own country, and he was more attractive in appearance than the others who were there. When she had finished playing, the flute girl sat down opposite him and looked at him intently. But he looked at no one at all and kept his eyes fixed on the ground, waiting for the time when he could depart from there.

But the wine pourer who had struck him went out to the well to draw water. It happened that there was a lion in that place. It killed him and left him lying there with his limbs torn apart. Immediately some dogs came and seized his limbs, and one of them, a black dog, took the right hand in his mouth and carried it into the banquet.

(9) When they saw this, everyone was shocked and asked which of them was missing. It became apparent to all that it was the wine pourer who had struck the apostle. The flute girl then broke her flute and threw it down and went to sit at the feet of the apostle. She said: "This man is either a god or an apostle of God. For I heard him say in Hebrew to the wine pourer: 'We shall now see this hand that has struck me dragged away by dogs.' This is what you have seen, for it has happened just as he said it would." And some of them believed her, but others did not.

When the king heard what had happened, he went to the apostle Thomas and said: "Arise, come with me and pray for my daughter, for she is my only child, and today I am giving her in marriage." The apostle did not want to go with him because the Lord had not yet been revealed to him there. But the king forced him to go to the bridal chamber to pray for them.

(10) Standing there the apostle began to pray in these words: "My Lord and my God, who accompanies his servants on their way, who guides and directs those who trust in him, refuge and resting place of the afflicted, hope of those who mourn and deliverer of captives, healer of sick souls and savior of all creation, who gives life to the world and strength to our souls! You know the future and for our sake you bring all things to completion. You, Lord, are the one who reveals hidden mysteries and who utters words that are unspeakable. You, Lord, are the one who plants the good tree and who causes all good things to arise by his hands. You, Lord, are the one who is in all things, who came through all things, who exists in all his works, and who reveals himself in the working of all things.

"Jesus Christ, son of compassion and perfect savior, Christ, son of the living God, the undaunted power that has overthrown the enemy, the voice heard by the rulers that has shaken all their powers, the ambassador sent from on high who has gone down even into hell, who has opened the gates and led out from there those who were shut up for many years in the power of darkness, and who has revealed to them the path that leads up on high: I beg you, Lord Jesus, offering you supplication on behalf of these young people, so that you may do to them whatever is helpful, advantageous, and profitable." After laying his hands on them and saying, "The Lord be with you," he left them there and departed.

(11) The king ordered the groomsmen to leave the bridal chamber. When everyone had left and the doors were shut, the bridegroom raised the curtain of the bridal chamber in order to take the bride to himself. Then he saw the Lord Jesus

conversing with the bride, bearing the appearance of Judas Thomas, the apostle who had just blessed them and departed. And the bridegroom said to him: "Did you not go out before all the others? How is it that you are now here?" But the Lord said to him: "I am not Judas, who is also Thomas, but I am his brother." Then the Lord sat down on the bed and ordered them also to sit down on the couches, and he began to speak to them:

(12) "Remember, my children, what my brother said to you and remember the one to whom he entrusted you. Know that if you refrain from this filthy intercourse, you will become holy temples, pure, free of trials and difficulties, known and unknown, and you will not be drowned in the cares of life and of children, who lead only to ruin. If you produce many children, you will become greedy and avaricious because of them, thrashing orphans and defrauding widows, and by doing so you will render yourselves liable to the harshest punishments. For many children become a liability, being harassed by demons, some openly, others covertly. Some become lunatics, other are half-withered or lame or deaf or mute or paralytic or idiots. Even if they are in good health, they will be do-nothings, committing useless and disgusting deeds. They will be caught either in adultery or in murder or in theft or in fornication, and you will be afflicted in all these cases. But if you are persuaded and keep your souls pure for God, living children will be born to you, who will suffer no harm. You will live an untroubled life, free from care and grief, while awaiting that true and incorruptible marriage. At that marriage you will be the attendants of the Bridegroom as you enter into that bridal chamber full of immortality and light."

(13) When the young people heard this, they believed in the Lord and dedicated themselves to him. They abstained from filthy desire and in this way remained in that place for the entire night. The Lord departed from them with these words: "The grace of the Lord will be with you." At daybreak the king arrived and, after filling the table, approached

the bridegroom and the bride. He found them sitting opposite each other, the bride with her face uncovered and the bridegroom with a joyful look. The mother approached the bride and said: "Why do you sit there so immodestly, child, as if you have been living with your husband for a long time?" Then her father said: "Is it because of your great love for your husband that you are uncovered?"

(14) The bride replied: "Truly, father, I am deeply in love and I pray to my Lord that the love which I have experienced tonight will continue, and I will claim for myself that husband whom I have experienced today. That is why I will no longer be veiled, since the mirror of shame has been taken from me. No longer am I ashamed or embarrassed, since the work of shame and embarrassment is far away from me. I am not afraid, since fear does not abide in me. I am cheerful and joyful, since the day of joy has not been shaken. I regard as nothing this husband and this marriage that have passed before my eyes, since I have been given in another marriage. I have had no intercourse with a temporary husband, which ends only in lust and bitterness of soul, since I have been united with a true husband."

(15) As the bride was still speaking, the bridegroom answered in these words: "I give thanks to you, O Lord, who have been proclaimed by a stranger and have been found in us. You have put me far from corruption and sown life in me. You have delivered me from this disease, which is difficult to cure and hard to heal and lasts forever, and you have established me in good health. You have shown yourself to me and have revealed to me all that pertains to me and the circumstances of my existence. You have saved me from destruction and led me to the better path. You have freed me from what is temporary and made me worthy of what is immortal and eternal. You have lowered yourself to me and to my smallness, so that you might lift me up to your greatness and unite me to yourself. You did not withhold your compassion from me when I was lost, but you have shown me how to search for myself and how to know who I was, and who and in what

state I am now, so that I might once again become what I was. I did not know you, but you sought me out; I did not understand you, but you took hold of me, you whom I now experience and cannot forget. Love of you seethes in me, and I cannot speak as I should. Whatever I can say about him turns out to be too brief, too little, and falls short of his glory. But he does not find fault with me for not being ashamed to say to him even what I do not know, for it is through his love that I say even this."

(16) When the king heard this from the bridegroom and the bride, he tore his clothing and said to those standing near him: "Go out quickly and search the whole city. Capture and bring to me that man, the magician, who is a wicked presence in the city. I led him into my house with my own hands and I told him to pray for my unfortunate daughter. Whoever finds him and brings him to me will receive whatever he asks of me." They went out and searched everywhere for him, but did not find him because he had set sail. They also went into the inn where he had stayed, and there they found the flute girl weeping and upset because he had not taken her with him. But when they told her what had happened to the young couple, she was delighted by the news and put aside her grief, saying, "Now I too have found rest here."

Then she got up and went to them and stayed with them a long time, until they had instructed the king as well. Many of the brothers also gathered there until they heard a report that the apostle had reached the cities of India and was teaching there. And they went away and joined him.

9.

Methodius of Olympus

Little is known about Methodius, who lived in the second half of the third century. He seems to have been a teacher in Lycia in Asia Minor and may have been bishop or presbyter in the town of Olympus. Some sources indicate that he died as a martyr, possibly around the year 312. Methodius's discussion of marriage is especially interesting because it occurs in a text primarily devoted to the subject of virginity. Methodius's *Symposium* was intended as an imitation and inversion of Plato's *Symposium*. Instead of a group of aristocratic Athenian males discussing the virtues and varieties of *erōs*, the characters in Methodius's dialogue are ten Christian virgins who have gathered to sing the praises of virginity.

The second discourse, which is translated here, is a defense of marriage by the virgin Theophila. The very presence of such a speech in a treatise devoted to virginity is significant. It indicates Methodius's awareness that Christian enthusiasm for asceticism often led to the repudiation of marriage. To guard against this interpretation of his work, Methodius included a vigorous defense of the goodness of marriage and procreation, and his work has aptly been characterized as "a handbook against Encratism and Gnosticism."[1] Methodius was strongly influenced by the anti-Encratite writings of Irenaeus and Clement of Alexandria, and he subsequently influenced other anti-heretical writers, such as Epiphanius of Salamis.[2]

SYMPOSIUM OF THE TEN VIRGINS, DISCOURSE 2

(1) Then Theophila spoke as follows: "Since Marcella has made such a fine start on the discussion without adequately finishing it, it is necessary, I believe, that I should try to complete the discussion. I think that she has properly described how humanity has made progress by degrees toward virginity, as God has given assistance from time to time. But her suggestion that it is no longer necessary to produce children is mistaken. It is very clear to me from Scripture that with the coming of virginity the Logos did not completely abolish procreation. Simply because the moon's light is brighter than that of the stars does not mean that the light of the stars is extinguished.

"We will begin with Genesis in order to pay the highest respect to Scripture. God's declaration and command regarding procreation, all agree, is still being accomplished even now, since the Creator is still fashioning human beings. Everyone can see that God the artist at this very moment is at work on the universe, as the Lord himself has taught us: *My father is at work even now*.[3] But when the rivers cease to flow into the channels of the sea, and when the light has been completely separated from the darkness—for now the separation is still going on—and when the dry land stops producing fruit and reptiles and other creatures, and when the predetermined number of human beings is fulfilled, only then must there be no more procreation.

1. Herbert Musurillo, *St. Methodius: The Symposium: A Treatise on Chastity*, Ancient Christian Writers 27 (New York: Newman, 1958), 16.

2. For an excellent overview of Methodius's theology, see L. G. Patterson, *Methodius of Olympus: Divine Sovereignty, Human Freedom, and Life in Christ* (Washington, DC: Catholic University of America Press, 1997).

3. John 5:17.

"But now it is necessary that human beings cooperate in producing the image of God, since the universe continues to exist and to be created. *Increase and multiply,*[4] Scripture says. We must not recoil from the commandment of the Creator, from whom we too have received our existence. Human reproduction begins with the sowing of seed into the furrows of the womb, in such a way that *bone from bone* and *flesh from flesh* is taken by an invisible power and fashioned by the Craftsman himself into another human being. In this way, we must believe, that saying is fulfilled: *This is now bone from my bone and flesh from my flesh.*[5]

(2) "This perhaps is what was signified by that ecstasy which fell upon the first man in his sleep;[6] it prefigured the enchantment that man would find in love, when thirsting for children he falls into ecstasy and is lulled to sleep by the pleasures of procreation, so that once more another person might be created from the bit that was torn from his bone and from his flesh. First the harmony of the body is greatly agitated in the excitement of intercourse (so I have learned from those who have consummated the marriage rite); then all the marrow in the blood, which has generative power and is liquid bone, is gathered from every part of the body, worked into a foam and coagulated, and then rushes out through the reproductive organs into the living soil of the woman. For this reason, it is well said that *a man will leave his father and mother,*[7] because a man forgets everything else when he is joined to a woman in tender embraces, overwhelmed with a desire for children. He offers his rib to the divine Creator to be removed, so that he the father might reappear again in his son.

"Since, then, even now God is still fashioning human beings, would it not be arrogant of us to loathe procreation, which the Almighty himself is not ashamed to accomplish

4. Gen 1:28.
5. Gen 2:23.
6. Cf. Gen 2:21.
7. Gen 2:24.

with undefiled hands? *Before I formed you in your mother's womb, I knew you,* he says to Jeremiah.[8] And to Job: *Was it you who took clay and formed a living being and placed it on the earth to speak?*[9] Job approached God with this prayer: *Your hands have made me and fashioned me.*[10] Would it not be foolish to repudiate marital unions, when we still expect that there will be people after us to be martyrs and to oppose the evil one? It was for their sake that the Logos announced that the days would be shortened.[11] If, as you have said, God now regards the begetting of children as something evil, how is it possible for people who are born contrary to the will and design of God to be pleasing to God? Logic dictates that God would despise them and consider them spurious, if they have been created, like counterfeit coins, in opposition to the intention and decree of his authority. It follows, then, that people have the right to produce children."

(3) At this point Marcella interrupted her and said: "Theophila, I see a great contradiction in what you have said. Do you think that it escapes our notice because of the great cloud you have cast over the matter? This is the question, my wise friend, which anyone might ask of you: What do you say about persons who are born illegitimately as a result of adultery? You have taught us that it is unthinkable, even impossible, for anyone to come into the world unless he is directly brought in by the will of the Almighty, since it is God himself who has prepared the dwelling place.[12] Do not try to escape, as it were, behind a wall, by citing as a proof that Scripture passage: *The children of adulterers will not come to perfection.*[13] You will be gently refuted with these words: Do we not quite frequently see people, who were conceived in illegitimate unions, come to term fully developed, like ripe fruit?

8. Jer 1:5.
9. Job 38:14, according to the Septuagint reading.
10. Job 10:8.
11. Cf. Matt 24:22.
12. By "dwelling place" Methodius means the body.
13. Wis 3:16.

"If, on the other hand, you try to play the sophist and answer: 'O, what I meant by not coming to perfection was not being perfected in the righteousness taught by Christ,' the reply will be: But surely, my dear, very many people born of illegitimate unions have nonetheless not only been deemed worthy to be numbered among the flock of the faithful but even in many cases have been chosen to lead them. Therefore, since it is plain and since all agree that people conceived in adultery do grow to maturity, we must not believe that the Spirit was uttering prophecies about conception and childbirth; rather, it was probably speaking about those who adulterate the truth, who bastardize the Scriptures with specious doctrines, and who beget imperfect wisdom, mixing error with piety.

"Well, now that you have been denied this avenue of escape, come and answer the question: Are people conceived in adultery born with God's approval? For you said that it was impossible for the offspring of a human being to come to perfection, unless the Lord formed it and gave it life."

(4) Then Theophila grew faint, as if she had been grasped around the waist by a worthy opponent, but after recovering her breath with great difficulty, she responded: "You are asking a question, my dear, that must be explained by means of an example, so that you may understand even better how the creative power of God that governs all things is at work in a special way in the conception of human beings, causing the seed that is planted in the fruitful soil to grow. For it is not the seed that is to blame, but rather the person who sows in another's field by fraudulent acts of intercourse, shamelessly hiring out his own seed in exchange for a little pleasure.

"Imagine that our birth into this world can be compared to a house that has an entrance that lies in front of high mountains; and that the house extends for quite a distance away from this entrance, with a great number of windows in the back; imagine also that this back part is circular."

"I can picture it," said Marcella.

"Now, suppose that sitting inside there is a craftsman making many statues in the shape of human beings. Imagine that he is constantly being supplied with his material, the clay, from the outside through the windows by a number of men who cannot see the artisan. Also imagine that the house is covered with mist and clouds, and that no one on the outside can see anything but the windows."

"I can imagine this too," she said.

"And each of those who are working together to supply the clay has been assigned a single window; only to this window may he bring and deposit his clay, and he is not to touch another window. If he should try to interfere and to open one that belongs to another, he is to be threatened with fire and scourging."

"Let him be so threatened."

"Now, then, see what happens next. Inside the house the craftsman goes around to all the windows and takes the clay that he finds in each and molds it individually. After molding each for several months, he gives back the finished product through the same window. Having this mandate, he must fashion the clay indiscriminately, even if someone acts wickedly and places clay in another's window. The clay has done nothing wrong; since it is guiltless, it must be molded and fashioned. But the person who put the clay into another's window contrary to the prescribed procedure should be punished as a damnable transgressor. The clay must not be blamed, but rather the man who acted so impiously. Because of his lack of self-control, he has secretly and violently taken and placed his clay in another's window."

"You have spoken the truth."

(5) "Well, then, now that I have provided this preamble, it is time for you, my wise friend, to apply this whole picture to our previous topic of conversation. The house is an image for the invisible process of our generation, and the entrance facing the mountains stands for the descent of souls from heaven and their entry into bodies. The windows refer to the female sex; and the craftsman represents the creative power of God that, under the cover of our procreative activities, as I have

said, makes use of nature and shapes human beings within us in an invisible way, fashioning garments for the souls. Those who supply the material of clay must refer to those of the male sex who, whenever they desire children, deposit their seed into the female channels in a natural manner, just as the men we have described placed their clay into the windows.

"The seed shares, so to speak, in the creative activity of God and, therefore, it must not be considered guilty of the impulses of unchastity. A craft always operates on the material submitted to it. Nothing should be regarded as evil in itself; it only becomes evil through the actions of those who use it. A thing that is used wisely and properly turns out to be good; if it is used wickedly or improperly, it turns out to be bad. Is it the iron that does wrong when—though it was discovered for the benefit of farming and crafts—it is sharpened and used by people to kill each other in battle? Is gold or silver or bronze or any part of the beneficent earth at fault, when people offend their Creator by ungratefully promoting the glittering idols made of these materials?

"And if someone should provide the craft of weaving with wool that has been stolen, the craft will work on the material submitted to it, since it is concerned only with one thing: whether the material receives the formation involved. It will reject nothing that is useful to it, since the stolen material, being inanimate, is not culpable. Therefore, the material should be worked with and fashioned, but the wicked thief should be punished. Thus those who injure marriages and destroy life's harmony, men whose insides are inflamed with madness and aroused to pursue adultery, should be tortured and punished. They cause disaster by stealing procreative embraces from other people's gardens, but the seed itself, like the wool, must be given form and life.

(6) "But there is no need to prolong the discussion with further examples. For nature could not have accomplished such a work in so little time without God's help. Who compacted the uncompacted nature of the bones? Who, for instance, caused the bone to solidify, when it is by nature liq-

uid? Who bound together the body's limbs with sinews so that they flex and relax as they turn at the joints? What God has mixed the body's fluids into the blood and then placed it as leaven into the soft flesh that was taken from the earth? Who but the Master Craftsman, who has fashioned us, that is, humanity, to be his rational, living images, molding us like wax in the womb out of moist and tiny seeds? Who is it whose providence ensures that the embryo is not suffocated when it is deluged with fluids and pressed within the confines of the narrow blood vessels? After the child has been delivered and brought into the light, who transforms it from a weak and tiny thing into something tall, beautiful, and strong? Who but the Master Craftsman, as I said, God, who by his creative power refashions and remodels the forms in Christ?

"That is why we have been taught by the divinely inspired Scriptures that all infants are entrusted to guardian angels, even those conceived in adultery.[14] If their existence were contrary to the will and ordinance of that blessed nature of God, how could they be entrusted to angels to be raised with great gentleness and care? How could they accuse their own parents, confidently summoning them to the judgment seat of Christ and saying, 'You, O Lord, did not deny us this common light. But these are the ones who exposed us to death, despising your commandment?' For Scripture says: *Children born of illicit unions will be witnesses against their parents' wickedness at the judgment.*[15]

(7) "Now, if you were speaking to uncritical and imprudent men, you could perhaps argue persuasively that the fleshly garment of the soul, which is implanted by human beings acting on their own, is formed in opposition to God's decree. But no one would believe you, if you taught that the essence of the soul is sown together with the mortal body. Only the Almighty can infuse what is immortal and ageless, since he alone is the maker of what is invisible and imperish-

14. Cf. Matt 18:10.
15. Wis 4:6.

able. As Scripture says: *He breathed into his face the breath of life, and man became a living being.*[16] See how the Logos blames those craftsmen who forget their own Creator and fashion idols in human form that defile humanity. Speaking in that most excellent book of Wisdom, he says: *Their heart is ashes, and their hope less substantial than the earth. Their life is more worthless than clay, since they do not know the one who made them, the one who breathed into them the soul that works within them, the one who implanted in them a living spirit.*[17] Thus God is the Creator of all human beings. Hence, too, as the apostle says: *He wishes all humankind to be saved and to come to knowledge of the truth.*[18]

"Now, since we have almost come to the end, one further point must be discussed. If anyone makes a thorough examination of human affairs, he will learn not to despise procreation, even while praising and giving greater honor to chastity (*hagneia*). Although honey is sweeter and more appealing than any other food, it would not be right to regard everything else as bitter, such as foods that possess natural sweetness like fruit. To support what I have said, I will present Paul as a witness: *The person who marries his virgin,* he says, *does right, and the one who does not marry does better.*[19] Surely, by presenting the better and sweeter way, the Logos did not intend to criticize or to forbid the other way, but rather to rank them, assigning to each its particular characteristic and advantage.

"To some people he has not yet granted that they should achieve virginity; for others, he wishes that they no longer defile themselves, growing red with stimulations, but rather strive henceforth to manifest the angelic transformation of the body, in which *they neither marry nor are given in marriage,*[20] according to the trustworthy oracles of the Lord. Not to

16. Gen 2:7.
17. Wis 15:10–11.
18. 1 Tim 2:4.
19. 1 Cor 7:38.
20. Matt 22:30.

everyone has the ability to be an immaculate *eunuch for the kingdom of heaven*[21] been entrusted, but only to those who are able to keep the blossom of virginity ever fresh and undefiled. The prophetic Logos is able to compare the church to a bright and multicolored meadow, adorned and decked out not only with the blossoms of chastity, but also with those of childbearing and of continence. For *on the right hand of the Bridegroom stands the queen, adorned in gold and embroidered garments.*[22] This, Arete, is what I am able to contribute to our discussion of chastity."

21. Cf. Matt 19:12.
22. Ps 45:9, 13.

10.

Lactantius

The life of Lucius Caelius Firmianus Lactantius (the "Christian Cicero") spanned the last half of the third century and the opening decades of the fourth (ca. 250–326). Born in North Africa, he was a brilliant orator who held a chair in Latin rhetoric at Nicomedia during the reign of the emperor Diocletian (284–304). Driven into exile during Diocletian's persecution, Lactantius eventually acquired the patronage of the emperor Constantine, who in the year 317 enlisted the aged orator to tutor his son Crispus.

The *Divine Institutes* is the earliest attempt at a Latin *summa* of Christian theology. It was begun about the year 304 and completed sometime before 313. Cast as an apology in seven books, the work aims both to refute non-Christian notions of the gods and to demonstrate the truth of Christianity. Book 6, from which the extract translated here is taken, deals with the true worship to be offered to God (*religio*) and the proper relations owed to fellow human beings (*humanitas*). Much of book 6 treats the passions and the senses, and Lactantius's discussion of marriage occurs within his discussion of the sense of touch.

Lactantius focuses on sexual desire (*libido*), which he considers a God-given capacity, but one liable to be distorted by the devil (6.23). Lactantius regards sexual relations as given solely for procreation, and the enjoyment of pleasure as legitimate when it accompanies the proper use of sex. All sexual relations outside marriage are to be condemned, and adultery is considered blameworthy in both men and women. Lactantius concludes his discussion by acknowledging that complete chastity is "the peak and summit of all virtues," although he points out that it is no requirement.

DIVINE INSTITUTES, BOOK 6

(23) I come now to that pleasure which is experienced through touch, which is a sense of the whole body. But I think that I should speak not about cosmetics or clothes, but only about sexual desire (*libido*). That desire must be controlled with the greatest diligence, since it does the greatest harm.

When God had formulated the plan of the two sexes, he instilled in them the desire for each other along with delight in intercourse. He therefore mixed into the bodies of all living things a most ardent desire, so that they would rush with the greatest zeal into those affections and thereby be able to procreate and multiply their species. This desire and longing appears to be sharper and more vehement in human beings, either because God wished human beings to be greater in number or because only to human beings did God grant virtue, so that they might receive praise and glory for controlling the pleasures and practicing abstinence.

Our adversary knows, then, how great is the power of this desire, which some prefer to call "necessity," and he causes it to change from something right and good to something evil and depraved. For he instills illicit desires, so that the foreign desires contaminate the proper ones that are themselves sinless. He presents titillating images to the eyes and offers kindling and nourishment to vices. Then, in the very depths of the person, he stirs up and sets in motion every kind of stimulation; he incites and inflames that natural ardor, until he has deceived the person who is caught in his net. To ensure that no one would abstain even from a stranger out of fear of punishment, he established houses of prostitution and made public the shame of unfortunate women, so that he might have a good laugh both at the men who do this and at the women who must suffer it.

He took souls that were born for holiness and drowned them in these obscenities, as if in a pool of filth; he extinguished shame and castigated modesty. He even joined males to males and invented wicked forms of intercourse that violate nature and God's order. In this way he trained the human race and armed it for every crime. What can be holy to those who have submitted the tender and vulnerable age of youth to be pillaged and defiled by their lust? Because of its magnitude this crime can be described no further. I can call them nothing more than impious parricides, these men who are not content with the sex that God has given them, but who also take unholy and wanton pleasure in their own sex.

Yet these men consider it an insignificant thing, or even something honorable. What can I say about those who indulge this abominable desire, or rather, this madness? I am ashamed to speak, but what should we believe will happen to those who are not ashamed to act this way? And yet, we must speak, since it happens. I am referring to those whose most shameful lust and execrable madness does not spare even the head! With what words or with what indignation shall I prosecute such a crime as this? The magnitude of this offense surpasses my ability to describe it!

So, then, whenever desire (*libido*) brings forth these works and conceives these crimes, we must fortify ourselves against it with the greatest virtue. If someone cannot restrain these impulses, he should control them within the prescribed limit of a legitimate marriage. In this way he will attain what he eagerly desires and yet not fall into sin. For why is it that people wish to be destroyed? Certainly pleasure is a consequence of honorable works; if they seek it properly, they are permitted to enjoy right and legitimate pleasure.

But if some necessity prevents it, then the greatest virtue must be exercised so that lust (*cupiditas*) may be restrained by continence. Not only is it forbidden to touch another person's spouse, but God even enjoins and teaches us to abstain from bodies that have been made public and common.[1] When two bodies have been joined together, they make one body.[2] So anyone who immerses himself in filth necessarily becomes covered with filth. Although a body can be quickly washed, a mind that has been defiled by the pollution of an impure body cannot be purged of the filth that clings to it, except by the application of good works over a long period of time.

It is necessary, therefore, that each person recognize that the union of the two sexes has been given to living creatures for the sake of procreation and that this law has been imposed on these desires to produce a succession. Just as God did not give us eyes so that we may gaze at and grasp at pleasure, but rather so that we may see and thereby do what is necessary to live, so also we have received that part of the body called the genitals, for no other reason than to generate offspring, as the very name teaches us.[3] We must obey this divine law with the utmost devotion. All who profess that they are disciples of God should be so raised and educated that they are able to control themselves. Those who indulge in pleasure, who yield to lust, subject the soul to the body and condemn it to death, for they have enslaved themselves to the body, in which death has power.

Each person, then, to the best of his ability should train himself in modesty, cultivate chastity, and guard purity with the conscience and mind. The person who follows God's law should not only obey public law but should be above all laws. If he becomes accustomed to these goods, he will be ashamed to deviate to worse things. Only right and honorable things

---

1. Lactantius refers here to public prostitution, which was common in the ancient world.

2. Cf. 1 Cor 6:16.

3. Lactantius notes that the *genitalem corporis partem* is so called because *genitalis* derives from the Latin verb *gigno*, "to give birth."

should give pleasure, for these are more pleasing to the better people than wicked and ignoble things are to the worse people.

I have not yet gone through all the duties of chastity that God has limited not merely to the confines of the private home but even to the marriage bed. In other words, the man who has a wife may not wish to have a mistress, either slave or free, and he must keep the marriage contract (*fides*). For it is not the case, as happens in public law, that only the woman who has taken another lover is guilty of adultery, whereas the husband is free of the charge of adultery, even if he has several concubines.[4] No, divine law joins the two under equal legal obligation into matrimony, that is, into one body, in such a way that either partner who divides the unity of the body is considered an adulterer.

It was for this reason that God made the woman, alone of all the animals, submit to her husband, although he willed that the other female animals should retreat from the males after conceiving a fetus. This was done so that desire would not force the men to look elsewhere, if their wives rejected them, and thus forfeit the glory of chastity. Furthermore, the woman would not achieve the virtue of purity, if she were unable to sin. For who would say that a dumb animal is chaste, when it rejects the male after conceiving a fetus? The animal does this because it will experience pain and danger if it allows penetration. There is no praise in not doing what you are unable to do. That is why people are praised for purity, because it is not natural but voluntary.

So, then, both partners must keep the marriage contract (*fides*); in fact, the husband's example of continence should teach the wife to act chastely. For it is wicked to demand what you are not able yourself to provide. This wickedness no doubt has produced adulteries by creating ill will in women who themselves kept faith, while their husbands did not show reciprocal charity. Finally, no adulteress is so

---

4. Roman law defined adultery as any extramarital sex by or with a married woman. Extramarital sex by men was not considered adultery.

shameless that she does not offer this excuse for her vices: that by sinning she is not inflicting an injury, but rather repaying one. Quintilian expressed this very well when he said, "A man who does not keep away from another's marriage also neglects his own."[5] By nature the two things are connected. A man who is busy seducing other men's wives has no time to attend to the sanctity of his own home; and the woman who falls into such a marriage, being aroused by his example, believes that she should either imitate it or take revenge.

We must be careful, then, not to create occasions for vice by our intemperance. Rather, let the behavior of the two spouses begin to influence one another, let them bear the yoke with equal commitment. Let us imagine ourselves in the other's place. For this is virtually the summit of justice: not to do to another what you yourself do not wish to suffer from another.[6]

These are the commands that God has enjoined regarding continence. But in order that no one may believe that he can circumvent the divine precepts, the following are added to remove every occasion for evasion or deceit: whoever takes a wife who has been dismissed by another is an adulterer; so is he who dismisses his wife to take another, except for the crime of adultery.[7] God does not want the body to be divided and torn apart. Moreover, not only must adultery be avoided, but even the very thought of it, lest anyone see another's wife and desire her in the heart.[8] The mind becomes adulterous, if it even conjures up an image of that pleasure. Indeed, it is the mind that sins, when it embraces in thought the fruit of immoderate desire; in this consists every crime, every fault. Even if the body is not stained by any spot, the essence of purity will not be present, if the heart is defiled. Nor can chastity appear undiminished, when lust has defiled the conscience.

5. Quintilian (ca. 35–100 CE) was a prominent Roman orator, whose book, *Institutio Oratoria*, became a classic study of rhetorical theory and practice.

6. Cf. Tob 4:15; Matt 7:12.

7. Cf. Matt 19:9.

8. Cf. Matt 5:28.

Nevertheless, no one should consider it difficult to rein in pleasure and to enclose its errant, wandering ways within the bounds of chastity and purity, since human beings have been challenged to conquer it and since many people have kept the integrity of their body in blessed incorruption. For there are many people who enjoy this heavenly way of life in the greatest happiness. Now God does not command that this be done, as if it were an obligation, since it is necessary that human beings be created, but he allows it. For he knows what a great constraint he has placed upon the emotions. If anyone can do this, he said, he will receive a great and incomparable reward.[9]

This type of continence is the peak and summit, as it were, of all virtues. If someone is able to struggle and ascend to it, the Lord will acknowledge him as his servant, the Master will recognize his disciple. He will triumph over the earth; he will be like God by seizing the virtue of God. Certainly, these things appear to be difficult, but we are speaking about a person for whom a path to heaven is being prepared by the trampling underfoot of earthly things. Since virtue consists in the knowledge of God, all things are difficult as long as you are ignorant, but they are easy when you have gained this knowledge. These are the difficulties we must undergo, as we head toward the highest good.

9. 1 Cor 7:7–8; Matt 19:12.

11.

John Chrysostom

Among the most prolific and most eloquent preachers of the patristic era, John Chrysostom was born and raised a Christian (ca. 349) in the city of Antioch. After a brief attempt to live an ascetic life on Mt. Silpios near Antioch, Chrysostom returned to the city and entered the clergy, eventually receiving ordination as deacon and presbyter. Trained in classical oratory by Libanius, the famous pagan sophist of Antioch, Chrysostom became an extraordinarily successful preacher. Eventually recruited to be bishop of Constantinople, he ended his life in exile as a result of conflicts with the empress Eudocia.

Homily 20 on Ephesians, which is translated here, is an excellent example of Chrysostom's attempt to Christianize the marital mores of Antiochene men. Oddly, the sermon is addressed only to men, although a high proportion of his congregation probably were women. The reading of the day is from Ephesians 5:22–33, and the image of man and woman as "one flesh," together with the notion of the marriage of Christ and the church, shape Chrysostom's discussion at every point. Although he endorses the Pauline injunction that wives should submit to their husbands, Chrysostom places a much greater emphasis on the love that husbands must show to their wives.

But Chrysostom's main aim in the sermon is to urge the husband to impose a quasi-ascetic regimen on his wife and household, particularly in respect to money. Here Chrysostom evidences little of the mistrust of human sexuality that characterizes so much of the Christian literature of this period (and that characterized Chrysostom's own early writings). On the contrary, Chrysostom speaks of the desire (*erōs*) that draws two human beings together as the creation of God and as the highest form of human love. Rather than emphasizing sexual asceticism, Chrysostom focuses on the problem of attachment to money. By doing so, he is able to promote an ascetic ideal of marriage that does not destroy marriage itself: by renouncing wealth, he writes, the Christian couple can approach even the ascetic virtue of the monk.

HOMILY 20 ON EPHESIANS

(1) A certain wise man who was compiling a list of blessings numbered this one among them: *A wife who agrees with her husband.*[1] In another place he listed as a blessing that a wife should live in harmony with her husband.[2] Indeed, from the very beginning God seems to have shown a special concern for this union. Speaking of the two as if they were one, he said: *Male and female he created them.*[3] And, in another place: *There is neither male nor female.*[4] For no relationship between two men is as close as that between a man and a woman, if they are joined together as they should be. When another blessed man wished to describe the highest form of love, as he was grieving over someone who was dear to him and, so to speak, one soul with him, he did not mention father, or

1. Sir 25:1.
2. Cf. Sir 40:23.
3. Gen 1:27.
4. Gal 3:28.

mother, or child, or brother, or friend. No, he said: *Your love to me was wonderful, more wonderful than that of women.*[5]

Truly, this love is more tyrannical than any tyrant. Other passions may be strong; this passion is not only strong but also imperishable. For deeply implanted in our nature there is a certain desire (*erōs*) that, without our noticing it, knits together these bodies of ours. That is why from the beginning woman came from man, and later man and woman came from man and woman. Do you see the bond and the connection, and how God did not allow any other substance from the outside to come between them? Notice how many providential arrangements he has made. The man was allowed to marry his own sister; or rather, not his sister but his daughter; no, not his daughter but rather something more than his daughter, his very own flesh. From the beginning God constructed the whole edifice, like a building made of stones, gathering them together into one. On the one hand, he did not create the woman apart from the man, lest the man regard her as something alien to himself. Nor, on the other hand, did he restrict marriage solely to the woman, lest by withdrawing and turning in on herself, she should be cut off from the rest.

Consider the case of plants: the best ones are those that have one stem that spreads out into many branches. If the branches were placed only around the root, they would all be superfluous; but if the tree had many roots, it would no longer be something marvelous to see. It is the same in this case. God made the entire race to grow from one, that is, from Adam, and he imposed the greatest restrictions to prevent it from being separated or divided. And making even further restrictions, no longer did he allow men to take their sisters and daughters as wives; this was done so that we might not restrict our love to one point and thereby be cut off from each other. That is why he said: *In the beginning the Creator made them male and female.*[6]

5. 2 Sam 1:26.
6. Matt 19:4.

Great evils are produced from this, as well as great benefits, both for households and cities. For nothing so welds our lives together as the love of man and woman. For the sake of love, many will lay aside even their weapons; for the sake of love, many will even give their lives. It was not without good reason that Paul showed so much concern about this matter when he said: *Wives, be submissive to your husbands, as to the Lord.*[7] Why is this? Because if they are in harmony, the children will be brought up well, the household will be properly ordered, and neighbors, friends, and relatives will enjoy the sweet fragrance. But if the opposite happens, everything will be turned upside down and thrown into confusion. When the leaders of an army are at peace with each other, everything goes according to plan; but if they are at odds, all will be chaos. So it is in this case. That is why he says: *Wives, be submissive to your husbands, as to the Lord.*[8]

How strange! Why does he say in another place: *If a person does not reject wife and husband, he cannot be my disciple?*[9] If it is necessary to be subject to a husband *as to the Lord,* why does he say that the husband must be rejected because of the Lord? The duty of submission is clear, but the word *as* should not be taken to mean that there is an equivalence of honor at all times and in every way. He could mean *as* in the sense of "knowing that you are serving the Lord." This is what he says elsewhere,[10] meaning that a woman should do for the sake of the Lord what she would not do for the sake of her husband. But he may mean, "When you obey your husband, know that in doing so you are serving the Lord." For if *the person who resists these external authorities resists what God has established,*[11] how much more so does this apply to the woman who does not submit to her husband! From the beginning God ordained it to be this way, he says. Therefore, let us take

7. Eph 5:22.
8. Eph 5:22.
9. Luke 14:26.
10. Cf. Eph 6:7, where Paul is speaking of slavery.
11. Rom 13:2.

it as a basic principle that the husband occupies the position of "head" and the woman the position of "body."

Then Paul offers these arguments: *For the husband is head of the wife,* he says, *just as Christ is head of the church and savior of his body. But just as the church is subject to Christ, so too wives must be subject to their husbands in everything.*[12] Notice how, after saying *the husband is head of the wife, just as Christ is head of the church,* he adds the words *and savior of his body.* For the head of the body is also its salvation. He had already laid down for the man and the woman the underlying reason and purpose of their love, assigning to each their proper place, to the husband the duty to lead and provide, to the woman the duty to obey.

(2) *Just as the church is subject to Christ* (that is, husbands and wives), *so too wives must be subject to their husbands as to God. Husbands, love your wives, as Christ has loved the church.*[13] You have heard the highest form of subjection. You have praised and marveled at Paul, such an amazing and spiritual man, because he has welded all our lives together. That is fine. But now hear what he demands of you, for he repeats the same example. *Husbands,* he says, *love your wives, as Christ has loved the church.* You have seen the measure of obedience; now hear the measure of love. Would you like your wife to obey you, as the church obeys Christ? Then you must care for her, as Christ does for the church. Even if it is necessary to give your life for her, even if you must be cut into a thousand pieces, even if you must endure any suffering whatever, do not refuse it.

Even if you do suffer like this, you will never suffer as much as Christ did. For you are doing it for one with whom you are already joined, but he did it for one who rejected him and hated him. Just as he took the one who had rejected him and hated him and spat on him and despised him, and laid her at his feet, not with threats or violence or fear or anything like that, but with great kindness, so you must behave in a

12. Eph 5:23–24.
13. Eph 5:24–25.

similar way toward your wife. Even if you see her looking down on you and despising you and holding you in disdain, you will be able to lay her at your feet by showing great care and love and affection for her. For nothing has greater power than these bonds, especially between husband and wife.

You may be able to restrain a servant by fear; no, not even a servant, for he will soon be off and away. But she who is your life's partner, the mother of your children, the very reason for your happiness, she must not be restrained by fear and threats, but by love and a gentle disposition. What sort of union is it, when the wife trembles before her husband? What sort of pleasure will the husband himself enjoy, if he lives with a wife who is more a slave than a free woman? Even if you suffer in some ways because of her, do not criticize her, for Christ has done nothing of the sort.

And he gave himself up for her, Paul says, *to make her holy, cleansing her.*[14] So, then, she was unclean, she had flaws, she was ugly, she was worthless. Whatever kind of wife you take, you will never take a bride like the one Christ took when he took the church; you will never have one so far removed from you as the church was from Christ. Yet he did not abhor or detest her because of her great ugliness. Would you like to hear about her ugliness? Listen to what Paul says: *For once you were darkness.*[15] Do you see her blackness? What is blacker than darkness? Notice also her arrogance: *living in malice and envy,* he says. And see her impurity: *disobedient and foolish.*[16] What is my point? Although she was foolish and slanderous, although such things were true, yet he gave himself up for her in her ugliness, as if she were beautiful, as if she were deeply lovable, as if she were something admirable. Paul spoke in admiration of this when he said: *Rarely will someone die for a righteous man,*[17] and *When we were still sinners Christ died for*

14. Eph 5:26.
15. Eph 5:8.
16. Titus 3:3.
17. Rom 5:7.

us.[18] Christ took her, adorned her, washed her, and did not refuse even this.

To make her holy, Paul says, *cleansing her by the washing of water in the word, to present her to himself as a radiant church, without stain or wrinkle or any other blemish, that she may be holy and spotless.*[19] He washes her impurity by the washing in the word, he says. What word? *In the name of the Father and of the Son and of the Holy Spirit.*[20] He has not adorned her in a simple way, but he has made her radiant. *Without stain or wrinkle or any other blemish.* We, too, should strive for this beauty and we will be able to create it ourselves. Do not seek from your wife that which is not hers. Know that the church has received everything from the Master. From him comes her splendor, from him her spotlessness. Do not reject your wife because of her ugliness. Hear what Scripture says: *The bee is the smallest of the flying creatures, but its fruit is the sweetest.*[21] She is God's creation; you are not criticizing her, but the one who made her. Why should the wife suffer?

Do not praise her for her beauty. That sort of praise and hatred and even love is typical of intemperate souls. You should seek after the beauty of the soul. Imitate the Bridegroom of the church. External beauty is full of arrogance and foolishness; it leads to jealousy and often makes you suspect that something foul is afoot. Perhaps external beauty gives pleasure? For the first month or two, or at most for one year, but no longer. After a while, familiarity will cause your interest to wane. Yet the evils bred by her beauty will remain: the vanity, foolishness, and contempt. But if your love is not based on that sort of beauty, this will not happen. If love has begun properly, that is, if it is love of the soul's beauty and not of the body's, it will remain strong.

(3) Tell me, what is better than heaven? What is better than the stars? No body you could describe is so luminous. No

18. Rom 5:8.
19. Eph 5:26–27.
20. Matt 28:19.
21. Sir 11:3.

eyes you could describe are so bright. When the stars were created, even the angels marveled, and now we marvel, but not as much as we did at first. This is the result of familiarity; things no longer strike us as they once did. How much more is this the case when it comes to wives. If disease approaches as well, everything takes flight. Let us look for kindness in a wife, and moderation and modesty. These are the true marks of beauty. We should not look for physical beauty; we should not blame her for what is beyond her control. In fact, we should not blame her at all, for that is arrogant. Nor should we be critical or ill-tempered. Do you not see how many men have lived with beautiful women, only to end their lives in misery? And how many, who have lived with women of no great beauty, have arrived at a ripe old age with great pleasure?

We should wipe away the stain that is within, we should smooth out the inner wrinkles, we should eliminate blemishes of the soul. This is the beauty that God seeks. We should make her beautiful for God, not for ourselves. Let us not seek money, or noble birth in the external sense, but noble birth in the soul. No one should expect to get rich from a wife, for that kind of wealth is base and disgraceful. By no means should anyone seek to grow rich in this way. *People who want to get rich*, he says, *fall into temptation and into useless and harmful desires, and into snares and ruin and destruction.*[22] So, then, do not seek an abundance of wealth from a wife, and you will find that all will go well for you.

Who, tell me, would abandon more important business to attend to lesser matters? But this, I fear, is what we do all the time. If we have a son, we do not concern ourselves with his becoming good, but with getting him a wealthy wife. Our aim is that he should thrive not in morals but in money. If we are engaged in business, our overwhelming concern is not how to avoid sin but how to turn a huge profit. Everything has become money! Everything has become corrupted because that passion possesses us!

22. 1 Tim 6:9.

In this way, he says, *husbands ought to love their wives, as their own bodies.*[23] What does this mean? He has now arrived at a better analogy and a more forceful example. And not only that, but it is another justification, one that is both nearer to us and clearer. The prior example was not very compelling, since someone could say, "That was Christ, and he was God, and he gave himself." From another perspective he deals with the same point, saying: *In this way husbands ought*, for it is not a matter of grace, but of obligation. He said: *as their own bodies*, and then added: *For no one hates his own flesh, but he nourishes it and cherishes it.*[24] That is to say, he cares for it with great devotion. How is she his flesh? Listen: *This now is bone of my bone,* he says, *and flesh of my flesh.*[25] Not only that, but also this: *They will be two in one flesh,*[26] for in this way did Christ love the church.[27]

***

(4) Just as the Son of God took our nature, so we share in his substance. Just as he holds us in himself, so we, too, hold him in us. *For this reason a man will leave his father and mother and be united to his wife, and they will be two in one flesh.*[28] Here is a third type of argument. He is showing that the person who has left those who begot him and nourished him will be joined to his wife. Then the *one flesh* is the father, the mother, and the child that is conceived from their intercourse. For the child is formed when the seeds mingle together; in this way they are three in *one flesh*. Similarly, we become one flesh with Christ by participation, and in an even greater way than the human child. How is this? Because it was this way from the beginning.

Do not tell me that things are this way or that. Do you not see that we have in our flesh many defects? One person

23. Eph 5:28.
24. Eph 5:29.
25. Gen 2:23.
26. Gen 2:24.
27. Cf. Eph 5:25.
28. Gen 2:24; Eph 5:31.

is lame, another has twisted feet, another withered hands, and another some other weakened limb. Yet he does not grieve about it or cut it off; in fact, often he values the defective part more highly than the other, and rightly so, because it is his own. The apostle wants each man to have as much love for his wife as he has for himself. It is not because we share one nature; no, the responsibility toward a wife is greater than that. It is because they are no longer two bodies, but one; he is the head and she is the body. And what did he mean in that other passage: *But the head of Christ is God?*[29] I would say that this means that just as we are one body, so too Christ and the Father are one. Therefore, the Father is also found to be our head. He gives us two examples, then, that of the body and that of Christ.

Then he adds: *This is a great mystery, but I am speaking of Christ and the church.*[30] What is this? He calls it a great mystery because it was a great and marvelous mystery that blessed Moses (or, rather, God) had signified. But, for the moment, he says, *I am speaking of Christ,* because he, too, left his Father and came down and took a bride and became one spirit with her. *The person who is joined to the Lord is one spirit.*[31] He does well to call it a great mystery, as if to say, "The allegory does not destroy the love." However, each of you also must love his own wife as he loves himself, and the wife must fear her husband.[32]

Truly, truly, it is a mystery, and a great mystery that a man should leave the father who begat him, who gave him birth, who raised him, and the mother who went through labor for him, the parents who provided him with such benefits and who lived in such intimacy with him, that he should be joined to someone whom he has never seen, with whom he has nothing in common, and that he should honor her above all others. Truly, it is a mystery! And the parents are not upset when this happens, but only when it does not hap-

29. 1 Cor 11:3.
30. Eph 5:32.
31. 1 Cor 6:17.
32. Eph 5:33.

pen, and they are delighted to spend vast sums of money on this. Truly, it is a great mystery, but one that contains some ineffable wisdom. From the beginning Moses revealed this in prophecy, and now Paul proclaims it in these words: *I am speaking of Christ and the church.*[33]

But he is not speaking only for the sake of the husband, but also for the wife, so that he might cherish her, just as Christ does the church. *And the wife must fear her husband.*[34] No longer is he speaking only about love, but about another duty. *She must fear her husband.* The wife is a second authority. Therefore, she must not demand equality, for she is under a head. But the husband must not despise her because she is subordinate. For she is the body, and if the head despises the body, it too will perish. Rather, he must balance her obedience with his love. As the head does, so should the body. The body should offer its hands, feet, and all its other members for service to the head, but the head should care for the body, since it has in itself all sense perception. Nothing is better than a union such as this!

How can there be love, you ask, where there is fear? But it is especially there that you will find it. For she who fears also loves. She who loves fears him as her head, but loves him as a member, since the head is also a member of the whole body. That is why the woman is placed in submission and the man in charge, so that there may be peace. Where there is equality of honor, there can never be peace; nor can a household be a democracy or a place where all are leaders, but there must be a single authority. This is always the case in matters that pertain to the body. For if men were spiritual, there would be peace. There were five thousand souls, and *not one of them claimed that any of his possessions was his own,*[35] but they were subject to one another. This is an example of wisdom and fear of God. He has shown how love behaves, but not yet how fear behaves.

33. Eph 5:32.
34. Eph 5:33. The word for "fear" found in Eph 5:33 could also mean "profound respect" or "reverence."
35. Acts 4:32.

(5) See how Paul expands on the topic of love, when he speaks about Christ and about his own flesh: *For this reason a man will leave his father and mother.*[36] He does not yet say anything about fear. Why not? Because he prefers that the principle of love prevail. Where there is love, everything else follows. Where there is fear, this is by no means the case. The man who loves his wife, even if she is not very obedient, will nevertheless endure it all. Harmony is so unmanageable and difficult to attain when the partners are not bound together by the tyranny of love. Certainly, fear can do nothing to rectify the situation. That is why Paul prefers to dwell on that which is the stronger bond. Moreover, the wife, who seems to be the loser because she is ordered to fear, actually gains, because the husband is given the more important command, to love.

But what if the wife does not fear, you ask? Love her, fulfill your duty. Even if others do not do their part, we must still do ours. This is what I mean: *Submit to one another,* he says, *in the fear of Christ.*[37] What if the other person does not submit? You must still obey God's law. The same rule applies in this case. Even if she is not loved, the wife must fear, so that she does all that is required of her. Even if his wife does not fear him, the husband must still love her, so that he does not fall short in any respect. Both have received their own tasks.

This, then, is a marriage that is according to Christ, a spiritual marriage and spiritual procreation, not one in blood and the pain of labor. Such was the birth of Isaac, as Scripture describes it: *It had ceased to be with Sarah after the manner of women.*[38] This is a marriage, not of passion and of bodies, but one that is entirely spiritual, when the soul is united to God in an ineffable union, which he alone knows. That is why Paul says: *The person who is united to the Lord is one spirit.*[39] See how eager he is to unite flesh to flesh and spirit to spirit.

36. Eph 5:31.
37. Eph 5:21.
38. Gen 18:11.
39. 1 Cor 6:17.

Where are the heretics? If marriage is to be condemned, surely he would not have called Christ a bridegroom and the church a bride. Nor would he have proclaimed by way of exhortation: *A man will leave his father and mother,* and then have added: *I am speaking of Christ and the church.*[40] Even the psalmist speaks about the bride: *Listen, O daughter, consider and give ear. Forget your people and your father's house. The king desires your beauty.*[41] That is why Christ said: *I have gone forth from the Father and I have come.*[42] But when I say that he went forth from the Father, do not think that he changed places in the way humans do. He is said to have gone forth, not in the sense of departing, but in reference to the incarnation; this is what is meant by his going forth from the Father.

Why did he not say that the wife "will be joined to her husband"? Why? Because he was speaking about love and was addressing the husband. To the wife he spoke about fear, when he said: *The husband is head of the wife and Christ is head of the church.*[43] He addressed the husband on the topic of love and he entrusted to the husband the duties of love. He spoke loudly and clearly to the husband regarding love, in order to unite and bind the man to the woman. If a man should leave his father because of his wife and then leave his wife and abandon her, would he deserve any pardon? Do you not see how much honor God wishes her to enjoy, when you leave your father to be joined to her?

"But what if we do our part," you say, "and still she does not follow?" *If the unbeliever leaves, let him leave. The brother or sister is not bound in such cases.*[44] But whenever you hear of fear, you should demand the fear that is proper to a free woman, not what you would expect from a slave. For she is your body; if you treat her improperly, you abuse yourself and dishonor your own body. What kind of fear is appropriate? If she does not contradict you, if she does not rebel,

40. Eph 5:31–32.
41. Ps 45:10–11.
42. John 16:28.
43. Eph 5:23.
44. 1 Cor 7:15.

if she does not desire to be in charge, this is sufficient fear. But if you love her, as you have been ordered to do, you will produce something even better. No longer will you produce it by fear, but rather love itself will have its effect. The human race is somewhat weak; it requires much help and much indulgence.

What will those who have contracted second marriages say? I will not condemn them, far from it! For the apostle himself allows it, though only by way of concession.[45] Provide everything for her, do everything for her, suffer every hardship. This is required of you. In this case Paul does not think it is right to offer advice by means of external examples, as he often does. The example of Christ is great and forceful enough, especially on the question of subjection: *He will leave his father and mother.* See, this is an external example. He does not say, "And he will live with his wife," but *he will be joined to her,* in order to show a complete union and an intense love. Not content with this, he goes on to explain the subjection in such a way that the two no longer appear to be two. He does not say that they will be "one spirit," nor does he say that they will be "one soul," for obviously that sort of union is possible for anyone. Rather, he says: *They will be one flesh.*[46]

(6) The wife is a second authority; she has authority and honor equal to the husband's in many respects. But the husband has something more. His special concern is the well-being of the household. This responsibility, which he received from Christ, requires not only that the husband love his wife but also that he govern her. *So that she may,* he says, *be holy and spotless.*[47] But the word *flesh* refers to love, and the words *he will be joined to her* likewise refer to love. For if you make her *holy and spotless,* everything else will follow. Seek what is God's, and what is human will follow with great ease. Govern your wife, and your household will thus be put in order. Listen to what Paul says: *If they want to know something,*

45. Cf. 1 Cor 7:6.
46. Eph 5:31.
47. Eph 5:27.

they should ask their husbands at home.[48] If we administer our
own households in this way, we will be suitable also to govern the church. For the household is a little church. In this
way it is possible for those who are good husbands and wives
to surpass all others.

Consider Abraham, Sarah, Isaac, and the 318 born in his
household.[49] Consider how the entire household was well-
ordered, how it was full of devotion. Sarah fulfilled the apostolic injunction and feared her husband. Listen to what she
says: *Until now it has not yet happened to me, and my lord is
old as well.*[50] And Abraham loved her so much that he obeyed
all her commands.[51] Their child was virtuous, and even their
household slaves were so admirable that they did not refuse to
undergo danger with their master. They did not hesitate or
ask why. One of them, the chief servant, was so remarkable
that he was entrusted with the task of travelling a great distance to arrange a marriage for the only son.[52] When a general has his soldiers well organized, the enemy can make no
incursion.

It is the same in this case. When the husband, wife, children, and household servants are intent on the same things,
there is great harmony in the household. Where this does not
happen, the entire household is often overturned and dissi-
pated by one wicked servant; one person will often destroy
and corrupt the whole. Therefore, let us take great care of our
wives and children and servants, knowing that we will make
the task of governing them easier and that we will not be subject to a strict accounting when we say: *Here I am and the children that God has given me.*[53] If a man is an admirable husband
and a good head, the rest of the body will suffer no harm.

Paul has now stated precisely what is the proper behavior
for a wife and for a husband; he has exhorted the woman to

48. 1 Cor 14:35.
49. Cf. Gen 14:14.
50. Gen 18:12.
51. Cf. Gen 21:12.
52. Cf. Gen 24.
53. Isa 8:18.

fear her husband as the head and the husband to love her as a wife. But how can all of this be realized, you may ask? He has shown what ought to be done, but now I will tell you how it can be done. If we despise money, if we look to one thing only, the virtue of the soul, if we keep the fear of God before our eyes. What Paul said to slaves is also relevant here: *The Lord will reward everyone for whatever good or evil he does.*[54] So, then, you should love your wife, not so much for her sake as for the sake of Christ. Paul indicated this when he said *as to the Lord.*[55] You should do all things *as to the Lord,* that is, for his sake. This should be enough to induce us and persuade us, and not to allow any mocking and dissension.

Do not believe anyone who slanders a husband to his wife. A husband should not believe any random accusations against his wife, nor should a wife be overly inquisitive about his comings and goings. In no case should a husband ever render himself worthy of suspicion. Why is it, tell me, that after spending the whole day with your friends and devoting the evening to your wife, you are still unable to ease her mind and free her of suspicion? Even if your wife accuses you, do not be angry. It is affection, not foolishness, that causes this; her complaints come from fervent affection, burning desire, and fear. She is afraid that someone might rob her marriage bed, that someone might harm her in respect to her most cherished goods, that someone might steal him who is her head, that someone might break into her marriage chamber.

There is yet another reason for petty quarreling. No one should make immoderate use of the servants, neither the husband with the maids, nor the wife with the male servants. This is the sort of behavior that creates suspicions. Consider the righteous ones whom I mentioned earlier. Sarah herself ordered the patriarch to take Hagar. She commanded him; no one forced her to, and he did not approach her himself. Although he had been childless for a long time, he preferred never to become a father rather than to cause grief to his wife.

54. Eph 6:8.
55. Eph 5:22.

Nevertheless, after all this, what did Sarah say to him? *May God judge between you and me.*[56]

Now, if he had been anyone else, would he not have become angry? Would he not have lifted his hands, as if to say, "What do you mean? I did not want to become involved with the woman. It was all your doing, and now you are blaming me!" But Abraham said nothing of the sort, but simply replied: *Your servant is in your hands. Do with her whatever you think best.*[57] He gave up the woman who shared his bed in order not to grieve Sarah, although nothing is more likely to produce benevolence than this. If sharing a meal produces unanimity even between robbers and their enemies (for the psalmist says: *He shared sweet food with me*[58]), how much more will the sharing of one flesh—for that is what it means to share a bed—be able to draw us together. None of this, however, was able to overcome the righteous one, but he gave Hagar up to his wife, showing that he was not at fault. And he did something even greater: he sent her forth when she was pregnant. Who would not have taken pity on a woman bearing his own child? Yet, the righteous man remained unmoved, for he valued the love of his wife more highly than everything else.

(7) We, too, should imitate this man. No one should reproach his neighbor's poverty; no one should lust for money; then everything will be at peace. A wife should not say to her husband, "You unmanly coward! You timid, sleepy dolt! I know a man from a low-class background, who has amassed a fortune by taking risks and travelling abroad. His wife wears gold and goes out on a pair of white mules. She rides everywhere, surrounded by a crowd of slaves and a swarm of eunuchs. But you stay put and live a useless life!" A wife should not say this or anything like this. For she is the body and she is not to give orders to the head, but to listen and obey.

---

56. Gen 16:5.
57. Gen 16:6.
58. Ps 55:14.

"But how will she bear poverty?" you ask. "Where will she find consolation?" She should associate with those who are poorer than she is, she should think about the great number of highborn and noble young women who not only have received nothing from their husbands, but who have even given away all that they have.[59] Let her reflect on the dangers that wealth produces and she will welcome a life free from such business. In a word, if she feels affection for her husband, she will say nothing of this sort. She will prefer to have him near her, without gaining a thing, than to have a thousand talents of gold along with the anxiety and worry that women inevitably experience when their husbands go on long journeys.

If the husband hears words like these, he should not resort to threats and violence because he is the authority. No, he should exhort and admonish her, as one who is less perfect than he. He should offer words of persuasion and never extend a hand in anger, for this sort of behavior is not appropriate for a free soul. There should be no threats or insults or abuse; rather, he should direct and guide her, since she has less wisdom than he. How will this be done? If she comes to know the true wealth, the heavenly philosophy,[60] she will make no complaints like that. The husband should teach her that poverty is not an evil; he should teach her not only by his words, but also by his deeds. He should teach her to despise glory, and the wife will neither speak about nor desire such things.

The husband should act like a man who has been entrusted with the care of a sacred image. From the very first evening that he receives her into the bridal chamber, he should teach her self-restraint, moderation, how to live a holy life, rejecting the desire for money at the very outset, as soon as she comes through the door. He should instruct her in philosophy and advise her not to have pieces of gold dangling

59. Chrysostom probably has in mind women who have given over their dowries to their husbands.

60. Chrysostom often refers to the ascetic life, and even Christianity itself, as the "true philosophy."

from her ears or down her cheeks or around her shoulders or strewn about the bedroom, nor should she have costly, golden clothing stored away. Let her be dressed elegantly, but the elegance should not degenerate into extravagance. Leave that sort of thing to the stage!

He should decorate the house with great propriety, so that it breathes temperance rather than perfume. Two, or even three, benefits will result from this. First, the bride will not be upset when the bridal chamber is opened and the clothes and the gold and silver vessels are returned to their proper owners. Second, the bridegroom will not have to worry about losing or protecting this pile of treasure. But the third and most important benefit is that the husband will be revealing his own attitude, showing that he takes pleasure in none of these things and that he will do away with all the rest. Nor will he show any tolerance at all for dances or indecent songs.

I know that I will appear ridiculous to some when I give this advice. But if you listen to me, as time goes on and as you reap the benefit of the practice, you will know the reward. The laughter will pass away, and you will laugh at what is now the custom. You will see that the current practice is the work of foolish children and drunken men. What I am urging is a work of moderation, philosophy, and a sublime way of life. What, then, do I say is necessary? Banish from marriage all those shameful and satanic songs, all those obscene odes, those bands of unchaste young people.[61] This will be enough to teach the bride moderation. Straightaway she will say to herself: "How wonderful! What a philosopher my husband is! He cares nothing for the present life. He has taken me into his house to bear and raise his children, to manage his household." Are these things distasteful to a bride? For the first or second day, but no longer than this. She will even derive the greatest pleasure from these activities and free herself from all suspicion. For the man who cannot endure either flute players or dancers or effeminate songs, even on his wed-

---

61. Chrysostom has in mind the erotic songs and plays that normally accompanied marriage rites in the Greco-Roman city.

ding day, will certainly never allow himself to do or say anything that is shameful.

Then, after you have removed all of this from the marriage,
take her and mold her well. Allow her modesty to last for a
long time, do not destroy it suddenly. For even if a young
woman is without shame, she knows that she should keep
silent for a time out of respect for her husband, while she is
still a stranger in the situation. You should not destroy this
show of reserve too soon, as intemperate husbands do, but
you should extend it for a long time. This will bring you a
great reward. Meanwhile, she will not criticize or complain
about any of the rules you set.

(8) Now, this is the time to lay down all your laws, while
modesty, like a bridle upon her soul, prevents her from criticizing or complaining about what you are doing. For when
she acquires confidence, she will overturn and disrupt everything without any fear at all. What better time is there to
mold a wife than when she is still respectful, reverent, and
timid in the presence of her husband? Then you should lay
all the laws upon her, and she will obey, willingly or unwillingly. How can you preserve her modesty? By showing that
you yourself are no less modest, by conversing with her in a
few words filled with all dignity and seriousness. Then you
should speak to her about philosophy, for her soul will be
receptive. You must establish in her that most beautiful disposition: I mean modesty.

But, if you wish, I will also provide you with an example
of how you should speak to her. If Paul was willing to say:
Do not deprive each other,[62] and to speak the words of a bridesmaid—no, not of a bridesmaid, but of a spiritual soul—then
we have all the more reason to speak this way ourselves.
What, then, should you say to her? With great kindness say to
her: "I have taken you, my child, to be the partner of my life,
and I have brought you in to share with me the most honorable and most necessary tasks, the bearing of my children and

---

62. 1 Cor 7:5.

the management of my household. What appeal, then, do I make to you?"

Better yet, speak to her first about love. Nothing is so effective at persuading someone to listen to what you say as the knowledge that the words are spoken with great love. How can you show this love? By saying, "I could have married many women who are richer than you, or from a noble family, but I chose not to. No, I was in love with you, and with your way of life, your decorum, your modesty, and your moderation." Then, immediately after this, you should prepare a path to speak about philosophy, and in a roundabout way you should denounce wealth. For if you hold a prolonged discourse directly against wealth, you will be tiresome. But if you mention it in passing, you will succeed. For you will appear to be doing it apologetically, not like someone who is austere, miserly, or petty. But if you take the opportunity to speak in reference to her, she will even be pleased.

Let us begin the speech again: "I could have married a wealthy, prosperous wife, but I could not bear it. Why not? Because I have been taught, quite properly and reasonably, that the possession of wealth is something to be despised, something that belongs to thieves, prostitutes, and grave robbers. That is why I have abandoned these things and approached the virtue of your soul, which I value more highly than gold. A young woman who is wise and free and devoted to piety is worth the whole world. That is why I have embraced you, that is why I love you and prefer you to my very own soul.

"The present life is nothing. I pray and beg and would do anything so that we may be counted worthy to live in the present life in such a way that we will also be able to be securely united to each other in the future life. Our time here is brief and fleeting. But if we are counted worthy to live this life in a manner pleasing to God, we will be together forever with Christ and with each other and we will enjoy even greater pleasure. I value your love more than anything; nothing is more bitter or painful to me than ever to be at odds with you. Even if I lose everything and become poorer than Irus,[63] even if I have to undergo the greatest dangers and all manner of suffering, I can endure anything, as long as your affection for me is secure. My children will be dear to me, as long as you feel kindly toward us. But you, too, must also do these things."

Then mix into the conversation the words of the apostle about how God wants us to have our affections united: "Listen to what Scripture says: *For this reason man will leave his father and mother and be joined to his wife.*[64] There should be no excuse for pettiness between us. Let us dispose of money and crowds of servants and outward honors. Your love is worth more to me than anything else."

What gold, what treasure will be more precious to a wife than these words? Do not be afraid that when she is loved she will turn away from you, but confess that you love her. Certainly concubines, who attach themselves to one man after another, would feel contempt for their lovers if they heard words like these. But a freeborn or noble young woman would never be puffed up by these words; no, she would be all the more won over by them. Show her how much you value her company by staying home with her rather than going out in the marketplace. Cherish her more than all your friends, more than the children born of her, and love the children for her sake. If she does anything good, praise and admire it. If she does something wrong, as young girls sometimes do, encourage her and give her advice. On every occasion you should denounce wealth and extravagance, show her the sort of beauty that comes from proper behavior and holiness, and constantly teach her what is profitable.

(9) You ought to pray together. Both should go to church, and at home the husband should ask the wife, and the wife should ask the husband, about what was said and read there. If you should experience poverty, call to mind the holy men

63. Cf. Homer, *Odyssey* 18.1–125.
64. Eph 5:31.

Paul and Peter, who were more highly esteemed than wealthy men or kings. Remember how they spent their lives in hunger and thirst. Teach her that there is nothing in this life to fear, except offending God. If you marry in this way and with these aims, you will be not much inferior to the monks; the married person will be not much less than the unmarried.

If you want to give dinner parties or banquets, there should be no disorderly or improper behavior. Rather, if you should find some poor, holy person who is able to bless your house, who is able to bestow all God's blessings simply by setting foot inside, invite him in. Let me add something else. None of you should be eager to marry a wealthy woman; choose instead someone much poorer. A wealthy wife actually causes more pain than pleasure by her wealth, because of the insults, because of her demands for more than she brought to the marriage, because of the arrogance and extravagance and vulgar language.

Perhaps she will say, "I have not yet spent any of your money. I am still wearing my own clothes, the ones my parents gave me." What are you saying, woman? Still wearing your own clothes? What could be more pitiful than such talk? You no longer have your own body and you have your own money? After marriage you are no longer two bodies, but you have become one. The two sets of possessions, are they not also one? Oh, the love of money! The two have become one person, one living being, and still you say "mine"? That word is a curse, a foul invention of the devil. God has created things to be shared that are much more important than money. Should not money also be shared? No one can say, "This is my light, or my sun, or my water." All the better things are shared. Should not money be shared as well? Let money perish a thousand times! Or, rather, not money itself, but the choices that people make, not knowing how to use money and valuing it above all things.

Teach her this along with everything else, but do so with great kindness. Since the very exhortation to virtue contains within itself much that is harsh, especially for a young and tender maiden, whenever you speak about philosophy you should be intent on showing kindness. You must especially rid her of that "yours" and "mine." If she says that something is hers, tell her: "Why are you saying it is 'yours'? I do not know what you mean. I have nothing that is my own. Why do you say 'mine', when all things are yours?" Grant her the word. Do you not see that we do the same thing with children? When a child snatches something we are holding and then wishes to grab something else, we let the child do it and we say, "Yes, this is yours and that is yours."

We should do the same thing with a wife, since her mind is something like a child's.[65] If she says "mine," say to her, "Everything is yours; even I am yours." This is not the language of flattery, but of wisdom. In this way you will be able to calm her anger and quench her sadness. It is flattery when you do something improper for the wrong reason, but this is the height of philosophy. Say, then: "And I am yours, my child. This is the advice that Paul gave me when he said: *The husband's body does not belong to him, but to his wife.*[66] If I have no power over my own body, but you have, this is much more the case with regard to money." You will have quieted her, if you say this; you will have quenched the fire and put the devil to shame. You will have bound her to you with these words and made her more your slave than one bought with money.

By your own speech, then, you must teach her never to say "mine" and "yours." You should never call her simply by her name, but always add expressions of endearment and honor and much love. Honor her, and she will not need honor from others; nor will she need glory from others, if she enjoys it from you. Cherish her above all things and for the sake of all things, both for her beauty and wisdom, and praise her. In this way you will persuade her not to pay attention to any-

---

65. Chrysostom's condescending attitude toward the young wife is only partially justified by the fact that Roman women usually married at a considerably younger age than Roman men.

66. 1 Cor 7:4.

one on the outside, but to laugh at them all. Teach her to fear God, and all will flow from this as from a fountain, and your household will be filled with countless blessings. If we seek what is incorruptible, what is corruptible will follow. *Seek first,* he says, *the kingdom of God, and all these things will be given to you.*[67]

What sort of children do you think will come from such parents? What sort of servants will such masters have? What will happen to everyone else who comes near them? Surely, they too will be filled with countless blessings. For the most part, slaves receive their moral formation from the character of their masters: they imitate their masters' desires; they love the same things, since that is what they have been taught; they say the same things; they are involved in the same activities. If we train ourselves properly and pay close attention to the Scriptures, we will learn even greater things. In this way we will be able to please God, to live all of the present life in virtue, and to enjoy all the blessings that have been promised to those who love him. May God grant that all of us will be counted worthy, through the grace and loving kindness of Jesus Christ. To God the Father together with Christ and the Holy Spirit may all glory, power, and honor be, now and forever and for endless ages! Amen.

67. Matt 6:33.

12.

Ambrosiaster

The named "Ambrosiaster" ("Pseudo-Ambrose") was coined in the early modern period to refer to the author of the first complete Latin commentary on the Pauline epistles. Subsequent scholars attributed to the same author a collection of *Questions on the Old and New Testaments*. While Ambrosiaster's true identity has never been determined, several facts about him can be known with certainty. In the Pauline commentary he attests that he was writing at Rome during the episcopate of Pope Damasus (366–384). Recent scholarship has suggested that his writings date from the later years of Damasus's reign, during the period of Jerome's sojourn there (382–385). He was most likely a member of the Roman clergy, perhaps a presbyter at one of the suburban churches.[1] Both the Pauline commentary and the *Questions* exist in multiple versions, all apparently from Ambrosiaster's own hand.

Paul's examination of marriage, divorce, and remarriage in 1 Corinthians 7 was the most extensive discussion of these issues in the New Testament. Christian opinion on marriage and celibacy often diverged over the interpretation of these verses, and Ambrosiaster offered a careful, literal reading of

---

1. For this suggestion, see Sophie Lunn-Rockliffe, *Ambrosiaster's Political Theology* (Oxford: Oxford University Press, 2007), 80–86.

the text. It reflects the moderate opinion of the Roman clergy on marriage, in contrast, for example, to Jerome, whose zealous promotion of virginity and ascetic discipline provoked opposition from several quarters, both clerical and lay. Ambrosiaster's commentary also had influence on subsequent writers, including Augustine and Pelagius. Because the Pauline commentary was usually attributed to Ambrose, and because the *Questions* were often ascribed to Augustine, the writings of Ambrosiaster exerted enormous influence in the Middle Ages under the names of these venerable Fathers of the Church.

COMMENTARY ON THE FIRST LETTER OF PAUL TO THE CORINTHIANS, CHAPTER 7

7:1 *Now concerning the matters about which you wrote to me: It is good for a man not to touch a woman.* Disturbed by the corrupt opinions of the pseudo-apostles, who were teaching hypocritically that marriage should be rejected, in order to appear purer than other people, the Corinthians wrote to the apostle seeking answers on these matters. Since they were not pleased by this way of thinking, they were asking only about this matter and left out other matters. Nevertheless, he responded to them that it is indeed good not to touch a woman, although they should not assert this without qualification.

7:2 *Yet on account of fornication.* That is, in order to avoid committing anything contrary to the law, whenever that which the law does not prohibit is avoided, he says: *Each man should have his own wife and each woman should have her own husband.* For those who seek a simple answer usually err.[2] For how could it happen that they would be able to abstain from their own wives, when Paul found them committing so many vices? Therefore he does not permit it, in order to prevent

---

2. Ambrosiaster suggests that "it is good not to touch a woman" is too simple (and dangerous) a solution to the problem of sexual desire.

them from partaking of what is forbidden, while abstaining from what is lawful, as the Manichaeans do.

7:3 *A husband should give to his wife her conjugal rights, and likewise the wife to her husband.* In this matter they are subject to one another, in order that, since they are one body, their will may also be one, in accordance with the law of nature.

7:4 *The wife does not have power over her own body, but her husband does; likewise, the husband does not have power over his own body, but his wife does.* He says this because it is not lawful for either the man or the woman to give their bodies over to someone else. For in this matter they are in debt to each other, so that no opportunity to sin may be given.

7:5 *Do not deprive one another.* (1) He says this so that they may be of one mind in the matters that pertain to the married state, lest dissension should give rise to fornication. *Except by agreement for a time.* That is, they may abstain by mutual consent in order to give thanks. *So that you may be free for prayer.* Although one ought to pray without ceasing—for one should engage in this practice every day—nevertheless, so that there may be a focus on prayer, he advises that space be made for it by setting aside specific times in order to be worthy of the Lord. For one must pray in a purer state in order to receive mercy. Although marriages are pure, one still ought to abstain from what is lawful, so that one's prayer may more easily be rendered effective. For even under the Law those who wished to be sanctified abstained from the fruit of the grapevine at the command of the Lord, so that they might become more holy.[3] For when someone does not touch even what is lawful, he shows that he wishes to receive that for which he prays.

But then come together again. (2) He gives the advice that after the day of prayer they should return to the natural practice.[4] *Lest Satan tempt you on account of your lack of self-control.* He warns that one should abstain only on the days set apart,

---

3. Cf. Num 6:4. Ambrosiaster refers to ancient Jews who took the Nazirite vow.

4. The sentence translated here comes from the second edition of Ambrosiaster's commentary. In the first edition he had stated that temporary abstinence made the

so that an opportunity may not be given to the devil, as the apostle Peter says: *Behold, the devil roams around like a roaring lion, seeking someone to devour.*[5] For if one takes a wife in order to produce children, it does not seem that much time has been given for this purpose, since festival days and days of religious procession and the very nature of conception and birth show that, according to the law, one ought to abstain during these times.

7:6 *But I say this by way of concession, not a command.* It is clear that he gives this advice in order to banish fornication, not to prevent anyone from pursuing the path to a better life.

7:7 *But I wish that all were as I myself am.* Just like any kind and concerned teacher, he desired that everyone would be like him, if it were possible. And in the next lines he soon showed what sort of person he was:

But each person has his own gift from God, one of one kind and one of another. That is, each person has his own gift from God, in accordance with his own desire,[6] so that with God's assent each person's will makes his choice possible.[7] For this reason, no one should be constrained, lest being prohibited from what is lawful, he should commit that which is unlawful, but each person should choose for himself which path to follow.

7:8 *But to the unmarried and to the widows I say this: it is good for them, if they remain as they are, just as I do.* He would not say, "it is good for the unmarried to be just as I am," if he were not untainted in the body, nor would he say: *I wish that all were as I myself am.* For if he had a wife and said this, then he did not desire that there be any virgins, but this is not so. From his youth he was so fired with zeal in his spirit that he did not have an interest in this matter,[8] since as a young man

---

married couple "worthy to receive the body of Lord," but he eliminated this in his revised version.

5. 1 Pet 5:8.

6. The word translated here as "desire" (*votum*) could also refer to a "vow" or religious commitment.

7. Literally, "with God's assent his willing achieves the possibility."

8. That is, Paul had no desire for the married life, according to Ambrosiaster.

he had been seized in advance by the grace of God. After he said that each person has his own gift from God, he showed why it is better that a person should be more willing, since each person is assisted in the direction that he seems to pursue with the passion of his mind.

7:9 *But if they are not exercising self-control, they should marry.* (1) He desires that they imitate him and strive to exercise self-control. But if they see that they are not able to persevere due to the incitement of the flesh, since they are not willing enough in that matter to be assisted by God—for God helps the person, whom he sees striving with all his power—they should marry, therefore, if they are afraid of burning. Perhaps at a later time they will be able to obtain this. For after a hindrance has been removed, the will restores itself to greater strength.

For it is better to marry than to burn. (2) He did not say: *It is better to marry than to burn,* as if it is good to burn and, therefore, it is better to marry; but he has followed our customary language. For we are accustomed to say: it is better to acquire wealth than to lose it. To "burn," then, is to be driven by desires or to be conquered by them. So when the will consents to the heat of the flesh, it burns, whereas to suffer desires and not to be conquered by them is characteristic of a distinguished and perfect man.

7:10 *But to those who have been joined in marriage, I give charge, not I but the Lord.* After he spoke to the unmarried and the widows, he addressed with the Lord's words those who were married:

7:11 *A wife should not separate from her husband; but if she does separate, she should remain unmarried.* (1) This is the apostle's advice: that if the wife leaves her husband because of his bad behavior, she should remain unmarried. *Or be reconciled to her husband.* But if she cannot exercise self-control, he says, since she does not desire to struggle against the flesh, she should be reconciled to her husband. For it is not permitted for a woman to remarry, if she divorces her own husband on account of fornication or apostasy or if he seeks to use her under the compulsion of his lewd desires, since the woman, as the inferior party, does not enjoy the same rights as the man, who is the superior.[9] But if her husband commits apostasy or desires to enjoy his wife in a perverted manner, the woman can neither marry another man nor return to her husband.

And a husband should not divorce his wife. He says that a husband should not divorce his wife. (2) But the following words are to be understood: *Except on account of fornication.*[10] He did not add what he wrote concerning the woman: *But if she separates, she should remain as she is*, because it is lawful for a man to marry another woman, if he divorces a wife who sins. For a man is not bound by the law in the same way as a woman is, for *the man is the head of the woman.*[11]

7:12 *To the rest I say, not the Lord.* He said this to show the distinction between what the Lord had ordered in his own words and what the Lord conceded to his authority, since the Lord also speaks through him. For he says: *Do you seek proof that Christ is speaking in me?*[12]

If any brother has a wife who is an unbeliever, and she consents to live with him, he should not divorce her.

7:13 *And if any woman has a husband who is an unbeliever, and he consents to live with her, she should not divorce her husband.* He said this because in the very beginning, when both were clearly pagans, it happened that one of the spouses would come to believe. And since unbelievers were repelled by the worship of God and, similarly, believers feared the

9. Ambrosiaster offers a stunning account of gender inequalities, which he based both on legal custom and on biblical interpretation. See my discussion in "The Paradise of Patriarchy: Ambrosiaster on Woman as (Not) God's Image," *Journal of Theological Studies* n.s. 43 (1992): 447–69.

10. Matt 5:32. Ambrosiaster reads the Pauline verse in the light of the famous "Matthean Exception," which allowed divorce in the case of adultery.

11. 1 Cor 11:3. Ambrosiaster's promotion of a double standard on the matter of divorce and remarriage is unusually explicit. Some scholars believe, however, that his view may represent the usual practice in the Western church prior to Augustine. See Philip Lyndon Reynolds, *How Marriage Became One of the Sacraments: The Sacramental Theology of Marriage from Its Medieval Origins to the Council of Trent* (Cambridge: Cambridge University Press, 2016), 150.

12. 2 Cor 13:3.

contamination of their previous error, Paul ordered the believers to live contentedly with them, if the unbelievers were content to live with those who had changed.

7:14 *For the unbelieving husband is sanctified in the believing wife, and the unbelieving wife is sanctified in the believing husband.* He shows that they have the benefit of a good will, since they do not dread the name of Christ. This also extends to the protection of the household, where the sign of the cross is made, by which death has been conquered, for this is sanctification.

Otherwise your children would be unclean. Their children would be unclean, if they divorced those who desired to live with them and then had intercourse with other people. For they would be adulterers; because of this their children would be illegitimate and, therefore, unclean.

But now, they are holy. They are holy because they were born from a lawful marriage and because they were born under the worship of the Creator since one of the parents was well-disposed. Just as whatever happens through reverence to the idols is unclean, so, too, whatever happens under the profession of God the Creator is holy.

7:15 *But if the unbelieving partner separates, let him separate.* (1) He preserves religious commitment by ordering Christians not to leave marriages. But if the unbeliever separates out of hatred of God, the believer will not be guilty of dissolving the marriage, for the rights of God are greater than the rights of matrimony.

For a brother or a sister is not bound to servitude in a situation of this kind. (2) This means: one does not owe the respect of marriage to the person who despises the author of marriage. For a marriage has no legal validity where there is no devotion to God; because of this, it is not a sin for a person who is divorced on account of God to marry someone else. For the insult against the Creator dissolves the law of marriage in respect to the one who was abandoned; the result is that there can be no accusation if the one abandoned marries another. But the unbeliever, who departs, evidently sins against both God and matrimony, since he did not wish to have a marriage under devotion to God. And so, there is no duty of conjugal fidelity to the person who departed so that he would not hear that the God of the Christians is the author of marriage. (3) For if Esdras demanded that unbelieving wives and husbands be divorced,[13] so that God might become more propitious, and if God was not angered by them taking other wives from among their own people—for they were not commanded not to take other wives, after divorcing the unbelieving ones—how much more, if the unbeliever has departed, will a woman have freedom of choice, if she wishes to marry a man of her own law. For that which has been made outside of the decree of God should not be considered a marriage. But when, at a later time, he acknowledges this and regrets that he left, he corrects himself in order to merit forgiveness. But if they both believe, they confirm the marriage by acknowledging God.

But God has called us to peace. (4) It is true that if someone leaves the marriage, he should not be taken to court, since he left out of hatred of God and thereby should not even be considered worthy of the marriage bond.

7:16 *For how do you know, wife, if you will save your husband? Or how do you know, husband, if you will save your wife?* He says this because those who do not abhor the name of Christ can perhaps believe.

7:17 *Only, to each person let it be as the Lord has assigned.* (1) The Lord has assigned to each person when he will be saved, that is, he knows when a person has the ability to believe, and he supports him. So, too, here he teaches that [the believers] should wait for them [i.e., the unbelieving spouses], and that [the believers] should not suffer scandal because of them, since hope for them must be preserved. But, if [the unbelievers] depart, they should pay it no attention.

Let each person walk as God has called him. (2) That is, if a believer is married, whether he is a man or a woman, he should not leave the marriage, but should remain as he is, whether Jew or Greek.

---

13. Cf. Ezra 9 and 10. "Esdras" is the Latin name for Ezra the scribe.

Just as I teach in all the churches. In order to persuade them, he says that he did not hand down to them anything other than what he handed down to others, so that when they hear that others of the same faith were taught this, they would more readily follow. For if someone sees that his companion agrees with him, he is more easily influenced.

***

7:25 *Now concerning virgins, I do not have a command from the Lord.* He responds to their writings, just as he did above: *Now concerning the matters about which you wrote to me.*[14]

But I give advice as one who having obtained the Lord's mercy is trustworthy. He denies that he had received a command concerning virgins, since the author of marriage could not order something contrary to marriage, lest he might criticize his original creation. *But I give advice,* that is, advice which is neither displeasing nor decked out with flattery, since he has received the grace to be capable of giving sound advice.

7:26 *Therefore I think that on account of the present distress it is best that a person should remain as he is.* (1) He says that it is good to remain a virgin. And in order to show this without qualification, he said: *On account of the present distress it is best that a person should remain as he is,* so that it would be clear that between the good and the best there is nothing as excellent and valuable as virginity. For he teaches that virginity is more acceptable not only in the sight of God but also in the present life, since it does not experience the difficulties of the present life, which marriage suffers, and the pains of childbirth, as well as the deaths of children. (2) Therefore, in order to encourage them to aspire to this, he teaches that women who love virginity benefit from the destruction of the present distress. As a result, when they learn that virginity has a better standing not only before God but also in the present, they should strive for it with all their strength. For there is only one thing for which the virgin labors: to conquer the desire

14. 1 Cor 7:1.

of the flesh, since she is free in all other respects. Since she is flesh in her origin and nature, the enjoyment of the flesh seems pleasant and its desire sweet; for this reason, it is no small glory to overcome these things.

7:27 *Are you bound to a wife? Do not seek release.* (1) His advice provides remedies, for he says that no one should be released from his wife except on account of fornication. Frequently it happens that after divorcing their wives under the pretext of continence, after their religious commitment grows cold, these men ensnare other women.[15] But if a man who is married desires to live a better life, he should encourage his wife, so that they may live more purely without scandal.

Are you free from a wife? Do not seek a wife. (2) Knowing that this is more pleasing to God and free from difficulty, a man should not seek a wife, yet in such a way that he also abstains from other women. If not, how is it beneficial to suppress the desire of the flesh, that is, to reject what is lawful and yet submit to what is unlawful?

7:28 *But if you take a wife, you have not sinned.* (1) He certainly does not sin, since he has done that which has been conceded. But if he considers marriage to be of little importance, he acquires for himself merit and a crown. For it takes great restraint not to touch that which has not been prohibited.

And if a virgin marries, she will not sin. She does not sin, since she is free before God in this matter.

But people of this kind will have worldly troubles.[16] (2) That is, even if they are free from sin, they will experience troubles in this life: the groaning of the womb, the rearing of children, nourishment, shelter, dowries, sickness, the management of the home, the needs of the wife, the domination of the husband.

But I am sparing you. He spares them, when he calls them

15. Ambrosiaster points to a problem that will be treated more fully by Pelagius and Augustine: the unilateral adoption of sexual continence by one of the married persons.

16. Literally, "tribulations of the flesh."

instead to the things that eliminate the aforementioned worldly troubles and anxieties. In this way he is able to appear to spare them, when he permits and does not oppose those who desire that which he shows to be burdensome.

7:29 *This is what I am saying, brethren: the time that is left is short.* (1) When he said that *the time that is left is short,* he indicated that the end of the world was near, although he knew that there was still time left. But he should not have written something else, for the sake of those who were going to read these things at that time when only a little time was to be left. This was to prevent them from thinking that the day of judgment was always far off and either not fearing it or thinking it was not real. But that which is said to be near, although it is still far off, has a great effect. For it instills in people a fear, which leads to living a better life. Moreover, even in the present life how anxious people are when they have cases to plead before the judges, when the day of the trial is said to be imminent! He is saying here that which he says in another place: *deceivers, but truthful.*[17]

Let those who have wives be as though they had none. (2) Since the end of the world is near, they should not be concerned about procreation nor preoccupied with its enjoyment, so that being more willing and more ready to do the works of God, and trained in the observance of the law, they may offer resistance when the battle is imminent. For there will be distress, and of such a kind that has never been, and many will fall into the snare of the devil. Furthermore, none of us desires that these things happen in our own time, fearing the distress predicted by our savior.[18] (3) For this reason, just as we choose for ourselves that we refrain from begetting many children, we also benefit others. Being devoted more to prayer and service to God, let us be on the lookout for the day of judgment, so that we may not be unprepared because of the hindrances of the present distress, and so that they may not encounter that which we fear. Therefore he desires that the believers

17. 2 Cor 6:8.
18. Cf. Matt 24:21.

abstain even from what is lawful, so that they may appear not only innocent but also glorious. For it is characteristic of the greatest virtue to forego what has been allowed, and not to desire what is prohibited is not far from it.

7:30 *And those who mourn, as though they were not mourning.* For when they know that the end of the world will happen soon, those who are perhaps oppressed on behalf of God's justice[19] console themselves with this hope.

And those who rejoice, as though they were not rejoicing. Those who rejoice in the present should know that grief will soon come, namely to those who rejoice in the world because they doubt God's judgment.

And those who buy, as though they had no possessions. Those who buy, believing that only a small time is left for the world, should act in such a way that they do not devote all their care to a business that will quickly pass away, but rather take care of their own souls, which they know are eternal.

7:31 *And those who make use of this world, as those they were not making use of it.* That is, that they should not have confidence in the use of the world, since it will quickly pass away when the world is destroyed. *For the form of this world is passing away.* Since he said that the world is ending, he shows that its form is passing away and this is the end; that is, its substance does not pass away, but its form does. And so, if the form of the world will perish, there is certainly no doubt that all things that are in the world will cease to exist. It is passing away because every day the world grows old.

7:32 *I want you to be without anxiety.* For when the anxiety of this world is diminished, a person is more eagerly vigilant toward the things of God. *He who does not have a wife thinks about the things of the Lord, how he may please God.* He shows how we may be without anxiety by saying: *He who does not have a wife thinks about the things of the Lord.* For after the anxiety of marriage is removed, which alone is more burdensome than all other things in the world, the spirit is taught to

19. Cf. Matt 5:10.

be worthy of God, but only if the spirit divests itself of these troubles in the hope that it may serve God more.

7:33 *But he who has a wife is anxious about the things of the world, how he may please his wife.*[20] For the world is concerned about the care of one's wife and children. For, among other things, it is their custom, in certain circumstances, to permit actions which should be punished, so that they may not offend their wives. For example, Zerubbabel, one of the three bodyguards of Artaxerxes,[21] relates the following in the book of Esdras: *A sad wife causes great bitterness in the home.*[22]

7:34 [*There is a difference between a woman and a virgin.* (1) They certainly are not different in nature, but in behavior, since we read in the book of Numbers that virgins were called "women."[23] Therefore, a woman [i.e., a married woman] has one kind of anxiety, while a virgin has another kind. Yet when the word "woman" is used, it is not clear what he means, unless he subsequently clarifies it. But when he says "virgin," the meaning of the word is clear. In this case the apostle placed the word "virgin" after "woman," in order to signify that the "woman" was not a virgin; in this way, he wished to show that a virgin is free from the burdens and labors, which a woman suffers when she is united to a man.][24]

But the unmarried woman is anxious about the things of the Lord, that she may be holy in body and spirit. By "spirit," he means the mind (*animus*). (2) For when, out of hope for heavenly things, she does not take on the anxiety of a husband and children, she thinks about the Lord, how she can preserve her commitment to be devoted to the Lord, yet only if her mind,

20. The first version of Ambrosiaster's commentary had added the words "and he is divided" to the biblical quotation.

21. In 1 Esdras 3 and 4, it is clear that Darius was the king of the Persians at this time, not Artaxerxes.

22. The speech of Zerubbabel on the power of women is found in 1 Esd 4:14–32 LXX. The first version of Ambrosiaster's commentary contained the following comment on the biblical verse: "For this reason, it is said that he is divided, because he cannot both dwell upon divine things and do the will of his wife."

23. Cf. Num 31:9.

24. The portion of the comment on 1 Cor 7:34 in brackets was added in the later version of Ambrosiaster's commentary, based on a different version of the biblical text.

within her clean body, casts off earthly things and strives after heavenly ones. For it is the soul that either sanctifies or pollutes the body. For what benefit is it to have a clean body and a polluted soul, since it is the merit of the soul that brings either honor or damnation to the body?[25]

For the married woman thinks about worldly matters, how she may please her husband. (3) Restrained by the law of marriage, she is anxious about how she may fulfill her marital duty while subject to worldly difficulties.

7:35 *But I say this for your own benefit, not to place a restriction upon you, but to encourage you to that which is honorable.* (1) Since that which is more beneficial or better seems burdensome and harsh to certain people on account of the habit of worldly activity, after he has given a reason, out of his deep love, he simply reminds them that what he says is more beneficial and more honorable. It is honorable, because it is holy and pure, but beneficial, because it is respectable before God and without difficulty in this world. What, then, are we saying? If virgins think about God and married women think about the world, what hope before God remains for those who marry? If this is the way things are, their salvation is in doubt. (2) But we see virgins who think about this world and married people who are zealous for the Lord's works. Purity will not be attributed by God to these virgins, but there will be a reward before God for those married persons, since, although they were tied down by earthly things and obligations of the flesh, they put forth the effort so that in the future they would merit something of the eternal reward. But not only will those virgins not have virginity attributed to them, but they will also be subject to punishment, since under the pretext of a better hope they lived lives full of worldly concern and anxieties and were lazy in doing the works of God. As the prophet Jeremiah says: *Cursed is the one who does the works of God negligently.*[26] (3) These are the people about

---

25. Ambrosiaster insists that mere physical virginity is not enough to bring heavenly rewards to the Christian.

26. Jer 48:10.

whom the apostle speaks in another letter: *Indeed, they have the appearance of piety, but deny its power.*[27] But the apostle is speaking to those who desire to follow the heavenly commands with pure devotion, showing and teaching a shorter route by which to approach God more quickly. For she who desires to remain a virgin in order to be worthy of God, knowing what kind of reward she can receive, if she abstains from what is lawful in order to become better, simultaneously rejects all the obstacles of the flesh, in the knowledge that these things delay the advance of the runner, like the weight of shackles around her feet.

7:36 *But if someone sees that he is acting shamefully toward his virgin, she is beyond puberty, and thus it should happen, let him do what he desires. He does not sin, if she marries.* Because previously he exhorted them to maintain virginity and continence, presenting them with reasons, to such an extent that marriage almost appeared to be something to be rejected as harmful, now he shows that a virgin does not sin, if she marries, so that they would not think he is rejecting marriage; but she is undertaking a matter of great labor, which does not have a reward before God, just as it has no punishment. For he desires that Christians be better in every way. Therefore, if a woman desires marriage, and she is already sexually mature, it is better for her to marry publicly according to the law that has been conceded, rather than act wickedly in secret and be ashamed by this.

7:37 *But he does well who, being under no necessity, has established in his own heart, has power over his own will, and has decided in his own heart to keep her as a virgin*[28]. He says that the person who has a virgin whose mind is not set on marriage should keep her and not impose upon her the kindling[29] of

27. 2 Tim 3:5.
28. Scholars dispute whether it is the case of a man deciding to arrange the marriage of his daughter, or a man deciding to marry his fiancée. Ambrosiaster does not fully resolve the ambiguity of the biblical text, though the former interpretation is more likely.
29. The Latin word *fomes*, translated here as "kindling," usually refers to the kindling or fuel of a fire, but it can also refer to semen, the "fuel" of procreation. See

marriage, since he sees that she does not desire to marry. For if the benefits [of virginity] ought to be preferred, how much more should they not be removed!

7:38 *And so, he who gives his virgin in marriage, does well.* [He does well, since he does what is lawful.][30] *And he who does not give her in marriage does better.* He does better, since he acquires for her merit before God and frees her from the anxiety of this age.

7:39 *A wife is bound by law, as long as her husband lives.* (1) He follows up on these things in order to teach that a woman, even if she has been cast out by her husband, does not have the freedom to remarry.

But if her husband dies, she is free. This is also relevant to the matters he discussed above, since he is showing how blessed a virgin is, because she is subject to no one, except God alone. For she seems to overcome her natural subjugation, when she elevates that which has been humbled by nature.

She may marry whomever she wishes, but only in the Lord. (2) That is, she may marry the person whom she thinks is suitable for herself, since marriages against one's will often turn out badly. But *only in the Lord*; that is, she may marry without the suspicion of wickedness and marry a man of her own religion; this is what it means to marry in the Lord.

7:40 *But she will be more blessed, if she remains as she is, according to my advice.* When he says *she may marry*, he is speaking according to the natural law. Although first marriages are from God, second marriages are merely permitted. Furthermore, first marriages are performed in a lofty manner under the blessing of God, but second marriages lack glory even in the present.[31] But second marriages were conceded on account of incontinence and because younger women

---

Alexander Souter, *A Glossary of Later Latin to 600 A.D.* (Oxford: Oxford University Press, 1949), 151.

30. The sentence in brackets was added in the later version of Ambrosiaster's commentary.

31. Ambrosiaster seems to be referring to the offering of a nuptial blessing by a priest at a Christian marriage ceremony, a practice he mentioned on several occasions.

often fell into widowhood. Because of this, he allows second marriages. But since it is better that she remains continent, so that she may be more worthy in the future, he gives the advice, so outstanding in spiritual reason, that she should remain continent.

But I think that I also have the Spirit of God. In order to show that his advice is authoritative and provident, he recommends it in humble words that have a deep meaning.

13.

Jerome

About a decade after Ambrosiaster composed his *Commentary on the Pauline Epistles*, Jerome, the prominent scholar, penned his famous treatise *Against Jovinian*. Writing from Bethlehem in 393, Jerome was responding to a Roman monk, Jovinian, who had been preaching that marriage and celibacy were equally meritorious before God and that married Christians would receive an equal reward in heaven as their celibate brothers and sisters. In the same year that Jerome composed his treatise, Jovinian's views were also condemned as heresy by Siricius, bishop of Rome, and by Ambrose, bishop of Milan. Jovinian had composed certain writings, which seem to have been largely compilations of biblical texts that supported his views. Friends of Jerome at Rome had sent to him these writings and invited him to respond.

Jerome's response, as will be evident from the following excerpts, took an extreme position and verged on a complete rejection of marriage. Influenced by the most radical writings of Tertullian and, occasionally, those of Origen, Jerome left little room for a balanced approach to Scripture or the church's tradition. When his treatise arrived in Rome, it was roundly criticized for its extremism. A Roman presbyter, Domnio, who served as a distributor of Jerome's writings, copied out some of the more offensive passages and wrote to Jerome demanding an explanation. A distinguished aristocrat, Pammachius, also became involved, attempting to withdraw copies of *Against Jovinian* from circulation (unsuccessfully, Jerome tells us) and offering his own criticism of the treatise. During the next few decades a number of writers sought to counter the influence of Jerome's extremism, among them Augustine and Pelagius, as well as Jerome's one-time friend, Rufinus of Aquileia, although they did not support all of Jovinian's views.[1] Despite the hostile reception of *Against Jovinian* by many of Jerome's contemporaries, the book circulated widely in the Middle Ages.

AGAINST JOVINIAN, BOOK 1

(7) Let us return to the chief point of his testimony: *It is good*, he said, *for a man not to touch a woman.*[2] If it is good not to touch a woman, then it is evil to touch one, for there is no opposite to good except evil. But if it is evil and it is forgiven, the concession is made to prevent something worse than this evil from happening. But what kind of good is it, which is conceded because there is something worse? He would never have written: *Each man should have his own wife*, if he had not first written, *But on account of fornication.*[3] Take away fornication and he will not say, *Each man should have his own wife.* It is like someone saying, "It is good to feed upon wheat bread and to eat the purest wheat flour." Yet to prevent someone compelled by hunger from eating cow dung, I concede to him that he may also eat barley. Is it the case, then, that wheat grain does not have its own purity, if barley is preferred to manure? That thing is naturally good, which does not admit

---

1. For a full account of the controversy surrounding Jovinian, see David G. Hunter, *Marriage, Celibacy, and Heresy in Ancient Christianity: The Jovinianist Controversy* (Oxford: Oxford University Press, 2007).
2. 1 Cor 7:1.
3. 1 Cor 7:2.

of comparison with an evil, which is not overshadowed by a preference for something else.

At the same time, one should acknowledge the apostle's prudence. He did not say, "It is good not to have a woman," but *it is good not to touch a woman*, as if the danger lies in the touching, as if the person who touched her would not escape from that woman *who pillages the precious souls of men*,[4] who makes the hearts of young men to take flight. *Will someone carry fire in his bosom and not be burned? Or walk on coals of fire and not be scorched?*[5] So then, just as the man who touches fire is immediately burned, so the touch of a man and a woman perceives its own nature and understands the difference between the sexes. The myths of the pagans tell how Mithras and Ericthonius were generated from the ground by the heat of lust, one from rock, the other from earth.[6] That is why our Joseph fled from the hands of the Egyptian woman, when she wanted to touch him. He even threw away the cloak that she had touched, as if he were bitten by a most rabid dog and was afraid the poison would seep in bit by bit.[7]

But on account of fornication, each man should have his own wife and each woman her own husband.[8] He did not say, "Because of fornication each man should take a wife," or else with this excuse he would have given free rein to lust, so that every time a man's wife died, he would have to take another one to avoid fornication. But [he said] *each man should have his own wife*, that is, he should use the one he had before he became a believer, whom it was *good not to touch*. And after becoming a Christian, he should know her only as a sister, not as a wife, unless fornication made his touch excusable.

The wife does not have power over her own body, but her hus-

---

4. Prov 6:26.

5. Prov 6:27–28.

6. According to Greek mythology, Ericthonius was begotten of semen ejaculated on the ground (or on Gaia) by Hephaestus, the god of fire, who tried unsuccessfully to rape Athena. Iconography of the god Mithras often portrays him being born out of rock.

7. Cf. Gen 39:1–13.

8. 1 Cor 7:2.

band does. Likewise the husband does not have power over his own body, but his wife does.[9] This entire question concerns those who are already married, whether they are permitted to divorce their wives, which was something the Lord prohibited in the gospel.[10] That is why the apostle says: *It is good for a man not to touch his wife.*[11] But since once a man has taken a wife, he is not free to abstain *except by mutual agreement,*[12] nor to divorce his wife, unless she sins, he must pay the conjugal debt. Indeed, he has willingly bound himself so that he is forced to pay it. *Do not deprive one another, except perhaps by mutual agreement for a time, to be free for prayer.*[13] I ask you, what sort of good is it that prevents prayer? That does not allow one to receive the body of Christ? As long as I fulfill my marital duty, I do not fulfill the duty of continence.

The same apostle in another place orders us to pray always.[14] If one must pray always, one must never be enslaved to marriage, because as often as I pay the debt to my wife, I am unable to pray. See how the apostle Peter, who had experienced the chains of wedlock, molds the church and instructs Christians: *Likewise, you husbands, live with your wives in a thoughtful way, bestowing honor on the woman as the weaker vessel, and, as you are coheirs of a manifold grace, so that your prayers may not be obstructed.*[15] Notice that he says that prayers are obstructed by the conjugal duty—the same idea as in Paul, because spoken in the same spirit. But he says *likewise,* because he is challenging the men to imitate the women, since above he had already enjoined the wives, saying: *So that the men may see your chaste and reverent behavior, do not let your adornment be the outward braiding of hair, and decoration of gold, and the wearing of fine clothing. But let it be the hidden person of*

9. 1 Cor 7:4.

10. Cf. Matt 5:32, 19:9, and parallels.

11. Jerome has substituted "wife" (*uxorem*) for "woman" (*mulierem*) in this version of the quotation from 1 Cor 7:1.

12. Cf. 1 Cor 7:5.

13. 1 Cor 7:5.

14. Cf. 1 Thess 5:17.

15. 1 Pet 3:7.

the heart, in the incorruption of a meek and silent spirit. This is
what is pleasing in the sight of God.[16]

Do you see what sort of marriage he enjoins on husbands
and wives? Living together *in a thoughtful way*, so that they
know what God wishes, what God desires, so that they *bestow*
honor on the woman as the weaker vessel. If we abstain from sexual intercourse, we bestow honor on our wives. If we do not
abstain, it is clear that the opposite of honor is insult. And to
the wives he said: *So that the men may see your chaste and rev-*
erent behavior, do not let your adornment be the outward braiding
of hair, and decoration of gold, and the wearing of fine clothing.
But let it be the hidden person of the heart, in the corruption of a
meek and silent spirit. Words truly worthy of the apostle and of
the rock of Christ! He gives a law to husbands and wives, and
after condemning bodily ornament, he preaches chastity and
the ornament of the inner man, *in the incorruption of a meek*
and silent spirit. In a way he is saying this: "Since your outer
man has been corrupted and you have lost the blessed state
of incorruption that is proper to virgins, you should at least
imitate the incorruption of spirit through belated abstinence
and show forth in your mind what you cannot show in your
body."

(8) But when in the following words the apostle says, *to*
be free for prayer, and then come together again,[17] no one should
think that he was expressing a wish, rather than simply a
concession to prevent a greater disaster. For he immediately
added: *lest Satan tempt you because of your lack of self-control.*
This is truly a lovely concession: *then come together again!* That
which he is embarrassed to call by its own name, that which
he prefers only to the temptation of Satan, that which is the
reason for incontinence—we labor to explain it, as if it were
obscure, although he himself made it very clear when he
wrote: *I say this by way of concession, not as a command.*[18] And
do we still mutter that marriage is not called an indulgence,

16. 1 Pet 3:2–4.
17. 1 Cor 7:5.
18. 1 Cor 7:6.

but rather a command, as if second and third marriages are not given the same concession, as if the doors of the church are not open through penance even to fornicators, and—what is even greater—to the incestuous? Take, for example, that man who violated his stepmother, whom the apostle handed over to Satan in his First Letter to the Corinthians for the destruction of his flesh, so that his spirit would be saved.[19] In his second letter Paul received him back and worked to keep the man from being overwhelmed with sorrow.[20] What the apostle wished is one thing; what he forgives is another. In the case of his wish, we act meritoriously; in the case of pardon, we are acting improperly. Do you want to know what the apostle wishes? Add the words that follow: *But I wish that everyone were as I am.*[21] Blessed is the person who will be like Paul! Happy is the one who hears the apostle's command, and not his forgiveness! "This is what I wish," he says, "this is what I desire: that you *be imitators of me, as I am of Christ.*[22] He was a virgin born of a virgin, incorrupt from the incorrupt. Since we are human beings and cannot imitate the savior's birth, let us at least imitate his behavior. That state of his was one of divinity and blessedness, our state belongs to the human condition and requires labor. *I wish all people to be as I am,* so that by being like me they may become like Christ, whom I am like. *For whoever believes in Christ ought to walk in the way that Christ did.*[23] *But each one has his own gift from God, one of one kind and one of another.*[24] What I wish is clear," he says. "But since in the church there are diverse gifts, I also make a concession for marriage, lest I seem to condemn nature." At the same time, you must consider that the gift of virginity is one thing, that of marriage another. If marriage and virginity merited the same reward, he never would have said, after enjoining continence: *But each has his own gift from God, one*

19. Cf. 1 Cor 5:1–5.
20. Cf. 2 Cor 2:7.
21. 1 Cor 7:7.
22. 1 Cor 11:1.
23. 1 John 2:6.
24. 1 Cor 7:7.

of one kind and one of another. Where several things each have
their distinctive property, there is also room for diversity. I
grant that marriage is a gift of God, but there is a great difference between one gift and another. For the apostle also said
about the same man after he had done penance for incest: *You
should rather grant him forgiveness and console him*,[25] and *Anyone to whom you grant forgiveness, I also grant forgiveness.*[26] And
lest we should think that a human gift is something worthless, he added: *What I have forgiven, if I have forgiven anything,
I have granted to him for your sake in the presence of Christ.*[27]
The gifts of Christ are diverse. That is why Joseph, by way
of type, had a coat of many colors. And in the Forty-Fourth
Psalm we read: *The queen stood at your right hand, in a garment
of gold, woven in many colors.*[28] And the apostle Peter said: *as
coheirs of a manifold grace.*[29] The Greek word used here is *poik-
ilēs*, which means "varied."

(9) Then follows: *But I say to the unmarried and to widows,
it is good for them to remain as they are, as I have. But if they are
not practicing self-control, they may marry. For it is better to marry
than to burn.*[30] After he had conceded conjugal rights to the
married, and had shown what he himself wished or what he
conceded, he moves on to the unmarried and to widows, and
proposes the example of himself, and calls them happy, if they
remain as they are. *But if they are not practicing self-control, they
may marry*; this is the same thing he said earlier: *but on account
of fornication* and *lest Satan tempt you because of your lack of
self-control.* And he has given a reason for saying, *If they are
not practicing self-control, they may marry. For it is better to marry
than to burn.* The reason it is better to marry is that it is worse
to burn. Take away the fire of lust, and he will not say *it is
better to marry.* For the word "better" also means a compari-

25. 2 Cor 2:7.
26. 2 Cor 2:10.
27. 2 Cor 2:10.
28. Ps 45 (44):13–14.
29. 1 Pet 3:7.
30. 1 Cor 7:8–9.

son with something worse, not a simple reference to a thing that is good in itself without any comparison. It is as if he were to say, "It is better to have one eye than to have none; or better to stand on one foot and support the rest of the body with a stick than to crawl on broken shins." What are you saying, apostle? I do not believe you when you say, *Even if I am unskilled in speech, yet I do not lack knowledge.*[31] Just as the following statements derived from his humility: *since I am not worthy to be called an apostle*;[32] and *to me who am the least of the apostles*;[33] and *as to one untimely born*,[34] so, too, I think this is a statement of humility. You know the proper meanings of words, which is why you cite the testimonies of Epimenides, Menander, and Aratus.[35] When you speak about virginity and continence, you say: *It is good for a man not to touch a woman*; and *It is good for them to remain as they are*; and *I think this is good on account the pressing distress*; and *It is good for a man to remain as he is*. But when you come to marriage, you do not say, "It is good to marry," because you cannot add the words "than to burn." But you say: *It is better to marry than to burn.* If marriage is, in itself, good, do not compare it with burning, but simply say, "It is good to marry." I am suspicious of the good of that thing which the greatness of another evil forces to be a lesser evil. But I do not want a lesser evil, but something that is simply good in itself.

***

(26) Jovinian now comes to the gospel and places before us Zacharias and Elizabeth, Peter and his mother-in-law, and with his customary silliness he does not understand that they, too, should be numbered among those who follow the Law. For there was no gospel before the cross of Christ, since the gospel was consecrated by his passion and blood. Accord-

---

31. 2 Cor 11:6.
32. 1 Cor 15:9.
33. 1 Cor 15:9.
34. 1 Cor 15:8.
35. Jerome refers to the citations of these authors in Titus 1:2, 1 Cor 15:33, and Acts 17:28.

ing to this rule, Peter and the other apostles had wives—I will concede this to Jovinian out of my abundance—but they had married them at a time when they did not yet know the gospel. Later, when they were recruited to be apostles, they relinquished their conjugal duty. For when Peter, speaking on behalf of all the apostles, says to the Lord: *Behold, we have left everything and followed you,*[36] the Lord responds to him: *Amen; I say to you that there is no one who has left home, or parents, or brothers, or a wife, or children, for the sake of the kingdom of God, who will not receive much more in this age, and in the age to come eternal life.*[37] Now Jovinian may oppose us and attempt to prove that all the apostles had wives by citing this passage: *Do we not have the right to be accompanied by women* (or *wives,* since among the Greeks the word *gynē* signifies both), *just like the rest of the apostles and Cephas and the brothers of the Lord?*[38] Let him even add the words found in some Greek codices: *Do we not have the right to be accompanied by women who are sisters, or by wives?* From this it is clear that he was speaking about other holy women, who following Jewish custom ministered to teachers out of their own resources, as we read was the practice even of the Lord himself. For even the order of the words shows this: *Do we not have the right to our food, and drink, and to be accompanied by women as sisters?*[39] When he mentions food and drink and the distribution of expenses first, and then refers to women who are "sisters," it is quite clear that they should not be understood to be wives, but rather those women who, as we have said, ministered out of their own resources. This was also written in the old Law about that Shunammite woman, who was accustomed to welcome Elisha and prepare for him a table, and bread, and lamp, etc.[40] Or, certainly, if we take *gynaikes* to mean "wives" and not "women," the addition of the word

36. Matt 19:27.
37. Matt 19:29.
38. 1 Cor 9:5.
39. 1 Cor 9:4–5.
40. 2 Kgs 4:8–10.

"sisters" eliminates "wives" and shows that they were related in spirit, and not married. Although with the exception of Peter, it is not clearly stated that any of the other apostles were married. And since it was written only about one of them, and there is silence about the rest, we ought to understand that they were without wives, since Scripture indicates nothing of the sort about them.

And Jovinian, who places before us Zacharias and Elizabeth, Peter and his mother-in-law, ought to know that John was born from Zacharias and Elizabeth, that is, a virgin was born from marriage, the gospel from the Law, chastity from matrimony, so that the virgin Lord might be announced by a virgin prophet, and be baptized by him. But we can say about Peter that he had a mother-in-law at the time when he became a believer, and he no longer had a wife, although in the *Travels of Peter* both his wife and his daughter are mentioned.[41] But now our debate is based on the canon. And since he calls us to the apostles, because they, as the foremost authorities of our teaching and leaders of Christian dogma, were not virgins—in order to make us concede that they were not virgins, although it cannot be proven, except in the case of Peter—let him know that these apostles are the ones about whom Isaiah prophesied: *If the Lord of hosts had not left us descendants,*[42] *we would have been like Sodom, and become like Gomorrah.*[43] Therefore, they who were from the Jews could not restore in gospel that which they had lost in Judaism.

And yet one of the disciples, John, who is said to have been the youngest among the apostles and who was a virgin when he embraced the Christian faith, remained a virgin. Therefore he is loved more by the Lord and reclined on his breast.[44] And that which Peter, who had a wife, did not dare to ask,

41. In his *Commentary on Galatians* (1.18a) Jerome refers to the same book (*Periodos*) and attributes it to Clement of Rome. This may have been a source underlying the Pseudo-Clementine *Recognitions*.

42. Literally, "seed" (*semen*).

43. Isa 1:9.

44. Cf. John 13:23.

he requested John to ask.[45] And after the resurrection, after Mary Magdalene announced that the Lord had risen, both Peter and John ran to the tomb, but John got there first.[46] And when they were in the boat and were fishing in the lake of Gennesaret,[47] Jesus stood on the shore, and the apostles did not know the one whom they were looking at. Only the virgin recognized the virgin, and he said to Peter: *It is the Lord*.[48] Again, after Peter heard it said that he would be bound by another and led where he did not wish to go—his suffering on the cross had been prophesied—he asked: *Lord, what about this man?*[49] He did not wish to desert John because they had always been closely joined. The Lord said to Peter: *What is it to you, if I wish him to be as he is?*[50] And that is why the word spread among the faithful that this disciple would not die.[51] From this it is demonstrated that virginity does not die and that not even the blood of martyrdom washes away the defilement of marriage, but virginity remains with Christ, and its falling asleep is a transition, not a death.

---

45. Cf. John 13:24.
46. John 20:1–4.
47. Also known as the Sea of Galilee or the Sea of Tiberius.
48. John 21:7.
49. John 21:21.
50. John 21:22.
51. Cf. John 21:23.

14.

Pelagius

Best known as an opponent of Augustine's teaching on the necessity of divine grace, the monk Pelagius was also deeply involved in propagating ascetic ideals in the households of aristocratic women at Rome between the years 390 and 410. He was on especially intimate terms with members of the Anicii, one of the noblest Roman families. *His Letter to the Matron Celantia,* a portion of which is translated here, illustrates some of the problems that beset a Roman matron with ascetical leanings. Pelagius gave specific advice on how to balance the care of the household with the needs of the spiritual life. He also attempted to distinguish his views from those of Jovinian, on the one hand, and from those of the Manichaeans, on the other.

But Pelagius also had to face a more pressing problem. Celantia had undertaken a vow of sexual abstinence without the approval of her husband. Pelagius took a dim view of the matter, although he was careful not to condemn Celantia outright. Instead, he urged her to respect her husband and said that he would use his influence to persuade her husband freely to accept the vow himself. Pelagius's *Letter to the Matron Celantia* is an index of the degree to which ascetic enthusiasm had penetrated the highest levels of Roman society in the late fourth century. His own somewhat ambivalent attitude toward Celantia's renunciation of her marital relationship stands in marked contrast to the views of Augustine, who insisted that married persons owed each other fidelity in rendering sexual relations.[1]

LETTER TO THE MATRON CELANTIA

(24) Be concerned for the household in such a way as to allow some free time for your soul. You should find an appropriate place, somewhat removed from the clatter of the family, where you can find shelter, so to speak, from the great tempest of cares, a place where you can calm in the tranquility of your heart the disruptive thoughts that flow from the outside. This should be your place to pursue the reading of sacred Scripture, to take frequent opportunities for prayer, to think carefully and intensely about the future. This private time will then enable you to balance all the duties that occupy the rest of your time. I am not saying that you should withdraw from your family; on the contrary, my point is that you should take this time to learn and to meditate on how you ought to serve your family.

(25) You should rule and care for your family in a manner that reveals your desire to be a mother, not a domineering mistress, of your family. You should receive respect from them because of your kindness, not because of severity. Obedience is always freer and more faithful when it proceeds from love rather than from fear. Most of all, in a marriage that is spotless and worthy of respect, it is imperative to hold fast to the order laid down by the apostle.

(26) First of all, the husband should be given all authority, and the entire household should learn from you how much honor is owed to him. Show by your obedience that he is lord, by your humility that he is great. The greater the honor you give to him, the more you also will be held in honor. For

1. See, e.g., Augustine, Letter 262 to Ecdicia, as well as Sermon 354A translated below.

the head of a woman, as the apostle says, *is her husband,*[2] and the dignity of the head is a source of adornment for the rest of the body. That is why he says in another place: *Wives, be subject to your husbands, as is fitting in the Lord.*[3] And the blessed apostle Peter says: *In the same way wives should be subject to their husbands, so that, if any of them do not believe the word, they may be won over without words by the behavior of their wives.*[4] If, therefore, honor is owed even to non-Christian husbands because of the right of marriage, how much more ought such honor to be rendered to Christian husbands!

(27) In order to show how married women must adorn themselves, he said: *Your beauty should not come from outward adornment, such as braided hair, gold jewelry, and fine clothes, but it should be that of your inner self, in the incorruptibility of a quiet and modest spirit, which is of great worth in the sight of God. For this is the way the holy women of the past who put their hope in God used to make themselves beautiful. They were subject to their husbands, just as Sarah obeyed Abraham and called him "lord."*[5] Now by giving these commands he is not ordering women to wallow in filth and to be clothed in a horrid patchwork of rags. Rather, he is forbidding immoderate and excessively luxurious attire, and he is recommending simple ornament and dress. The chosen vessel [Paul] also spoke about this: *In like manner the women should adorn themselves with modesty and sobriety, not with braided hair or gold or pearls or expensive clothes, but with good works, which is appropriate for women who profess chastity.*[6]

(28) Remember that some years ago, kindled with a wonderful ardor of faith, you resolved to live in continence and consecrated the remainder of your life to purity. This is a sign of a great spirit and a mark of perfect virtue: suddenly to renounce the pleasure that one has experienced, to flee the

2. 1 Cor 11:3.
3. Col 3:18.
4. 1 Pet 3:1.
5. 1 Pet 3:3–6.
6. 1 Tim 2:9–10.

enticements of the flesh that one has known, and to quench with the love of faith the flames of a still burning youth. But at the same time I have learned something that troubles and disturbs me no small amount, namely, that you have begun to observe this great good without the consent and agreement of your husband. Now this is something that the authority of the apostle completely forbids; in fact, in this case at least, he has not only subjected the wife to her husband, but he has also subjected the husband to the power of his wife. *A wife,* he says, *does not have power over her own body, but her husband does; in the same way a husband does not have power over his own body, but his wife does.*[7]

Now you seem to have forgotten the marriage covenant and to have become unmindful of this agreement and right by making a vow of chastity to the Lord without consulting your husband. But it is a dangerous matter to promise what is in another's power, and I do not know how a gift can be pleasing, if that which one person offers really belongs to two. Now I have heard and seen for myself that many marriages have been severed through ignorance of this sort and that the practice of chastity, I am sorry to say, has simply led to adultery. For while one party abstains even from what is licit, the other party falls into what is illicit. In such a case I do not know who deserves the greater censure, who deserves the greater blame: the one who committed fornication after his wife rejected him, or the wife who by rejecting her husband presented him, in a certain way, with the opportunity for fornication.

In order that you may learn what is the whole truth in this case, I must offer a few words about the divine authority. The rule of apostolic teaching does not, with Jovinian, equate the works of marriage with continence, nor does it, with Manichaeus, condemn marriage. The chosen vessel and apostle to the Gentiles thus takes a moderate and middle position between the two, so that he allows a remedy for incontinence, while he calls forth continence to its reward. His

7. 1 Cor 7:4.

whole purpose is this: to propose chastity when both partners agree to it, or at least for both partners to pay the debt they owe to each other.

(29) But now let us present the exact words of the apostle and let us examine the whole case from the very beginning. For he says to the Corinthians: *Now for the matters you wrote about. It is good for a man not to touch a woman.*[8] Although in this place he has praised chastity, lest anyone think that he prohibits marriage, he adds: *But because of fornication each man should have his own wife and each woman her own husband. The husband should render to his wife what is due, and likewise the wife should render to the husband his due. For a woman does not have power over her own body, but her husband does; in the same way, a man does not have power over his body, but his wife does. Do not deprive one another.*[9] But, once again, in order not to appear to be excluding chastity by speaking so much about marriage, he adds: *except perhaps by mutual consent for a time, in order to be free for prayer.*[10] Immediately he seems to take back his words *for a time* in order not to appear to be teaching a brief and temporary continence rather than a permanent one. For he adds: *because of your incontinence. But I say this as an indulgence, not as a command.*[11] Therefore, the words *for a time* teach that there should occur periodic practice of chastity, so that over set intervals of time they both may test the strength of their continence and promise without danger that which they both must preserve. But he clearly states what he would really like: *But I wish that all people were as I am myself,*[12] that is, living under the yoke of perpetual chastity.

(30) Do you not see how cautiously and prudently, without giving rise to scandals, the teacher expressed his firm opinion regarding chastity? For he did not want so great a good, which requires the consent of both spouses, to fail because of

8. 1 Cor 7:1.
9. 1 Cor 7:2–5.
10. 1 Cor 7:5.
11. 1 Cor 7:5–7.
12. 1 Cor 7:7.

the rash conduct of one spouse. Indeed, what is more firm, what is more secure than that chastity that originates from the resolve of both partners and is preserved by both of them in common? Nor should either party be concerned only for himself or herself, but they should both urge each other on to persevere in virtue. For in this case, as in others, what is praiseworthy is not merely to have begun what is good, but to have accomplished it.

For some time now, as you realize, my discourse has been treating a difficult and sensitive subject, and I have not dared to come down on one side or the other, since I dread both of them equally. But my difficulty ought to give you a sense of your own predicament, for I would prefer to disturb you by speaking the truth than to deceive you with false praise. The evil, as you see, is twofold, and there is equal danger on either side; both sides hem you in. To disregard and despise your husband altogether is a clear violation of the apostle's decree. But to destroy a chastity that has endured so long and to fail to render to God what you promised is something to be feared and dreaded. As the saying goes, "You will easily make an enemy of a friend, if you do not pay what you promised." For Scripture says: *But if you make a vow to the Lord God, do not hesitate to fulfill it, for the Lord your God will surely demand it of you, and it will be a cause of sin for you.*[13]

Scripture is saying, therefore: Show your husband the honor that is owed to him, so that in both respects you may be able to give the Lord what you vowed. I have no doubts in respect to his conscience, if you had expected some small ones, not because I am taking the good of chastity away from you, but because I am exhorting his spirit with all my strength to make a sacred declaration of chastity, so that he may make a voluntary offering to God in the odor of sweetness, so that his mind may be stripped of all worldly bonds and bodily desires, and so that you may be able more fully to embrace the Lord's commandments. But lest you think that I have said anything carelessly, I have based my teaching on

13. Deut 23:21; cf. Eccl 5:4.

the testimony of the divine Scriptures, just as the apostle himself said: *And they will be two in one flesh; but now not one flesh,
but one spirit.*[14]

14. Cf. 1 Cor 6:16–17; Eph 5:31.

15.

Augustine

Augustine of Hippo (354–430 CE) is the author whose discussion of marriage and sexuality was the most extensive—and the most influential—of all the writings contained in this anthology. As noted in the introduction, his book *The Good of Marriage* (*De bono coniugali*) was composed ca. 404, largely in response to the debate between Jerome and Jovinian that had taken place a decade earlier. Although neither Jerome nor Jovinian was mentioned in the text itself, in his later review of his writings, the *Retractationes*, Augustine noted that he had written in response to "the heresy of Jovinian," because some people were still murmuring that Jovinian could not be answered by defending marriage, but only by condemning it. This remark was a not-very-subtle reference to Jerome's *Against Jovinian*, which had caused such consternation at Rome in the early 390s.

In *The Good of Marriage* Augustine set himself the task of refuting both Jovinian and Jerome. Against Jovinian, he argued that celibacy was, in itself, a higher state than that of marriage. In the service of this aim, Augustine also composed a companion treatise, *On Holy Virginity* (*De sancta virginitate*), which articulated both the advantages and the dangers of the celibate and virginal lives. Against Jerome, Augustine attempted to demonstrate that marriage was not merely a lesser evil than fornication (the argument that Tertullian and Jerome had persistently offered), but rather that marriage was a genuine good, albeit inferior to the good of virginity or sexual abstinence. In the course of his argument, Augustine developed the teaching that would become classic in Christian theology for more than a millennium, namely that there were "three goods" in marriage: the procreation of children (*proles*), sexual fidelity (*fides*), and the "sacrament" (*sacramentum*). By the last, Augustine referred to the indissolubility of the marital union, which lasted until the death of one of the spouses. Indissolubility, which disallowed remarriage after separation or divorce, was a characteristic of Christian marriages, Augustine maintained, because they contained a sacred sign or symbol (*sacramentum*) of the indissoluble union of Christ and the church.

About the same time that he was composing *The Good of Marriage*, Augustine delivered the sermon that is the second text presented here. But rather than dealing on a theoretical level with the various "goods" of marriage, Augustine focused on a problem that seems to have been widespread in Christian communities in late antiquity: the unilateral adoption of sexual continence by one spouse without the agreement of his or her partner. As we have seen, numerous Christian writers addressed this topic, including Ambrosiaster, Pelagius, and Jerome. But to a much greater degree than his more ascetic contemporaries, Augustine saw sexual abstinence within marriage as a problematic practice.

As he had argued in *The Good of Marriage*, one of the purposes of marriage was to serve as a channel for the "concupiscence of the flesh," that is, the disordered and disruptive desires that accompany human sexuality. Although Augustine regarded these desires as a symptom of original sin and considered it an "evil" (*malum*) to acquiesce to them, he believed that the apostle Paul had granted married people a "concession" (*indulgentia*)[1] for this behavior; to engage in

---

1. Cf. 1 Cor 7:6.

sex mainly out of lust (and not, for example, out of a desire for children) was "forgivable" (*venialis*), Augustine argued, because it took place within the confines of marriage and enabled the couple to avoid illicit, extramarital relations.

In Sermon 354A we see Augustine emphasizing ever more strongly the role of the second good of marriage, fidelity (*fides*), in the marital relationship. A married person who has the God-given ability to practice continence should not adopt continence unless his or her partner is able to do so as well. Like the patriarchs and matriarchs of the Old Testament, who were capable of continence but who engaged in sex out of their duty to obey God's command and to produce the people of Israel, married people today have the duty to engage in sex to assist their weaker partners, even if they themselves are capable of continence. More explicitly than in *The Good of Marriage*, in Sermon 354A Augustine argued that the act of engaging in sex to help one's partner was an act of mercy and charity.

The final selection from Augustine is taken from his correspondence: a letter to Atticus, patriarch of Constantinople. It dates from ca. 421 and shows Augustine engaging a new set of issues that were to preoccupy him for the remainder of his life. Augustine's sense of the pervasive character of human sinfulness and the absolute necessity of God's grace, already articulated in his famous *Confessions*, was not to the liking of all Christians. Early in the fifth century, the monk Pelagius is said to have been shocked by the implications of Augustine's teachings; it seemed to Pelagius that Augustine was robbing human beings of any agency of their own and eliminating any motive to improve themselves or to embrace the ascetic life. Pelagius, by contrast, insisted that human beings had the power to change their lives and adopt ascetic practices. He rejected Augustine's insistence on the essential weakness of the human will after the fall and believed that human beings were born in virtually the same state as Adam and Eve before their sin.

After the teachings of Pelagius were condemned in the

Tractoria of Pope Zosimus in 417, Julian, bishop of Eclanum in southern Italy, took up the mantle of the Pelagian cause. Deposed and exiled from Italy in the following year, Julian continued to attack Augustine's teaching and to search for support in the East. Julian's primary argument against Augustine was that his theology of original sin implied a "Manichaean" view of the natural world. Augustine's notion that human sexual desire had been corrupted by sin and that infants had been born sinful, from Julian's perspective, seemed to imply a condemnation of marriage and procreation. For more than ten years Augustine and Julian engaged in a literary debate on marriage and concupiscence. Julian's views have been preserved primarily in Augustine's several refutations of them: *On Marriage and Concupiscence*; *Against Two Letters of the Pelagians*; *Against Julian*; and the *Unfinished Work against Julian*.

Although Augustine wrote these lengthy treatises in response to the attacks of Julian, his most concise answer was given in Letter 6* to the bishop Atticus, which is found among the newly-discovered letters of Augustine, edited by Johannes Divjak. Letter 6* was written early in the controversy with Julian (ca. 421). After first defending himself against the charge that he condemns marriage, Augustine argued that the Pelagians failed to make a distinction between the natural good of marriage (sexual intercourse and the desire for children, that is, the "concupiscence of marriage"), on the one hand, and the effects of original sin (the "concupiscence of the flesh"), on the other hand. By defending the integrity of nature, and especially the innocence of newborn babies, Augustine claimed, the Pelagians denied the need of salvation through Christ.

THE GOOD OF MARRIAGE

(I.1) Every human being is part of the human race, and human nature is a social reality and possesses a great and natural good, the power of friendship. For this reason God wished to create all human beings from one, so that they would be held together in human society, not only by the similarity of race, but also by the bond of blood relationship. Therefore, the first natural union of human society is the husband and wife. God did not create even these as separate individuals and join them together as if they were alien to each other, but he created the one from the other. The power of the union was also signified in the side from which she was taken and formed, for they are joined to each other's side, when they walk together and together look where they are walking. The result is the bonding of society in children, who are the one honorable fruit, not of the union of male and female, but of sexual intercourse. For there could have been some kind of real and amiable union between the sexes even without sexual intercourse, a union in which the one rules and the other obeys.

(II.2) There is no need at this time for us to examine and set forth a definite opinion on the question of how the offspring of the first humans could have come into being, whom God had blessed, saying: *Increase and multiply, and fill the earth,*[2] if they had not sinned. For it was by their sin that their bodies deserved the condition of death, and there could be no intercourse except of mortal bodies. Many different views have been expressed on this subject, and if we were to examine which of them is most congruent with the truth of the divine Scriptures, there is matter for an extended discussion.

One possibility is that, if they had not sinned, they would have had children in some other way without any act of intercourse, by a gift of the almighty Creator, who was able to create the first human beings without parents, who was able to form the flesh of Christ in a virgin's womb, and—to speak now even to unbelievers—who was able to give offspring to bees without intercourse.

Another possibility is that much of that passage should be interpreted in a mystical and figurative way. For example, *Fill*

---

2. Gen 1:28.

the earth and master it[3] could refer to a fullness and perfection of life and power, so that the increase and multiplication that is expressed in the text, *Increase and multiply*, would mean a development of the intellect and an abundance of virtue, just as it is said in the psalm: *You have increased my soul in virtue.*[4] In this case the human race would not have received a succession of offspring, if sin had not caused there to be a succession unto death.

Yet another possibility is that the bodies of the first human beings were originally created as animal, not spiritual, so that later by the merit of obedience they would have become spiritual in order to achieve immortality. This would have happened not after death, since death entered the world through the envy of the devil[5] and became the punishment for sin, but through that transformation which the apostle describes when he says: *Then those of us who are still alive and left will be caught up with them in the clouds to meet Christ in the air.*[6] In this interpretation the bodies of the first married couple would have been created mortal in their initial formation, but would not have died, if they had not sinned, just as God had threatened. It is just as if God might threaten a wound, since the body is vulnerable to wounding, although the wounding would not have happened unless his commands were violated.

So, then, generations of bodies such as these could have come into being through sexual intercourse. They would have developed up to a certain point, but would not have advanced to old age; or they would have grown to old age, but would not have died, until the earth was filled by the multiplication that was promised in the blessing. If God allowed the clothes of the Israelites to retain their proper state without decay for forty years,[7] how much more would he have rendered to the bodies of those who obey his com-

3. Gen 1:28.
4. Ps 138:3.
5. Cf. Wis 2:24.
6. 1 Thess 4:17.
7. Cf. Deut 29:5.

mands a kind of happy equilibrium of a fixed state until they were changed into something better, not by human death, in which the soul deserts the body, but by a blessed transformation from mortality to immortality, from an animal to a spiritual quality.

(III) It would take too long to investigate and to discuss which of these opinions is true, or whether the text is susceptible of one or more other interpretations.

(3) This is what we now say: according to that state of birth and death, which we experience and in which we were created, the union of male and female is something good. The divine Scripture commends this alliance to such an extent that a woman who is divorced by her husband is not allowed to marry another, while her husband is still alive; and a man who is divorced by his wife may not take another, unless the wife who has left him has died. It is right, therefore, to inquire why the good of marriage is a good, which even the Lord confirmed in the gospel, not only because he prohibited divorce, except in cases of fornication,[8] but also because when he was invited to the wedding, he attended.[9]

I do not believe that marriage is a good solely because of the procreation of children; there is also the natural association (*societas*) between the sexes. Otherwise, we would no longer speak of a marriage between elderly people, especially if they had lost or had never produced children. But now in a good marriage, even if it has lasted for many years and even if the youthful ardor between the male and female has faded, the order of charity between husband and wife still thrives. The earlier they begin to refrain from sexual intercourse, by mutual consent, the better they will be. This is not because they will eventually be unable to do what they wish, but because it is praiseworthy not to wish to do what they are able to do.

If, therefore, they remain faithful to the honor and the conjugal duties that each sex owes the other, even if both of their

8. Cf. Matt 19:9.
9. Cf. John 2:1–11.

bodies grow weak and almost corpselike, yet the chastity of spirits joined in a proper marriage will endure; the more it is tested, the more genuine it will be; the more it is calmed, the more secure it will be. There is an additional good in marriage, namely the fact that carnal or youthful incontinence, even if it is wicked, is directed toward the honorable task of procreating children. As a result, conjugal intercourse makes something good out of the evil of lust (*libido*), since the concupiscence of the flesh, which parental affection moderates, is then suppressed and in a certain way burns more modestly. For a sort of dignity prevails over the fire of pleasure, when in the act of uniting as husband and wife the couple regard themselves as father and mother.

(IV.4) To this we would add that in the very act of paying the conjugal debt, even if they demand it somewhat intemperately and incontinently, the spouses still owe to each other mutual fidelity (*fides*). The apostle attributed to this fidelity so much authority that he called it a "power," saying: *A wife does not have power over her body, but her husband does; likewise, a husband has no power over his body, but his wife does.*[10] The violation of this fidelity is called adultery, when one has intercourse with another man or woman contrary to the marriage agreement, either at the instigation of one's own lust or out of consent to another's lust. In this way fidelity, which is a great good of the spirit even in the insignificant affairs of the body, is broken. Therefore, it is certain that fidelity ought to be preferred even to the health of the body, by which life itself is sustained. A little straw may be almost nothing compared to a great amount of gold; yet, when fidelity is genuinely preserved in a matter of straw as if in one of gold, it is no less valuable because it is preserved in a thing that is less valuable.

When fidelity is used to commit sin, of course, we wonder whether it should still be called fidelity. But whatever it is, if one acts contrary to it, one becomes worse, unless one is abandoning it in order to return to a true and legitimate fidelity, that is, in order to make amends for a sin by correct-

10. 1 Cor 7:4.

ing the wickedness of the will. Take, for example, someone who is unable to rob a man by himself and so finds an accomplice and agrees with him that they will commit the crime together and then share the loot; but after the crime is committed, he takes it all himself. The accomplice, of course, will be sad and will complain that fidelity to him was not kept. But in his very complaint he ought to realize that he should have kept his fidelity to human society by leading a good life and by not unjustly plundering another human being, if he recognizes how unjust it was that fidelity to him in the society of sin was not preserved.

Of course, the first robber, who is guilty of infidelity on two counts, should be judged the guiltier of the two. But if the first regretted the evil they had done and for this reason refused to share the loot with his accomplice, in order to return it to the man from whom it was stolen, not even the unfaithful accomplice would call him unfaithful. Thus, if a wife who has violated the fidelity of marriage keeps her fidelity to the adulterer, she is still evil: but if she is not faithful even to the adulterer, she is worse. Yet if she repents of her wickedness and returns to her marital chastity, thereby repudiating her adulterous agreements and purposes, I do not think that even the adulterer will regard her as violating fidelity.

(V.5) It is often asked whether this situation should be called a marriage: when a man and a woman, neither of whom is married to another, have intercourse with each other, not in order to have children, but out of incontinence solely to have sex, and yet faithfully pledge not to do this with anyone else. Perhaps it would not be absurd to call this a marriage, if they made this agreement to last until the death of one of them, and if, although they have not come together for the sake of procreation, they at least do not avoid it, either by not wishing to have children or by acting in an evil way to prevent children from being born. But if one or both of these conditions are absent, I do not see how we could call this a marriage.

For if a man is living with a woman only until he finds someone else who is worthy either of his position or of his wealth, whom he can marry as an equal, in his heart he is an adulterer, not with the woman whom he would like to find, but with the woman with whom he is living but not in a marital union. The same applies to the woman, if she is aware of this and is still willing to have unchaste intercourse with a man, with whom she does not have a commitment as a wife. But if she preserves her fidelity to him as to a spouse after he has taken a wife, and if she refuses to marry and decides to remain completely continent, I would not find it easy to call her an adulteress. Yet who would not call it a sin, knowing that she had intercourse with a man who was not her husband?[11]

But if the only thing the woman wanted from the sexual relations was to have children, and if she unwillingly bore whatever else was involved beyond the desire for procreation, surely this woman ranks higher than many matrons. Some of them, even if they are not guilty of adultery, force their husbands, who often desire to be continent, to pay the debt of the flesh. They make intemperate use of their right, not out of a desire for offspring, but solely out of the passion of concupiscence. Nonetheless, in the marriages of such women there is this good, namely that they are married. For this is why they were married, so that concupiscence itself might be directed toward a legitimate bond and thereby cease to flow in a disordered and disgraceful way. Concupiscence has in itself a weakness of the flesh that cannot be restrained, but in marriage it has an association of fidelity that cannot be dissolved. On its own, concupiscence leads to immoderate intercourse, but in marriage it finds a means of chaste procreation. Even if it is shameful to use a husband in a lustful way, nevertheless it is honorable to choose to have sex only with a husband and to bear children only with a husband.

(VI) Likewise, there are men who are so incontinent that they do not spare their wives even during pregnancy. But

---

11. Augustine is describing the situation in which he lived for many years.

whatever immodest, shameful, and sordid acts are committed by married persons with each other, these are the result of human vice, not the fault of marriage itself.

(6) Furthermore, even when people make an excessive demand for the payment of the carnal debt—which the apostle did not give to them as a command but granted as a concession[12]—so that they engage in intercourse even without intending procreation, even if immoral conduct leads them to this sort of intercourse, nevertheless marriage protects them from adultery and fornication. It is not that this sort of behavior is permitted because of marriage; rather, it is forgiven because of marriage. Therefore, not only do married people owe each other the fidelity of sexual intercourse for the sake of procreation, which is the first association of the human race in this mortal life, but they also owe each other a sort of mutual service for the sustaining of each other's weakness, so that they may avoid illicit intercourse. As a result, even if one of them would prefer to adopt perpetual continence, it is not permitted without the consent of the partner. For in this matter *a wife does not have power over her body, but her husband does; likewise, a husband has no power over his body, but his wife does.*[13]

Therefore, they should not deny one another that which the husband seeks from matrimony and that which the wife seeks from her husband, even if this proceeds not from a desire to have children but only from weakness and incontinence. This is to prevent them from falling into damnable seductions at the temptation of Satan because of the incontinence of one or both of them. Conjugal intercourse for the sake of procreation carries no fault; intercourse for the sake of satisfying lust, provided that it takes place with a spouse, carries a forgivable fault (*venialis culpa*) because of marital fidelity; but adultery or fornication carries a mortal fault. Therefore, abstention from all intercourse is better even

---

12. Cf. 1 Cor 7:6.
13. 1 Cor 7:4.

than marital intercourse that takes place for the sake of procreation.

(VII) But while continence has greater merit, it is no sin
to pay the conjugal debt; and although to demand it beyond
the need for procreation is a forgivable fault, certainly fornication and adultery are crimes that must be punished. Therefore, the charity of marriage must be careful that, in seeking
greater honor for itself, it does not create a situation in which
a spouse incurs damnation. For *whoever divorces his wife, except
in the case of fornication, makes her commit adultery*.[14] Once the
nuptial agreement has been made, it is a kind of sacrament
to such an extent that it is not made void even by separation,
since as long as the husband who left her still lives, she commits adultery if she marries someone else, and the husband
who left her is the cause of this evil.

(7) Since it is permissible to divorce an adulterous wife, I
wonder whether it is also permissible to marry again after
the divorce.[15] In this case sacred Scripture creates a difficult
problem, since the apostle cites a precept of the Lord saying
that a woman ought not to leave her husband, but that if
she leaves him, she should remain unmarried or be reconciled
to her husband.[16] She definitely should not withdraw and
remain unmarried, except in the case of an adulterous husband, because by withdrawing from a husband who is not
adulterous she may cause him to commit adultery. But, perhaps, she can be justly reconciled to her husband, either by
tolerating him, if she is unable to restrain herself, or after he
has been corrected. But I do not see how a man can be permitted to marry another woman when he leaves an adulterous wife, if a woman is not permitted to marry again when
she leaves an adulterous husband.

If this is the case, the unifying bond of marriage is so strong
that, although it is created for the purpose of procreation, it
may not be dissolved for the purpose of procreation. A man

14. Matt 5:32.

15. Augustine is describing the case, which Ambrosiaster justified above, in which
a man was allowed to remarry after divorcing his first wife for adultery.

16. Cf. 1 Cor 7:10–11.

may be able to divorce a barren wife and marry someone
who can bear his children, but in our times and according to
Roman law, a man is not permitted to take a second wife, as
long as he still has one wife who is alive. Certainly, when an
adulterous wife or husband has been abandoned, it would be
possible for many human beings to be born, if the woman
or the man chose to marry again. But if this is not permitted, as the divine law seems to prescribe, who could fail to
acknowledge the demands that the great strength of the conjugal bond makes for itself?

I do not think that it could be so powerful if there were
not attached to it a kind of sacred significance (*sacramentum*)
of something greater than could arise from our feeble mortality, something that remains unshaken in order to punish
those who abandon or wish to dissolve this bond. For even
when there is a divorce, the nuptial alliance is not abolished,
and the persons involved remain spouses, even when they are
separated. Furthermore, they commit adultery if they have
intercourse with anyone else after the divorce, and this applies
both to the man and to the woman. This is not the case for
the woman, however, except *in the city of our God, on his holy
mountain.*[17]

(VIII) But who does not know that the laws of the non-
Christians are different? Among them when a divorce has
been issued, both the woman and the man are free to marry
whomever they wish, without any liability to human punishment. This custom is similar to something that Moses apparently permitted regarding a written notice of divorce because
of the Israelites' hardness of heart.[18] In this case there appears
to be more of a rebuke than an approval given to divorce.

(8) *Let marriage be held in honor by all and the marriage bed
be undefiled.*[19] We do not say that marriage is a good merely
in comparison with fornication; in that case there would be
two evils, one of which is worse. In that sense even fornica-

---

17. Ps 48:1. Again Augustine counters the view that a woman's adultery effectively
dissolved the marriage bond.
18. Cf. Deut 24:1; Matt 19:8.
19. Heb 13:4.

tion would be a good because adultery is worse—since to violate another person's marriage is worse than to have sex with
a prostitute; and adultery would be a good because incest is
worse—since it is worse to have intercourse with your mother
than with another man's wife; and on it would go until you
reach things which, as the apostle said, *it is disgraceful even
to mention.*[20] On this rendering all things would be good in
comparison with something worse. But who has any doubts
that this is false?

Marriage and fornication, therefore, are not two evils, one
of which is worse, but marriage and continence are two
goods, one of which is better. Similarly, bodily health and
sickness are not two evils, one of which is worse, but health
and immortality are two goods, one of which is better. Likewise, knowledge and vanity are not two evils, of which vanity is the worse, but knowledge and love are two goods, of
which love is the better. For *knowledge will be destroyed,* the
apostle says, and yet it is a necessity in the present life; but *love
will never fail.*[21] In the same way, the procreation of mortal
bodies, which is the purpose of marriage, will be destroyed;
but freedom from all sexual relations is an angelic practice
here and now, and it will remain so forever.

Just as the feasting of the just is better than the fasting of the
sacrilegious, so the marriages of the faithful are to be ranked
higher than the virginity of the impious. But this does not
mean that feasting is preferable to fasting, only that justice is
preferable to sacrilege; similarly, marriage is not preferable to
virginity, but faith is preferable to impiety. For the just will
feast when it is necessary in order to give to their bodies what
is right and proper, as good masters do to their servants, but
the sacrilegious fast in order to serve demons. The faithful
marry in order to have chaste intercourse with their spouses,
but the impious adopt virginity in order to commit fornication against the true God.

Therefore, just as Martha did something good when she

20. Eph 5:12.
21. 1 Cor 13:8.

ministered to the saints, but her sister Mary did something
better when she sat at the Lord's feet and listened to his
words,[22] so likewise we praise the good of Susanna in her
conjugal chastity,[23] and yet we rank more highly the good
of the widow Anna,[24] and much more highly the good of
the virgin Mary. It was a good thing that they did, when
they supplied Christ and his disciples with the necessities out
of their own resources; but those who abandoned all their
resources in order to follow the same Lord more readily did
an even better thing. Yet, in both of these goods, whether
that of Martha and Mary or that of the disciples, the better
thing could not be done without bypassing or abandoning
the lesser good.

It must be understood, therefore, that marriage is not to
be regarded as an evil simply because abstention from it is
necessary in order to achieve the chastity of a widow or the
integrity of a virgin. It is not the case that what Martha did
was an evil simply because her sister had to abstain from it in
order to do the better thing. Nor is it an evil to invite a just
man or a prophet into one's house simply because the person
who wishes to follow Christ perfectly is required to abandon
his house in order to do the better thing.

(IX.9) Surely, it must be acknowledged that God gave us
some goods to be sought for their own sake, such as wisdom,
good health, and friendship, and other goods that are necessary for the sake of something else, such as learning, food,
drink, sleep, marriage, and sexual intercourse. Some of these
goods are necessary for wisdom, such as learning; some are
necessary for good health, such as food and drink and sleep;
and some are necessary for friendship, such as marriage and
sexual intercourse, for these lead to the propagation of the
human race, in which a friendly association is a great good.

Thus the person who does not use these goods, which
are necessary because of something else, for the purpose for
which they were intended, sometimes sins in a forgivable

22. Cf. Luke 10:38–42.
23. Cf. Sus 22–23.
24. Cf. Luke 2:37.

way, sometimes in a damnable way. But the person who uses them for the purpose for which they were given does well. Therefore, the person who abstains from using things that are unnecessary does better. In the same way, when we have need of these things, we do well to want them; but we do better not to want them than to want them, since I am doing well when I do not consider them necessary.

For this reason, it is good to marry, since it is good to produce children, to be the mother of a family. But it is better not to marry, since it is better, even in regard to human society itself, not to have any need of marriage. For the state of the human race is such that not only do some make use of marriage because they are unable to be continent, but also many others indulge in illicit intercourse. Since the good Creator sees to it that good comes of their evils, numerous offspring are born and an abundant succession is produced, out of which holy friendships may be sought.

This leads me to conclude that in the earliest times of the human race the saints were required to make use of the good of marriage, not as something to be sought for its own sake, but as a good necessary for something else, namely the propagation of the people of God, through which the Prince and Savior of all peoples was both prophesied and born. But in the present, since there is abundant opportunity for spiritual kinsmen to enter into holy and genuine associations everywhere and among all nations, even those people who wish to marry solely for the sake of procreation are urged to practice the better good of continence.

(X.10) But I know what they will murmur: "What if all people wish to abstain completely from sexual intercourse? How would the human race survive?" If only all people had this desire, as long as it proceeds from *a pure heart and a good conscience and a sincere faith!*[25] The City of God would be filled up much more quickly, and the end of time would be hastened. What else does the apostle seem to encourage when he

---

25. 1 Tim 1:5.

says: *I would like everyone to be as I am?*[26] Or, in another place: *What I mean, my friends, is that the time is short. From now on even those who have wives should live as if they had none; those who mourn, as if they were not mourning; those who rejoice, as if they were not rejoicing; those who buy, as if they were not buying; and those who use this world, as if they were not using it. For the form of this world is passing away. I want you to be without care.* Then he adds: *The man without a wife is concerned about the Lord's affairs, how to please the Lord. But the married man is concerned about the affairs of the world, how to please his wife and he is divided. And the unmarried woman and virgin—she is concerned about the Lord's affairs, that she may be holy in body and spirit. But the married woman is concerned about the affairs of the world, how to please her husband.*[27] For this reason, it seems to me that in the present time only those who do not restrain themselves should marry, in accord with that saying of the same apostle: *But if they cannot control themselves, they should marry, for it is better to marry than to burn.*[28]

(11) Not even in this case, however, is marriage a sin. For if marriage were preferable only by comparison with fornication, it would be a lesser sin than fornication, but still it would be a sin. But, as it is now, what shall we say in response to the very clear message that the apostle declares: *He may do whatever he wishes; he does not sin; let him marry?*[29] And: *If you have taken a wife, you have not sinned; and if a virgin marries, she does not sin?*[30] This is now clear evidence that it is wrong to have any doubts about the sinlessness of marriage.

Therefore, it was not marriage that the apostle granted *as a concession*—for would it not be quite absurd to say that a concession is granted to those who did not sin? Rather, he granted *as a concession* that sexual union which takes place because of incontinence, not solely for the sake of procreation

26. 1 Cor 7:7.
27. 1 Cor 7:29-34.
28. 1 Cor 7:9.
29. 1 Cor 7:36.
30. 1 Cor 7:28.

and sometimes not even for the sake of procreation at all. Marriage does not force this sort of intercourse to occur, but it does obtain for it a pardon, as long as it is not so excessive that it impedes the times that ought to be set aside for prayer, and as long as it does not lead to that use which is contrary to nature.

The apostle was unable to remain silent about this when he spoke about the extreme depravities that impure and wicked people practice. The intercourse that is necessary for the sake of procreation is without fault, and only this belongs properly to marriage. Intercourse that goes beyond the need of procreation follows the dictates of lust (*libido*), not of reason. Nevertheless, to render this to a spouse (though not to demand it), so that the spouse may avoid the damnable sin of fornication, is a duty of the married person. But if both partners are subject to such a desire (*concupiscentia*), they are doing something that clearly does not belong to marriage.

Nevertheless, if in their union they love what is honorable more than what is dishonorable (that is, if they love what belongs to marriage more than they love what does not belong to marriage), this is granted to them as a concession by the authority of the apostle. Their marriage does not encourage this fault; rather, it intercedes for it, if they do not turn away from the mercy of God, either by failing to abstain on certain days in order to be free for prayer (since abstinence, like fasting, lends support to one's prayers) or by exchanging a natural use for one that is contrary to nature, for this is more damnable in a spouse.

(XI.12) For when the natural practice extends beyond the marriage pact (that is, beyond what is necessary for procreation), this is pardonable in a wife but damnable in a prostitute. Conversely, the use of sex beyond nature, which is abominable in a prostitute, becomes even more abominable in a wife. The ordinance of the Creator and the order of creation have such great force that an excessive use of something that is granted to be used is much more acceptable than even a single or rare excess in the use of something that has not been granted. That is why a spouse's immoderation must be tolerated when it is a question of licit sexual relations, so that lust will not erupt into illicit relations. This is also the reason why it is much less sinful to make constant demands of one's wife than to make even the most infrequent use of fornication.

But if a man wishes to use that part of his wife's body that has not been granted for this purpose, the wife is more shameful if she allows this to happen to herself than to another woman. The glory of marriage, therefore, is the chastity (*castitas*) of procreation and fidelity (*fides*) in rendering the duty of the flesh. This is the work of marriage, and this is what the apostle defends from all blame when he says: *If you have taken a wife, you have not sinned; and if a virgin marries, she does not sin.*[31] And: *He may do whatever he wishes; he does not sin; let him marry.*[32] Married persons are granted *as a concession* the right to demand from each other in a somewhat immoderate or excessive manner the payment of the conjugal debt, for the reasons that he gave above.

(13) Therefore, when the apostle says that *the unmarried woman thinks about the things of the Lord, that she may be holy in body and spirit,*[33] we should not take this to mean that the chaste Christian spouse is not holy in body. Indeed, this word was addressed to all the faithful: *Do you not know that your bodies are a temple of the Holy Spirit who is in you, whom you have received from God?*[34] Therefore, even the bodies of married people are holy when they keep faithful to each other and to the Lord. Even a spouse who is a nonbeliever is no obstacle to the holiness of either spouse; on the contrary, the apostle himself bears witness that the holiness of a wife benefits an unbelieving husband and the holiness of a husband benefits

---

31. 1 Cor 7:28.
32. 1 Cor 7:36.
33. 1 Cor 7:34.
34. 1 Cor 6:19.

an unbelieving wife: *For the unbelieving husband is sanctified in his wife, and the unbelieving wife is sanctified in her husband.*[35]

Therefore, in the previous passage Paul spoke of the greater holiness of the unmarried woman compared with that of the married woman, and indicated that a greater reward belonged to the unmarried because her good was greater than the other good, since the unmarried woman thinks only about how to please the Lord. This does not mean, however, that the Christian woman who preserves her conjugal purity does not think about how to please the Lord, but only that she thinks about this less, because she also thinks about the things of the world, how to please her husband. For Paul's intention was to let them know what marriage would require of them, namely that they would have to think about the things of the world, how to please their husbands.

***

(XIV.17) It is clear that a couple who have entered into an illicit union can still contract a valid marriage, if they subsequently make an honorable agreement.

(XV) But once they have entered into a marriage in the City of our God, where even from the very first intercourse of two human beings marriage derives a kind of sacramental quality (*quoddam sacramentum*), the marriage cannot be dissolved in any way, except by the death of one of the spouses. For the bond of marriage remains, even if children, for the sake of which the marriage was entered into, do not result because of a clear case of sterility. Therefore, it is not permissible for married persons who know that they will not have children to separate from each other and have intercourse with others, even for the sake of having children. If they do so, they commit adultery with those with whom they have intercourse, but they remain married persons.

Among the ancient fathers, of course, it was permissible to take another woman, with the permission of one's wife, and to produce children that were shared in common, the

35. 1 Cor 7:14.

husband providing the seed and the intercourse, the wife providing the right and authorization. Whether this is also permitted in our own day I would not be so rash as to say. For today there is not the same need of procreation that there was in the past. In those days it was even permissible for husbands who could have children to take other wives in order to produce more numerous progeny, which is something that is certainly not allowed today.

The mysterious difference in times brings with it such a great opportunity for doing or not doing a thing properly that today a man who does not marry even one wife does the better thing, unless he cannot remain continent. But in the past they took many wives blamelessly, even those who would have been able easily to remain continent, if piety had not demanded something else at the time. For just as that wise and just man, who desired for a long time *to be dissolved and to be with Christ*,[36] who took the greatest delight not in his desire to live but in his duty to serve, ate food in order to remain in the flesh (something that was necessary for the sake of other people), so also did the holy men in ancient times have intercourse with women, making use of the right of marriage not out of desire but out of duty.

(XVI.18) For sexual intercourse is to the health of the human race what food is to the health of a human being, and neither exists without some carnal pleasure (*delectatio carnalis*). When this pleasure is moderated and directed toward its natural use by the restraint of temperance, it cannot be lust (*libido*). Illicit food is to the sustaining of life, however, that which fornication or adulterous intercourse is to the desire for offspring. And what illicit food is in the indulgence of the stomach and the palate, illicit intercourse is in the lust that does not seek children. And an immoderate desire for licit food is to some people what to spouses is the pardonable use of intercourse. Therefore, just as it is better to die of hunger than to eat food that has been sacrificed to idols, so it is better

36. Cf. Phil 1:23.

to die without children than to seek to have children by illicit intercourse.

But from whatever source human beings may come, as long as they do not pursue the vices of their parents and as long as they worship God properly, they will be honorable and safe. For human seed is God's creation, no matter what sort of person it comes from, and it will be evil for the person who uses it in an evil way, although in itself it will never be evil. Just as the good children of adulterers cannot be used to defend adultery, so the wicked children born to married people cannot be used to disparage marriage.

In the same manner, just as the fathers in New Testament times took food because of their duty to care for others and just as they ate it while enjoying the natural pleasure of the flesh—although their pleasure was in no way comparable to the pleasure experienced by those who ate of sacrificial offerings or by those who consumed licit foods in an immoderate way—so, likewise, the fathers in Old Testament times had sexual intercourse because of their duty to care for others. The natural pleasure that they enjoyed did not give way to any sort of irrational or forbidden lust, nor should it be compared either to the wickedness of fornication or to the intemperance of married persons. Indeed, it was the same vein of charity, which once led them to produce children in a fleshly way, which now leads us to propagate in a spiritual way for the sake of our mother, Jerusalem. Only the difference of times caused the fathers to do different works. Just as it was necessary that the non-carnal prophets copulate in a carnal manner, so it was necessary that the non-carnal apostles eat in a carnal manner.

(XVII.19) Therefore, the married women of our own day, of whom it is said: *If they cannot control themselves, they should marry,*[37] ought not to be compared even to the holy women who married in ancient times. Marriage itself, of course, in all nations exists for the same purpose: the procreation of children. No matter how these children turn out in the end, mar-

37. 1 Cor 7:9.

riage was instituted in order that they might be born in an ordered and honorable way. Now people who are unable to control themselves have taken a step up in honor, as it were, by marrying; but those who without a doubt would have controlled themselves, had the conditions allowed this, have taken a step down in piety, so to speak, by marrying. Because of this, even though the marriages of both types of people are equally good, in respect to the marriage itself, since they both exist for the sake of procreation, nevertheless the married people of our day are not to be compared to the married people of ancient times.

Married people today have something that is granted to them *as a concession* because of the honorable state of marriage, although this concession does not pertain to the essence of marriage itself; I am referring to the use of intercourse beyond the need of procreation, something that was not conceded to the ancients. Even if some married people today desire and seek in marriage only that for which marriage was instituted, even these spouses cannot be compared to the people of ancient times. For in people today the very desire for children is carnal, whereas in the ancients it was spiritual because it was in harmony with the sacred mystery (*sacramentum*) of the times. In fact, in our day no one who is perfect in piety seeks to have children except in a spiritual way, whereas in the past to have children in a carnal way was itself an act of piety, since the propagation of that people was a proclamation of future events and participated in the dispensation of prophecy.

(20) That is why a man was allowed to have several wives, while a woman was not allowed to have several husbands, not even for the sake of offspring, if perhaps she was able to bear children when her husband was not able to beget them. For according to the mysterious law of nature, things that serve as ruling principles love singularity. In fact, it is fitting that subordinate things should be subject not only as individuals to individual rulers but also (if the natural and social conditions allow it) as a group to a single ruler. That is why one

servant does not have several masters, whereas several servants do have one master.

In the same manner, nowhere do we read that any of the holy women served two or more living husbands. But we do read that one husband had several wives, when the social customs of that people permitted it and when the character of the times required it, since this does not contradict the nature of marriage itself. For several women can become pregnant by one man, but one woman cannot become pregnant by several men—this is the power of the ruling principle—just as it is right that many souls should be subject to one God. For this reason the only true God of souls is one: although one soul is able to commit fornication through many false gods, it cannot be made fruitful by them.

(XVIII.21) Since there will be one City constructed out of the many souls who have one soul and one heart in God—this perfect state of unity will be achieved only after our pilgrimage in this life, when the thoughts of all will be revealed and all hostility will cease—the sacred symbolism (*sacramentum*) of marriage in our day has been restricted to one man and one woman, with the result that it is forbidden to ordain a man as a minister in the church, unless he is the *husband of one wife*.[38] Those who have rejected the ordination of a man, who as a catechumen or a pagan had taken another wife, understood this most perceptively. What is involved is not the matter of sin, but rather the nature of the sacred symbol (*sacramentum*). For in baptism all sins are forgiven. But when the apostle said: *If you have taken a wife, you have not sinned. And if a virgin marries, she does not sin*, and: *He may do whatever he wishes, he does not sin; let him marry*,[39] he declared clearly enough that marriage is no sin.

It is analogous to the case of a woman who has been corrupted while still a catechumen. Just as she cannot be consecrated among the virgins of God after her baptism on account of the holiness of the sacred symbol, so likewise it does not

38. Cf. 1 Tim 3:2; Titus 1:6.
39. 1 Cor 7:28, 36.

seem unfair that a man who has had more than one wife should have lost, as it were, the standard appropriate to the sacred symbol, even if he has committed no sin. This standard is not necessary for the merit of a good life, but it is required for the symbolism of ecclesiastical ordination.

For the very same reason, just as the several wives of the ancient fathers signified our churches that would come into being from the many nations and would be subject to the one man Christ, so our high priest, *a man of one wife,* signifies the unity that derives from the many nations and is subject to the one man Christ. This unity will be perfected in the future, when *he will reveal what is hidden in darkness and will make manifest the hidden motives of the heart, so that each will receive his praise from God.*[40] In the present, however, there are disagreements, both manifest and hidden, even among those who, if charity is preserved, are to be one and in One. In the future these disagreements will be no more.

Therefore, just as in the past the symbol (*sacramentum*) of multiple marriages signified the multitude that would be subject to God in all the lands of the Gentiles, so in our time the symbol of single marriages signifies the unity of all of us who will one day be subject to God in the heavenly City. Thus, just as servants do not serve two or more masters, so in the past it was forbidden, and is now forbidden, and will always be forbidden for a woman to marry another man while her husband is still alive. For it is always wrong to commit apostasy from the one God and to enter into the adulterous and superstitious worship of another god. Not even for the sake of more numerous offspring did our holy fathers do what the Roman Cato is said to have done, namely to have handed over his wife, while he was still alive, to fill the house of another man with children. Indeed, in the marriages of our women the holiness of the sacrament is more important than the fruitfulness of the womb.

(22) Therefore, even those who marry solely for the purpose of procreation, for which purpose marriage was insti-

---

40. 1 Cor 4:5.

tuted, are not to be compared to the ancient fathers, for they sought to have children in a manner quite different from those who live today. Take, for example, the devout and intrepid Abraham, who was ordered to sacrifice his son, whom he had received only after great desperation. Abraham, who had lifted his hand at God's command, would not have spared his only son, had not God himself prevented him and made him lower his hand.[41]

***

(XXIV.32) The good of marriage, therefore, among all nations and peoples lies in the purpose of procreation and in the faithful preservation of chastity. But for the people of God the good of marriage lies also in the holiness of the sacrament. Because of this holiness, it is wrong for a woman to marry another man, even if she leaves with a bill of divorce, as long as her husband is alive, even if she does this for the sake of having children. Even if the first marriage took place solely for the sake of procreation and even if that for the sake of which the marriage was made did not happen, the marriage bond is not dissolved until the spouse dies.

In a similar way, if a cleric is ordained in order to form a congregation and if the congregation does not come into being, nonetheless the sacramental sign of ordination remains in those who have been ordained. If a cleric is removed from office because of some fault, he will not lose the sacramental sign of the Lord that was imposed once and for all, although it remains as a mark of judgment.

The apostle, therefore, testifies that marriage was made for the purpose of procreation. *I want the younger widows to marry,* he said.[42] Then, as if someone had asked him, "But why?" he immediately added: *to bear children to become the mothers of the households.* This passage also pertains to the faithful preservation of chastity: *A wife does not have power over her body, but her husband does; likewise, a husband has no power over his body,*

---

41. Cf. Gen 22:1–14.
42. 1 Tim 5:14.

but his wife does.[43] This passage also speaks of the holiness of the sacrament: *A wife should not separate from her husband; but if she does separate, she must remain unmarried or else be reconciled to her husband, and a man may not divorce his wife.*[44] All of these are the goods on account of which marriage is a good: offspring, fidelity, sacrament.

Surely, it is better and holier in the present time not to seek after offspring in the flesh and thereby to keep oneself perpetually free, as it were, from all this activity and to be subject in a spiritual way to the one man Christ, but only if people use this freedom in order to *think about the things of the Lord, how to be pleasing to God.*[45] In other words, continence must constantly be on guard so that it does not fall short in respect to obedience. In their deeds the holy fathers of ancient times practiced the virtue of obedience as the root and mother, so to speak, of all their actions, whereas they possessed continence in the disposition of their souls. Indeed, through their obedience they even would have abstained from intercourse altogether, had they been ordered to, since they were righteous and holy people who were always prepared for every good work. For it would have been much easier for them to follow God's command or exhortation and to have abstained from sex, when they were able to sacrifice out of obedience the very offspring, whose propagation they were ensuring by their sexual intercourse.

SERMON 354A

(1) The Sunday readings, and the divine word in the sacred Scriptures which have just been read, and the heavenly authority exhort the human race to be mindful of its mortality because the end is approaching. For to every human being (that is, to each individual person) the end is near, even if perhaps the end of the human race itself is still far off. As I had

43. 1 Cor 7:4.
44. 1 Cor 7:10–11.
45. 1 Cor 7:32.

begun to say, the divine word seems to make this exhortation: that we should be mindful of our mortality since the end will come. But one should contemplate the life where there is no end. The person who remembers that he is mortal will deserve to gain immortal life.

(2) You have heard that the Pharisees, trying to test the Lord, asked him whether it was permissible for a man to divorce his wife for any reason.[46] His answer was true, because he is the Truth.[47] In their effort to test the Lord, they did not succeed in making him a liar; as a result both the faithful and the unfaithful learn the truth. The one testing hears the truth, so that the worshipper of God may be instructed. I have said this for this reason: so that people may not think that the Lord God said anything other than the way things are, since the Pharisees were not asking their question in a faithful manner, but in an effort to test him. For our purposes it does not matter what sort of people were asking the question; what matters is what he said. It does not matter what sort of person struck the rock, but rather what kind of water flowed from it.[48] Therefore in the Lord's response married people have something to learn; so, too, do those who are not yet married, or those who have already made a good resolution to reject marriage. Since, as they say, the time is running out, it urges us to say something in accordance with these words of the Lord.

(3) The words of the apostle pertain to us even more now, since they were spoken with greater diligence, more intense concern, and more abundant piety: *For the rest, my brothers and sisters, the time is short, and it remains for those who have wives to be as though they did not have them*, et cetera: *And those who buy as though they were not buying, and those who rejoice as though they were not rejoicing, and those who use the world as though they were not using the world. For the form of this world*

---

46. Cf. Matt 19:3.
47. Cf. John 14:6.
48. Cf. Num 20:9–11.

is passing away. I want you to be without worry.[49] And then
he added: *The man who does not have a wife thinks about the
things of God, how to please God; but the man who is bound in
marriage thinks about the things of the world, how to please his
wife.*[50] There is a great difference between thinking about the
things of God and thinking about the things of the world. It
is impossible for the comparison to unite what the thought
has thus divided. But is there some married man who is on
fire to devote himself to continence? Let him look to his own
side, let him see if she is following; if she is following, let
him lead the way. If she is not following, he may not separate
from her.[51] Perhaps he is able and she is not able, or she is able
and he is not; let him realize that they are *one flesh*. You have
heard not just any human, but the Lord of all humans in his
response to the Jews giving precepts to the Christians: *Have
you not read*, he said, *that in the beginning God made them male
and female?* And he said: *For this reason a man will leave his
father and mother and will cling to his wife, and they will be two
in one flesh. And so they are no longer two, but one flesh. What
God has joined*, he said, *man should not separate.*[52]

(4) It seems inappropriate to investigate this topic more
thoroughly, but we should not consider ourselves to be so
healthy that we do not have sympathy for those who are ill.
For what are we compared to the holiness of the apostle Paul?
And yet, with pious humility, with health-bearing speech,
with divine medicine, he entered human bedrooms. And such
great holiness approached the beds of married people, gazed
upon them lying there, and did not lay aside the garment of
his holiness, but rather gave advice to weakness: *The husband
should pay the debt to his wife.* It is a debt; he must pay it. *Likewise, the wife to her husband. The wife does not have power over*

49. 1 Cor 7:29–31.
50. 1 Cor 7:32–33.
51. The verb Augustine uses at this point (*dimittat*) is the usual Latin word for
"divorce."
52. Matt 19:4–5.

her own body, but her husband does.[53] This is no surprise, for the wife is subordinate to her husband. The man decides; the woman obeys. Nevertheless, although in other matters the woman ought to be the servant to the man, in this case—that is, when it comes to the commingling of the two sexes—in this case, their condition is equal. For it was a small thing for the apostle to say *The wife does not have power over her own body, but her husband does*—he has respectfully referred to the sexual organs by the honorable word "body" in order to avoid obscenity—what he was saying he made clear: *The wife does not have power over her own body, but her husband does. Likewise the husband does not have power over his own body, but his wife does.* By saying "wife" Paul made it clear that he was referring to the man's sex. It is the property of another; it is owed to the woman.

(5) It is impossible, then, for a man to have so much freedom of choice that he says, "I am already able to be continent. If you are able, join me; if you are not able, you cannot stop me. I do what I am able to do." What then? Do you wish, sir, for your own side to perish? If the weaker flesh cannot be continent, the will that is more sluggish will fornicate, and by fornicating it will be damned. God forbid that your crown should be her punishment! "You are deceived. This will not happen; it will not be like this. It will not happen as you say. Since she will be condemned for fornication, it is better that she alone should perish, rather than both of us." If you say this, you are deceived. For marriage is not condemned; *what God has joined together* is not condemned, but only *man should not separate.*[54] You are that man; by grasping at continence without the agreement of your wife, as a man, you wish to separate what God has deigned to join together. "But it is God," he says, "who does the separating, because I am doing this for God." Yes, this would be true, if you have read anywhere that God said, "If you have intercourse with your wife, I will condemn you." In that case, do what you will, so that

53. 1 Cor 7:3–4.
54. Matt 19:6.

you will not be condemned. But since you heard the apostle of Christ saying, *The wife does not have power over her own body, but her husband does. Likewise the husband does not have power over his own body, but his wife does. Do not deprive one another.*[55]

(6) He has said *deprive*, that is, by denying the debt, not by committing adultery. He was speaking about paying the debt, and he was binding them to pay the conjugal debts to one another. For he would not have permitted adultery in the following words, when he said: *Do not deprive one another*, he added, *except by mutual agreement for a time.* Should adultery be committed *by agreement*? If you think that the words *Do not deprive one another* refer to adultery, then what did he mean by *except by agreement*? God forbid that a husband and wife would permit each other to commit adultery *by agreement*! A modest and patient married woman is accustomed to put up with such things. It belongs to feminine chastity to tolerate such a husband. But that is no reason for the husband to feel confident; he should be wary lest at a later time he be condemned, when in the present it is said that he is tolerated. But the case is clear, and the word of the apostle needs no explanation. He says: *Do not deprive one another*, so that they will not deny conjugal debts to each other, *except by agreement for a time in order to be free for prayer.* You see, then, that the apostle prescribes a kind of continence—or, better, a brief respite of continence—in order to stimulate an offering of prayers, and with that solicitude with which such great holiness did not refuse to approach the beds of sick persons, [he added] *and then come together again.*[56]

(7) When you add, *for a time, in order to be free for prayer, and then come together again*, is this what you are commanding, apostle? "Yes, it is," he says. And where is your decency, where is the modesty that befits such great holiness? "But," he says, "I know the danger of weakness." Moreover, he did not

55. 1 Cor 7:4–5.
56. 1 Cor 7:5.

fail to mention the reason behind his advice. "Do you wish to hear," he says, "why I have said, *and then come together again? Lest Satan tempt you because of your lack of self-control.*"[57] Then he followed this up, so that he would not appear to have commanded this, rather than merely to have permitted it. For it is one thing to grant permission to weakness, something else to command the faith. "*But I say this as a concession,*"[58] he said. "When I say, *Come together again,* I am speaking in the form of a concession, not as a command. I am not giving a command to chastity, but I am granting permission to weakness." It is not praiseworthy, but it is forgivable: *as a concession, for I wish that everyone was like me; but each person has his own gift from God, one this one and another that one.*[59] And that is why the Lord also said: *Let the one who can receive it receive it.*[60]

(8) At this point someone might say: "If the apostle granted this *as a concession* and yielded to human weakness, then marriage is a sin. For one does not grant "concession" or "pardon" except to sin. Certainly, that which the apostle granted *as a concession* to weakness—I dare to say it—is a sin. But it is not there that the good of marriage lies. So, pay attention, brothers and sisters, and assist me by focusing your minds as I engage this most difficult passage and struggle for your sake before the Lord. He has granted *a concession* to such a deed. It is clear that he is referring to the sexual relations of married persons, not of adulterers. And yet he says, "*as a concession, not as a command.*[61] I am offering forgiveness, not issuing a command." The married person will say, "O apostle, if you are forgiving me, then I am sinning." And so I do not want the defender of the good of marriage to present this argument to me and to say: "Marriage is good so as to prevent adultery, for forgiveness is granted to marriage and a concession is given to marriage." This is to speak of two evils, not one

---

57. 1 Cor 7:5.
58. 1 Cor 7:6.
59. 1 Cor 7:6–7.
60. Matt 19:12.
61. 1 Cor 7:6.

good and one evil, but two evils: one of them small and the other great.[62]

(9) The apostle was not criticizing the good of marriage, but rather the evil of incontinence, that is, to make use of one's wife beyond what is necessary to produce children. To know why you have taken a wife, do not read my arguments, but your own marriage contracts. Read them, pay attention to them, and if you have done anything beyond them, blush! Read them, and I, too, will hear. I have to do this for your sake. This is certainly what you read: "for the sake of producing children."[63] Therefore, *anything that is beyond this is from the evil one.*[64] Take a close look at yourself, carefully scrutinize yourself, examine yourself. If you do nothing more than what must be done "for the sake of producing children," you do not have anything for the apostle to forgive. But if you do anything more than this, what you do is wrong; what you do is a sin. Nevertheless, do you wish to know what sort of good is the good of marriage? Through the good of marriage the evil of incontinence is forgivable. Lust is aroused, you are overcome, you are dragged along, but you have not been dragged away from your wife. You would have to be punished for having been conquered by incontinence, if marriage did not intercede for you. If, therefore, you are married and you do not wish to be subject to the apostle's grant of forgiveness, then do not exceed the limits of your marriage contracts.

(10) Have you not yet been conquered? Do not seek to be. For the man who is able to use his wife only "for the sake of producing children" is able also not to use her at all. He is victorious over lust; he controls the movements of the flesh; he boldly holds the reins of temperance; he directs that impulse, like a horse, wherever he wishes; he does not let go of the

62. Augustine's argument at this point is directed against the views of men, such as Tertullian and Jerome, who tended to characterize marriage as simply the lesser of two evils.

63. Augustine frequently appealed to the marriage contracts (*tabulae nuptiales*) to illustrate the purpose of human marriage.

64. Matt 5:37.

right to hold the reins. So, then, you are that sort of person and have not yet been conquered and are not yet bound: *If you are free of a wife, do not seek a wife.*[65] For if it is said to married persons: *The time is short, it remains that those who have wives should be as though they do not have them,*[66] why do you wish to have a wife, when you are able not to have one, while preserving your continence?

(11) For why should a people still have to be propagated for God, so that Christ, the salvation of the nations, may come? When that people was being propagated, men who could have practiced continence were compelled to take wives out of pious duty. The holy fathers produced children out of pious duty; the holy mothers gave birth to children out of pious duty, and they, too, were capable of continence. They were devoted to the propagation of the people; it was a duty. But now it is clear that in all places there is a large number of people, out of which spiritual children may be selected to form a holy people for Christ, adopted forever into a heavenly inheritance. Therefore, back then was the time to embrace; now is the time to refrain from embracing. The prophet speaks; let us listen: *There is a time for everything, a time to embrace and a time to refrain from embracing.*[67] The *time to embrace* was the time of prophecy; the *time to refrain from embracing* is the gospel time. *A time to throw stones, a time to gather them.*[68] The *time to throw stones* was the time of procreation of the human race; for *God is able to raise up children of Abraham from these stones.*[69] Why are stones still being thrown? Let those that have already been thrown be gathered. It was said that stones should be thrown: *Cursed be the one who does not raise up seed for Israel.*[70] Now it is said that stones should be gathered: *The time is short, it remains that*

---

65. 1 Cor 7:27.
66. 1 Cor 7:29.
67. Eccl 3:5.
68. Eccl 3:5.
69. Luke 3:8.

70. This saying is an *agraphon*, a passage cited as Scripture but not found in the canonical text. Faustus the Manichaean had cited the passage, and Augustine, accept-

those who have wives should be as though they do not have them.[71]
Now, therefore: *The one who can receive this, let him receive it.*[72]
In that former time the person who was able to receive the
duty of continence did not take it up; nevertheless, the virtue
was within them. They had their wives for the sake of God,
unless perhaps we think that Abraham, if he had been told to
be continent, could have hesitated out of fear, a man possessed
of such virtue and piety that he could offer his heir to be sacrificed at the Lord's command, the son whom God had given
to him to be raised.[73] But their time was different from ours.

(12) Therefore, let no one give commands, let no one think
that a requirement in this matter has been imposed upon him.
The one who can receive this, let him receive it. "But I am not
able," he says. You are not able? "I am not able." Then the
authority of the apostle, like a nursemaid, lifts you up, so that
if they are not able to practice continence, let them marry.[74] You
are allowed to do something to obtain pardon. The purpose
of pardon is to prevent you from rushing into eternal punishment. What is permitted should be done, so that what is
not permitted should be forgiven. What follows demonstrates
this: *I prefer that they marry rather than burn.*[75] "I have given a
concession," he said, "to incontinence, since I was afraid of
something worse; I was afraid of eternal punishments, I was
afraid of what awaits adulterers, what will befall them." Even
if married people, when overcome by concupiscence, make
use of one another beyond what is necessary to produce children, they should consider this one of the things for which it
is said each day: *Forgive us our debts, as we forgive our debtors.*[76]
But those who are able to receive this, let them receive this.
And in order that they may be able to receive it, let them

ing it as Scripture, responded to the passage in *Against Faustus the Manichaean* 14.13
and 32.14.
    71. 1 Cor 7:29.
    72. Matt 19:12.
    73. Cf. Gen 22:1–18.
    74. 1 Cor 7:9.
    75. 1 Cor 7:9.
    76. Matt 6:12.

pray. Faith procures even continence. *Since I knew*, the sacred
Scripture said, *since I knew that no one can be continent unless
God grants it, and this very thing requires wisdom: to know whose
gift it is.*[77] When you are afraid of continence, as if it were a
punishment, you do not knock on the door of grace. Do not
consider it a punishment. When you are capable of it, it will
not be a burden. He whose gifts must be sought will grant it
to you. Knock! You will receive. Ask, seek! You will find.[78]
The source is always flowing, do not let your faith be sluggish. And yet *the one who can receive this, let him receive it.* The
one who is not able, *If he is not being continent, let him marry.*

(13) Love one another. The husband is able and the wife is
not: do not exact the debt, but pay it. And in so far as you,
who are no longer exacting it, pay the debt, if you do not
exact it, you are doing a work of mercy. Indeed, I dare to
say it: it is a work of mercy. For if you do not pay the debt,
your wife may be overcome by concupiscence and become
an adulteress, or if you, woman, do not pay the debt to your
husband, he may be overcome by concupiscence and become
an adulterer. I do not want you to receive greater honor in
such a way that you are willing for him to be damned. But
if you are now not exacting the debt but only paying it, it
is counted as continence. For the debt is not being exacted
out of lust but being paid out of mercy. In short, say to your
God: Lord, you know in me what you have given, but I also
hear what you have advised, since you made both me and my
spouse, and you want neither of us to perish. Let us turn to
the Lord.

LETTER 6* TO ATTICUS

To my most blessed lord and esteemed brother, the fellow
bishop Atticus, Augustine sends greetings in the Lord.

(1) I have received no letters from your holiness through
the religious brother and fellow priest Innocent, although I

---

77. Wis 8:21.
78. Cf. Luke 11:9–10.

had expected that he would bring one to me. But when he informed me of the reason why this happened, I wrote this letter as if I had received something from Your Eminence. Because I am safe and sound by God's grace and the help of your prayers, I will pay my debt by writing. Innocent told me that a rumor had suggested something quite different, and naturally you believed it, since the report concerned a human being. For what is more credible than a message that a mortal man has died? Certainly this will happen at some time to everyone who lives in the flesh. But when he heard more recently from other messengers that I was still alive, and when he informed Your Grace, he told me that you were delighted and had given thanks to God, although you were not quite certain about it.

(2) Therefore, my lord, because I have no reason to doubt that you will be glad to receive my letter, I can more confidently and more eagerly ask by the laws of charity that you send a reply, thereby repaying the previous debt. I have, however, regarded the letters that your blessedness sent to my brother as if they had been sent to both of us, for we are united in spirit. Furthermore, I was glad to discover that in them your holiness exercised his pastoral care to correct the perversity of certain Pelagians and to warn of their craftiness.

(3) It is not surprising that they also slander the Catholics, if they are trying in this way to suppress whatever refutes their poisonous teachings. What Catholic defends the right faith against them to the extent of condemning marriage, which the Creator and Maker of the world has blessed? What Catholic would say that the concupiscence of marriage is a work of the devil, when it is clear that the human race would be propagated by it, even if no one had sinned, in order to fulfill that blessing: *Increase and multiply?*[79] The sin of the man, *in whom all have sinned,*[80] did not cause that blessing to lose the effect of its goodness, which is obvious to all in that clear, remarkable, and praiseworthy fecundity of nature.

79. Gen 1:28.
80. Rom 5:12.

What Catholic does not proclaim the works of God in every creature, both of spirit and of flesh? What Catholic is not led by a contemplation of creation to hymn the Creator, who not only made all things good before the fall, but who even now continues to make them good?

(4) With perverse reasoning and quarrelsome blindness they confuse those evils, which were rightly imposed upon nature because of its guilt, with the goods of nature. They praise the Creator of humankind to such an extent that they deny that little children need a savior, as if they had no evil; this is their damnable doctrine. They think that they can support this wicked error by praising marriage, saying that marriage is condemned if what is born of marriage is condemned, unless it is reborn. They do not see that there are two different things: one is the good of marriage, which continues to be present in marriage even after the fall; the other is the original sin, which marriage did not create and does not now create, but which marriage now finds to be a fact. Marriage can make a good use of this evil, if it does not do with it whatever it likes, but only what is permitted. These people refuse to consider this, because they have been convinced by an error that they prefer to defend rather than avoid.

(5) Because of this error they do not distinguish the concupiscence of marriage (*concupiscentia nuptiarum*), that is, the concupiscence of conjugal purity, the concupiscence for the legitimate procreation of children, from the concupiscence of the flesh (*concupiscentia carnis*), which lusts indiscriminately after licit and illicit things. The concupiscence of marriage, which makes good use of the concupiscence of the flesh, serves to restrain it from what is illicit and to channel it only toward what is licit. All chastity is a struggle against the power of the concupiscence of the flesh, which *resists the law of the mind,*[81] both the chastity of married people, who make a good use of it, and the chastity of holy and continent virgins, who in a better and more glorious way make no use of it.

Therefore, because they do not distinguish the concupis-

81. Cf. Rom 7:23.

cence of the flesh, in which there is only a desire for sexual intercourse, from the concupiscence of marriage, in which there is the duty to procreate, they praise in the most arrogant manner that concupiscence of the flesh, which caused the first human beings to blush, when they covered with fig leaves those bodily parts that caused no shame before the fall.[82] Indeed, they were naked and were not ashamed, so that we would understand that the impulse that did cause shame was conceived in human nature along with death. For it was then that they had reason to be ashamed, when they also began to suffer the necessity of death.

With great praises [the Pelagians] proclaim that a sober and prudent distinction must be made between this concupiscence of the flesh and the concupiscence of marriage; but they do so to such an extent that they believe that even if no one had sinned in paradise, it would still have been impossible to procreate children without that concupiscence in the body destined for life, just as now children are not procreated without that concupiscence in the body destined for death, from which body the apostle desires to be set free through Jesus Christ.[83]

(6) This opinion of theirs, proceeding as it does from ignorance and lack of reflection, leads to such a great absurdity that, no matter how arrogantly the human face is hardened by these things, not even they are able to sustain it completely. For if that concupiscence of the flesh, which we know contains so disordered an impulse that it must either be prevented from any use by the reins of chastity or be turned to a good use by the goodness of marriage, existed in paradise before the fall, then clearly in a place of such blessedness there are only two choices. Either a person would shamefully submit to the concupiscence, so that each time he felt the impulse he would have intercourse with his wife, without any need for procreation, but only to satisfy the appetite of his desire, even if she were already pregnant. Or he would struggle against

82. Cf. Gen 3:7.
83. Cf. Rom 7:24.

this concupiscence with the strength of abstinence to avoid being dragged by it into that sort of filthy conduct. Let them choose which of the two is preferable. If the concupiscence of the flesh dominated and was not resisted, then there was no true or honorable freedom in paradise; but if concupiscence was resisted and did not dominate, then there was no true peace or happiness there. Whichever you choose, either the blessed virtue or the virtuous blessedness of paradise is destroyed.

(7) Who does not see this? Who would contradict this most obvious truth, except out of the most arrogant stubbornness? Thus, the choice is left: Either in paradise there was no concupiscence of the flesh, which we feel at work in stormy, disordered desires against our will, even when there is no need. In this case, there still would have been the concupiscence of marriage there, which served the peaceful love of the spouses and commanded the genitals to procreate, just as the will commands the hands and feet to do their proper works. In this way children would have been conceived in paradise in a remarkable way, without the disruption of the lust of the flesh, just as they also would have been born in a remarkable way without the pains of labor. Or, if the concupiscence of the flesh did exist in paradise, it certainly would not have been the great and hateful burden that people now experience it to be, as they struggle against it with the chastity of marriage, widowhood, or virginity.

Concupiscence insinuates itself where it is not needed, and by its troublesome and even wicked desires it agitates even the hearts of the faithful and the saints. Even if we resist it and refuse to yield to its disturbing impulses with any conscious assent, we would still prefer by a holier desire that these impulses not be present in us at all, if it were possible; indeed, someday this will happen. For this is the completion of the good, which the apostle indicated the saints still lacked in this life, when he said: *I can will what is good, but I cannot bring it to completion.*[84] He does not say "do the good," but *bring*

---

84. Cf. Rom 7:24.

it to completion, because a person does good by not yielding to these desires, but he does not *bring it to completion* since the desires are still present. *I do not do the good that I want to,* he says, *but I do the evil that I do not want to do.*[85] Certainly, he did not do evil by offering his body to carry out wicked desires, but he was speaking about the very impulses of concupiscence; even if he did not yield to these impulses or commit the acts to which they were provoking him, nevertheless by having them he was doing what he did not wish to do. Finally, he adds: *But if I am doing what I do not wish to do,* that is, although I do not consent to concupiscence—although I do not want to experience concupiscence, I do so anyway—*it is no longer I who do it, but the sin that lives in me.*[86]

The guilt for this sin is passed on by generation; it is removed by regeneration, when the remission of all sins takes place. But some of its power and a kind of pernicious and contaminated disposition remain in the corruptible and mortal body, even when it has been absolved of guilt. The person who is regenerated must struggle against this, if he is to make progress. Even if he has embraced conjugal purity and not total continence, he will still struggle against this concupiscence of the flesh, in order to avoid adultery, fornication, and any other deadly and wicked vices. Lastly, he will have to struggle to avoid using even his wife intemperately, since he will have to abstain for a time from sexual relations, with her consent, in order to be free for prayer, and then return to them, so that Satan will not tempt them because of their lack of self-control, for the apostle says that this was granted to them *as a concession, not as a command.*[87]

Some people who have not given much thought to the matter believe that marriage itself was granted as a concession, but this is not true. If this were the case, God forbid, then marriage itself would be a sin. For when a concession is made, it is clear that a fault is being forgiven. But the con-

85. Rom 7:19.
86. Rom 7:20.
87. 1 Cor 7:5–6.

cession the apostle grants refers to sexual intercourse between spouses that takes place not for the sake of procreation, but in order to satisfy an incontinent desire; he grants it *as a concession,* so that damnable sins will not be committed, if the concession does not allow some laxity.

Even if some married people are so outstanding in the virtue of conjugal purity that they have intercourse solely for the purpose of procreation, and even if after their regeneration in baptism they continue to live in this way, each of their offspring born through that concupiscence of the flesh—which, though not good in itself, they make good use of through the good concupiscence of marriage—contracts original sin. For there is no doubt that that sin, which can be removed only by regeneration, accompanies anything that is born, unless it is also reborn, just as the foreskin, which can be removed only by circumcision, accompanies the son of a circumcised man, unless the son is also circumcised.

(8) If, therefore, this concupiscence of the flesh did exist in paradise, so that children were born through it to fulfill the blessing of marriage by increasing the human race, it certainly could not have been what it is now, that is, a thing whose impulses lust after licit and illicit objects indiscriminately. This concupiscence would lead to many of the foulest acts, if it were allowed to pursue any of these impulses, and we must struggle against it in order to preserve chastity. But if there was any concupiscence in paradise, it would have been the sort in which the flesh would never have lusted against the spirit, but would have obeyed the command of the will in a marvelous peace; it would never have been present, except when there was a need, and it would never have inflicted itself on the conscious mind with its disordered and illicit delights; it would have nothing wicked that would have to be restrained by the reins of temperance or resisted by efforts of virtue, but it would follow the person's will in an easy and harmonious obedience, whenever it was necessary.

In the present circumstances, therefore, since concupiscence is not like this, and since it is necessary that chastity oppose its enemy, they should admit that concupiscence has been vitiated by sin, so that by its impulses they, who were once naked and not ashamed, were put to shame. They should not be surprised that it was only the son of the Virgin, whom they cannot say was conceived by that concupiscence, who did not contract original sin.

Please forgive any tedium I may have caused for your holy senses by the length of this letter; I have done it not to make you more learned, but to refute the false accusations they are spreading around you.[88]

88. Augustine refers to the accusation of holding Manichaean views that Julian and others had directed against him.

16.

Paulinus of Nola

The following marriage poem or *epithalamium* (Carmen 25) was composed by the poet and ascetic writer Paulinus of Nola on the occasion of the wedding of Julian, future bishop of Eclanum, and his bride Titia (ca. 405). Paulinus was a prominent Roman aristocrat of Spanish origins, who eventually became bishop of Nola in southern Italy. After Paulinus and his wife, Therasia, lost their children, they resolved to live in sexual continence. Paulinus eventually became the patron of the shrine of Saint Felix at Nola and engaged in correspondence with numerous notable persons of his day, among them Augustine, Pelagius, and members of the Anician family.

The *epithalamium* was a well-known literary form in classical antiquity, and Paulinus made a conscious attempt to Christianize the genre. Rather than invoke the traditional goddesses of love, for example, Paulinus banished them from the scene (lines 9–10). Instead of the traditional erotic banter that usually characterized such wedding poems (cf. the *Nuptial Cento* of Ausonius, a teacher of Paulinus), Paulinus urged the young couple to share a desire for virginity or, at least, to produce children who will be virgins (lines 233–34).

More significant, however, than the rejection of pagan customs was Paulinus's acceptance of the fully Christian nature of marriage. The "yoke" of marriage is now assimilated to the "easy yoke" of Jesus (lines 4–6; cf. Matt 11:30). Paulinus appeals to the place of marriage within God's primal creative activity (lines 15–26). He urges the young couple to imitate the simplicity of Adam and Eve in paradise and tells them that their harmonious marriage will "bring to an end the servitude of Eve" (line 149). Although Paulinus himself had entered into a vow of continence with his wife, Therasia, and was thoroughly imbued with ascetic ideals, there is little place in his poem for the kind of pessimism regarding the sexual urge that so troubled Augustine. If anything, Paulinus portrayed marriage as fully compatible with the demands of Christian holiness.

CARMEN 25

(1) Harmonious souls are being united in chaste love,
A youth who is Christ's virgin, a maiden who is God's.

(3) Christ our God, lead to your reins these well-matched doves, and
Govern them under your easy yoke.[1]

(5) For your yoke, O Christ, is easy, when an eager will
Receives it, and when love bears it with ready obedience.

(7) The sacred duty of chastity is a heavy weight for the unwilling,
But to the pious it is a sweet task to conquer the work of the flesh.

(9) All vain and vulgar license must depart these wedding rites:
Juno, Cupid, Venus—the very essence of indulgence!

---

1. Cf. Matt 11:30.

(11) Holy offspring of a bishop are being joined in a sacred pact,
So peace, purity, and piety must enter the alliance.

(13) For the harmonious bond of marriage shares at once in the
Love of piety, the dignity of love, and the peace of God.

(15) With his own lips God made this union holy,
By the divine hand he established the human couple.

(17) He made the two abide in one flesh,[2]
In order to create a love more indivisible.

(19) For while Adam slept the rib was snatched from him.
But soon he received his partner made from his own bone.

(21) He experienced no harm, for his flesh was immediately replaced;
It was then that he realized a twin had been made from him.

(23) When he saw that another had been formed out of him in the union of their bodies,
He became a prophet of himself, speaking in a new voice.

(25) *This,* he said, *is flesh of my flesh, I see here the bone of my bone.*[3]
She is the rib from my side.

(27) So now, since the holy alliance of Aaron's children[4] was
Symbolized by that ancient couple,

2. Cf. Gen 2:24.
3. Gen 2:23.
4. This phrase suggests that both Julian and Titia were the children of bishops, that is, "priests," like the biblical Aaron. See above, line 11, and below, line 238.

(29) Let us celebrate with sober joys and quiet prayers,
And let the name of Christ resound everywhere on the lips of
pious people.

(31) Away with the crowds leaping in the decked-out streets.
Let no one strew the ground with flowers or cover the
doorsteps with garlands.

(33) There should be no mad procession in a Christian city.
I will have no profane display poison pious Christians.

(35) Let no wind blow a foreign stench, for everything should
Breathe the odor of purity and propriety.

(37) The saints have only one perfume, which is spread by the
name of Christ.
It breathes forth the fragrance of God with chastity.

(39) There should be no ornate trays heaped high with superfluous gifts;
The proper ornament is good morals, not money.

(41) The holy daughter-in-law of a bishop, the wife of a
young man already consecrated,[5]
Should receive a dowry of light.

(43) She should bristle at garments of gold or purple;
Her golden garment is the pure grace of God.

(45) She should also reject necklaces bedecked with jewels,
So that she herself may be a noble jewel for the Lord God.

(47) The weight of hateful avarice must not weigh down
The neck dedicated to bearing the yoke of Christ the Lord.

---

5. Julian was a lector at the time of his wedding.

(49) Rather, let her cultivate a pleasing inner beauty;
Let her adorn her character with a dowry that brings salvation.

(51) She must not desire to squander her income
On precious stones or Chinese silks.

(53) She should decorate her soul with chaste virtues,
That she may be an asset, not a liability, to her husband.

(55) When someone is eager to acquire the glory of bodily
extravagance,
That person is devalued and cheapened by vice.

(57) Badly blinded by lust for this shameful purpose,
The mind is corrupted by the body's gleaming booty.

(59) The wicked person does not realize how foul is the
adornment that he wears,
And the one who takes delight in his clothes becomes cheaper
than the clothes themselves.

(61) She who has become a daughter-in-law in the house of
an apostolic family,
Must never look like the daughter in a pagan temple.

(63) Her skin must never be poorly disguised with rouge,
Nor her eyes with black powder, nor her hair dyed with
color.

(65) The woman who despises the simple beauty of nature
Commits the sin of pride by condemning God's work in herself.

(67) In vain will such a woman claim that she is chaste,
When she adorns herself in such seductive guises.

(69) But you, youths of Christ, must flee from all that brings
Damnation as its prize, whose use leads to death.

(71) Believe what God's Word has said about such adorn-
    ments:
That they bring punishment on those who desire them.

(73) Isaiah warns that they will be bound with tight ropes,[6]
If they dare now to wear garments of white silk and purple
    silk tinged with purple,

(75) Or splendid tunics glowing with purple and glistening
    with gold,
That flow to the ankles with shapely folds.

(77) Bound with these ropes, they will wear sackcloth forever,
Pushing huge grindstones in their prison—a mill!

(79) And those who pile on their heads lengthy tresses
Will find a shameful bald spot on the top of their heads.

(81) O new bride of a holy man, avoid such adornments,
For these things delight only empty minds.

(83) You must not go out with perfumed clothes and hair,
Nor desire to be recognized by your smell when you pass.

(85) Do not sit with your hair piled high like a turret,
Layered and twisted with interwoven locks.

(87) Do not let your beauty cause many to worry;
Never become a source of deadly attraction.

(89) You should not even desire to please your own husband
By wickedly adding inches to your body.

---

6. Cf. Isa 3:24.

(91) And you, holy youth, so devoted to the sacred books,
Must also in your love reject bodily beauty.

(93) For Christ has generously rewarded you
By adorning your beautiful soul with everlasting riches.

(95) He has lavished you both with chaste wedding gifts:
Hope, Piety, Fidelity, Peace, Purity.

(97) The Word of God is your silver, and the Holy Spirit your
    gold;
Your jewels are good works shining in your hearts.

(99) If shabby clothing offends respectable people,
And if proud hearts delight in costly raiment,

(101) Then let the example of the saints and the chaste
Simplicity of the first human beings remove such shameful-
    ness.

(103) Take a look at our ancestors in their home in paradise:
Their whole world was one simple field.

(105) Their clothing was merely the skins of some sheep;
Are we now ashamed to wear woven wool?

(107) When lovely Rebekah came to marry the holy Isaac,
She was covered only with the veil of modesty.[7]

(109) It does not say that she came decked out in motley jew-
    els,
But only that she wrapped herself in a cloak.

(111) With this covering the virgin modestly concealed her
    face,
Afraid to look directly at her spouse's face.

7. Cf. Gen 24:65.

(113) Or will you take greater pleasure in the dancing girl
    Herodias,
Who obtained the death of the Baptist as the price of her
    dance?[8]

(115) The wicked girl took such vengeance for the sake of
    her mother's angry lust
That she gained a head to reward her indulgence.

(117) It was, of course, that head which proclaimed abroad
The news that God's own Lamb was near.

(119) What gained for her such a vile reward, if not her
    seductive attire?
The wicked dancer, a daughter worthy of her father!

(121) She forced him to the deed, although he was unwilling,
Winning him over to the crime by the enticements of her
    body.

(123) Even the guests, who were worthy of the wicked king's
    feast,
Were led to consent by the skillful movements of her feet.

(125) But if golden slippers had not covered her dainty feet,
So that she danced more wantonly with painted soles,

(127) And had she not worn a flowing garment with a
    swirling train,
And pulled back her hair to let the jewels on her forehead
    gleam,

---

8. Cf. Matt 14:6–8. In the biblical account, the dancing girl is the daughter of
Herodias.

(129) She would never have won over the depraved minds of
those who watched her,
Nor would her craftiness have achieved its unspeakable result.

(131) So, too, did Herod himself, puffed up in his regal vest-
ments,
Swell large with sacrilegious pride, ending up in madness.

(133) Forgetting the honor owed to God and inflated by his
attire,
He died most foully from a worm-infested wound.[9]

(135) The punishment fit the crime: he died covered with
sores,
For he believed that he was divine because of the dignity of
his clothes.

(137) But granted that such insane airs befit the hearts of
kings,
What business have we to do with the pomp of Pharaoh?

(139) The hollow glory of the world is a far cry from our
realms,
And the light of piety is incompatible with the shadows of the
enemy.

(141) A cleric should love a wife who adorns herself with
Christ,
Whose beauty lies in the light of her heart.

(143) A lector must learn from sacred history
That woman was made as God's gift to be a help to man.[10]

---

9. Cf. Acts 12:21–23.
10. Cf. Gen 2:18.

(145) In turn, a wife must in all humility receive Christ within
    her spouse,
So that she may be equal to the holiness of her husband.

(147) Thus she will grow into his holy body and be woven
    into his frame,
That her husband may become her head, just as Christ is his.

(149) Such a marriage brings to an end the servitude of Eve,
Just as Sarah became the free equal of pious Abraham.[11]

(151) When Jesus's friends were married in this manner, he
    himself served as the Groomsman,
And changed water into the nectar of the vine.[12]

(153) At a wedding such as this, it is fitting that Mary, the
    mother of the Lord, be present,
For she gave birth to God, while preserving her virginity.

(155) God himself built in this sacred virgin
A pleasing temple with a secret window open to the sky.

(157) Descending quietly, like rain from a high cloud,
He fell upon the fleece as silent dew.[13]

(159) For no one was ever aware of the mystery,
By which God assumed a human being from the Virgin
    Mother.

(161) What a strange new invention the Lord employed to
    save the human race:
A woman becomes pregnant without intercourse!

11. Cf. Gen 11:29; Gal 4:22.
12. Cf. John 2:1–11.
13. Perhaps an allusion to Gideon's fleece in Judg 6:36–38.

(163) A woman is married to a man, but does not submit to a husband;
She becomes a mother by giving birth, but not a wife by having sex.

(165) By covenant she was a spouse, but she was no wife in the body.
Untainted by a man, she was a mother to her son.

(167) By this great mystery (*sacramentum*) the church was wed to Christ,
And became at once both the spouse and sister of the Lord.

(169) She is his spouse, because she is wedded to him; she is his sister because she is not subordinate. . . .[14]

(171) She thus remains a mother, conceiving by the seed of the eternal Word,
Giving birth to nations.

(173) She is sister and wife since she has intercourse in the heart, not in the body,
For her husband is not man, but God.

(175) Old and young alike are born of this mother;
Her offspring have no age or sex.

(177) For this is the blessed progeny of God,
Which comes not from human seed, but from a heavenly generation.

(179) That is why the teacher says that in Christ *there is no male or female*,[15]
But one body and one faith.

---

14. Line 170 is missing in the Latin text.
15. Gal 3:28.

(181) For we are all one body, all members in Christ,
Who have Christ as our head.[16]

(183) Now that we have put on Christ, we have put away
Adam
And are at once being transformed into the likeness of
angels.[17]

(185) Therefore, all who have been born in baptism have this
task:
Both sexes must grasp the perfect Man.

(187) Christ must become the common Head, all things in all
people,
And as a king he will hand over his members to the Father in
the kingdom.[18]

(189) No longer will this fragile human life either marry or
be given in marriage,
When all of us have put on the eternal body.

(191) So, then, remember me and always live together in
purity;
Let the venerable cross be your yoke.

(193) As children of that mother, who is both sister and bride,
You must strive to make your hearts worthy of the names you
bear.

(195) As brother and sister, run together to meet Christ, your
spouse,
So that you may be one flesh in the eternal body.

16. Cf. 1 Cor 12:27.
17. Cf. Eph 4:22; Rom 13:14.
18. Cf. Eph 4:13; Col 3:11.

(197) May that love embrace you, which binds the church to
   Christ,
The same love by which Christ cherishes his church.

(199) May your father the bishop bless you,
May he chant chaste songs with the attending chorus.

(201) Kindly Memor, lead your children before the altar;
Entrust them to the Lord with a prayer and a blessing of the
   hand.

(203) But what is this fragrance slipping down from the sky
   and entering my nostrils?
What causes this unexpected light to blind my eyes?

(205) Who is this whose placid steps seem so far removed
   from human life?
Who is this whom Christ's manifold graces have pursued?

(207) Who is this surrounded by a blessed cohort of heavenly
   children,
Which resembles a band of angels?

(209) I recognize the man, accompanied by God's perfume,
Upon whose face the beauty of the stars now shines.

(211) This is the man, this is he, so rich in the many gifts of
   Christ our Lord,
A man of heavenly light—Aemilius![19]

(213) Arise, Memor, honor your father, embrace your
   brother;
The one Aemilius is both of these to you.

---

19. Aemilius, also a bishop, may have been the father of Julian's bride, Titia. Verses
213–15 suggest that Memor was the younger in age, but more senior in the episcopate.

(215) Memor is the younger and the elder.
What a marvelous work our great God has done: the younger
  man is the father.

(217) The one born later is the elder,
Because a bishop's heart bears the gray hairs of an apostle.

(219) Memor is both son and brother.
He rejoices that the father, whom he shares with his own
  children, is present.

(221) Justice and peace embrace,
When Memor and Aemilius are joined in one accord.

(223) The sacred band unites the two priests in divine
  honor,[20]
Piety unites them together in human love.

(225) Not forgetting his duty, Memor[21] in correct procedure
Entrusts his dear children into Aemilius's hands.

(227) Aemilius then joins their two heads in the marital peace.
Veiling them with his right hand, he sanctifies them with a
  prayer.

(229) Christ, O Christ, hear the pleas of your priests,
Give ear to the pious prayers of these holy suppliants.

(231) Christ, teach the newly married through the holy
  bishop;
Assist their pure hearts through his chaste hands,

(233) That the two of them may share a desire for virginity,
Or that they both may be the seed of holy virgins.

20. Paulinus refers to the *infula* or headband, which was a traditional marker of
priestly identity.
21. There is a pun in the Latin, which is difficult to communicate in English:
Memor, officii non immemor.

(235) The first of these prayers is the better one: to keep their
    bodies free of the flesh.
But if they unite in a physical way,

(237) May their chaste offspring become a priestly race.
May the whole house of Memor become a house of Aaron.

(239) May this house of Memor be a house of anointed ones.
Remember Paulinus and Therasia,

(241) And Christ will remember Memor forever.[22]

---

22. Another pun on the name Memor: *et memor aeternum Christus erit Memoris.*

17.

Ecclesiastical Legislation

One of the prominent features of the post-Constantinian church was the proliferation of meetings of bishops, known as councils or synods. Some of these dealt with pressing issues of doctrinal formulation, such as the Council of Nicaea in 325 or the Council of Chalcedon in 451. But in addition to these worldwide or "ecumenical" councils, a host of smaller regional councils were held to discuss disciplinary matters or other concerns of local interest; these councils then issued their rulings in the form of "canons." In other cases, prominent bishops, such as Basil of Caesarea, compiled his own collection of canons, distributing them by letter. The following texts give a range of canons from the eastern to the western parts of the Roman Empire. They provide a vivid picture of local bishops attempting to respond to a wide spectrum of issues: from divorce and remarriage to adultery, fornication, and incest.

The first set of texts derives from a collection known as the "Canons of the Council of Elvira." As early as the eighteenth century, some scholars had suggested that the eighty-one canons attributed to this council were actually a compilation of disciplinary regulations derived from several synods. In 1975 Maurice Meigne reopened the question of the unity of the canons, arguing that the great number and diversity of the canons, as well as their internal inconsistency, indicated that this collection was not from a single council.[1] Since the publication of Meigne's article, a vigorous debate has taken place, primarily within Spanish-speaking scholarship, over the question of whether the canons of Elvira were the unitary product of one council or a compilation from several synods.[2] Most recently, in a contribution to the *Zeitschrift für antikes Christentum*, Josep Vilella has presented compelling arguments for seeing the canons of Elvira (which he calls the "pseudo-Iliberritan canons") as a compilation of texts from widely differing times and places.[3] Caution, therefore, must be exercised when citing these canons as evidence of fourth-century Spanish practice.

The second set of legislative texts is taken from three letters of Basil, bishop of Caesarea in Cappadocia. Basil was one of the outstanding Greek patristic writers of the fourth century. Born into a wealthy Christian family (ca. 329) and well educated in classical culture, he played an active part in the theological struggles of the fourth century over the Creed of the Council of Nicaea. Basil and his fellow Cappadocian fathers, Gregory of Nazianzus and Gregory of Nyssa, were instrumental in the development of a consensus in favor of the Council. He also was a prominent leader of the monastic movement; his *Long Rules* and *Short Rules* remain to this day the principal monastic regulations of Greek Orthodox Christianity.

Between the years 374 and 375, Basil composed three letters to the bishop Amphilochius of Iconium. The purpose

1. M. Meigne, "Concile ou collection d'Elvire?" *Revue d'histoire ecclésiastique* 70 (1975): 361–87.

2. See Josep Vilella Masana, "Las sanciones de los cánones pseudoiliberritanos," *Sacris Erudiri* 46 (2007): 5–87; J. Vilella Masana and P. E. Barreda, "¿Cánones del Concilio de Elvira o cánones pseudoiliberritanos?" *Augustinianum* (2006): 285–373; and, most recently, Josep Vilella, "The Pseudo-Iliberritan Canon Texts," *Zeitschrift für antikes Christentum* 18 (2014): 210–59.

3. Vilella has based his analysis primarily on the fact that some of the canons employ vocabulary and witness to practices that are more characteristic of the late fourth and early fifth centuries.

of these letters was to give direction on the duration and modes of excommunication to be administered as penance in the church. Basil claims to be reproducing traditions on these matters that had been handed down by his predecessors, although on some occasions he feels free to modify the tradition in favor of leniency. In one instance (canon 9) he criticizes the anti-female bias of the custom, although he does not substantially alter it.

Basil's legislation gives further evidence of the marital rigorism of the early church. Second, third, and fourth marriages after the death of a spouse are not forbidden, although temporary excommunication is imposed on those who contract them. Penalties are established for adultery and fornication, as in the legislation of Elvira, although there is no evidence that Basil thought there should be only one opportunity for repentance. Basil also deals with cases of marriage within prohibited degrees of kinship, the marriage of slaves, and the sexual misconduct of the clergy. The wide array of problems treated in the legislative texts is evidence of the fact that then, as now, the ideals set in Christian theological treatises did not always match the realities of life.

CANONS OF THE COUNCIL OF ELVIRA

(7) If it happens that any of the faithful, after committing fornication, should be restored after doing penance and then should commit fornication again, he must be excluded from communion forever.

(8) Likewise, women who leave their husbands without any prior cause and who have intercourse with other men must be excluded from communion forever.

(9) Likewise, a Christian woman (*femina fidelis*) who leaves an adulterous Christian husband and who marries another has entered into a forbidden marriage. If she does marry, she may not receive communion until her first husband has died, unless the pressure of illness makes it necessary for communion to be given.

(10) If a woman who has been abandoned by a catechumen should take a husband, she can be admitted to the baptismal font. This also is the rule if the woman is a catechumen. But if the man married a Christian woman after he left his innocent wife, and if she knew that he had a wife whom he abandoned without cause, she must be given communion only at the end of her life.

(11) If that female catechumen should become seriously ill during the five-year period, she is not to be denied baptism.

***

(14) If young women have lost their virginity and if they take and keep as their husbands the men who violated them, they should be reconciled without penance after a year, because they have violated only the nuptials. But if they have had sex with other men, they must be admitted to communion only after a space of five years, after having completed the required penance, because they have committed fornication.

(15) Christian virgins are not to be given in marriage to pagans because of a surplus of girls, so that their youthful age, as it swells into a blossom, does not result in the soul's adultery.

(16) If heretics are unwilling to join the Catholic church, Catholic girls should not be given to them. They must be given neither to Jews nor to heretics, because there can be no association between the faithful and the unfaithful. But if their parents do what is forbidden, they must be excluded for five years.

(17) If any [parents] join their daughters to the priests of idols, they must be excluded from communion forever.

***

(64) If a woman remains in adultery to the very end of her life, she must be excluded from communion forever. But if she leaves the man, she may receive communion after ten years, after completing the required penance.

(65) If the wife of a cleric commits adultery and if her husband knows about the adultery and does not immediately put her away, he shall be excluded from communion forever, so that those who are supposed to be an example of good conduct do not appear to be teachers of vice.

(66) If a man marries his stepdaughter, he must be excluded from communion forever because he is incestuous.

***

(69) If a married man happens to fall once, he must do penance for five years and thus be reconciled, unless the pressure of illness makes it necessary for him to take communion before that time. This also is the regulation for women.

(70) If a wife has committed fornication with the knowledge of her husband, he must be excluded from communion forever. But if he puts her away, he may take communion after ten years, if he kept her in his house for any time after he learned of her adultery.

***

(72) If a widow commits fornication and later marries the same man, she may be reconciled to communion after a period of five years and after completing the required penance. But if she has abandoned him and married another man, she should be excluded from communion forever. If it was a Christian man that she married, he shall not receive communion except after ten years, after completing that required penance, unless illness makes it necessary for him to take communion before that time.

BASIL OF CAESAREA, LETTER 188 TO AMPHILOCHIUS

(4) On the subject of trigamists and polygamists, the ancient authorities laid down the same canon as for digamists, except in due proportion. In other words, one year for digamists, although some authorities say two years. Trigamists are

excluded for three years, and sometimes even four years. But we call this sort of thing polygamy, not marriage, or rather a restrained fornication. That is why the Lord said to the Samaritan woman who had five husbands in succession: *The one you have now is not your husband,*[4] because those who have surpassed the limit of digamy are no longer worthy to be called by the name of "husband" or "wife." For trigamists we have an exclusion for five years; this is a custom we have received not from the canons but from those who went before us. It is not necessary to exclude them from the church entirely, but they should be considered worthy to be hearers after two or three years; later, they may be permitted to stand with the rest of the congregation, but they must be excluded from the benefit of communion. When they have shown evidence of the fruit of repentance, they may be restored to the place of communion.

***

(9) The decree of the Lord that it is forbidden to withdraw from marriage *except in the case of fornication* [cf. Matt 5:32; 19:9] applies equally to men and to women, at least according to the logic of the idea. But the custom is different, and we find much stricter prescriptions for women, as when the apostle says: *The man who unites with a prostitute becomes one body with her;*[5] and when Jeremiah says: *If a wife goes to another man she will not return to her husband, but she will be a land defiled.*[6] In another place, it says: *He who keeps an adulteress is stupid and impious.*[7] But custom requires wives to keep their husbands, even if the husbands commit adultery and fornication.

Therefore, I do not know if a woman who lives with a man who has been divorced by his wife can be called an adulteress. The blame in this case falls upon the woman who divorced

4. John 4:18.
5. 1 Cor 6:16.
6. Jer 3:1.
7. Prov 18:22.

her husband and depends on the reason why she withdrew from the marriage. If she was being beaten and would not endure the blows, it would have been better for her to tolerate her husband than to separate from him. If she would not endure the loss of money, that is not an acceptable reason. But if her motivation was the man's living in fornication, this is not the customary observance of the church. Rather, a wife is instructed not to separate from an unbelieving husband, but to remain because it is uncertain what will result. *For how do you know, wife, whether you will save your husband?*[8]

For this reason a woman who leaves her husband is an adulteress if she goes to another man. But the man who has been abandoned may be pardoned, and the woman who lives with such a man is not condemned. If a man who has left his wife goes to another, however, he is an adulterer because he makes the woman commit adultery. The woman who lives with him is an adulteress because she has taken another woman's husband to herself.

BASIL OF CAESAREA, LETTER 199 TO AMPHILOCHIUS

(21) If a man who is living with a wife becomes dissatisfied with the marriage and falls into fornication, I judge him to be a fornicator and extend his period of punishment. We have, however, no canon to accuse him of adultery, if the sin is committed against an unmarried woman. For the adulteress *will become a land defiled*, it is said, *and she will not return to her husband.*[9] *And he who keeps an adulteress is stupid and impious.*[10] But the man who commits fornication is not to be excluded from cohabitation with his wife. Thus the wife will take back the husband who returns after fornication, but the husband will expel the defiled wife from his house. The logic of this is not clear, but this is the custom that is practiced.

8. 1 Cor 7:16.
9. Jer 3:1.
10. Prov 18:22.

(22) Men who have taken women by force, if they carried them off when they were betrothed to other men, must not be admitted until the women have been taken away and restored to the control of those to whom they were previously betrothed, whether or not these men wish to receive them. If a man has taken a woman who was at liberty [i.e., not yet betrothed], she must be removed and returned to her own family to be subject to the decision of her relatives, such as her parents or her brothers or whoever has authority over the girl. If they decide to give her to the man [who carried her off], then the cohabitation may stand; if they refuse, there must be no use of force.

If a man has taken a woman by seduction, whether covertly or by coercion, he must be held guilty of fornication. The punishment for fornication has been fixed at four years. During the first year they must be expelled from the prayers and weep at the doors of the church; during the second year they may be allowed to listen; during the third year they may be admitted to penance; and during the fourth year they may be allowed to stand with the congregation, but must be excluded from the offering. Finally, they may be admitted to the communion of the good [gift].

(23) Concerning men who marry two sisters or women who marry two brothers, I have issued a small letter, a copy of which I have sent to Your Reverence. A man who has taken his own brother's wife should not be received until he has separated from her.

(24) A widow who has been registered on the list of widows, that is, who is supported by the church, is ordered by the apostle no longer to be supported when she marries.[11] There is no law that pertains to a widower, but the penalty that applies to digamists is sufficient. If a widow who is sixty years of age decides to marry again, she should not be judged worthy of communion until she has put an end to her vice of impurity. But if she was registered [as a widow] before the age of sixty, the blame is ours, not hers.

11. Cf. 1 Tim 5:11–12.

(25) The man who keeps as his wife the woman whom he has violated is subject to the penalty of rape, but he is permitted to take her as his wife.

(26) Fornication is not marriage, nor is it the beginning of marriage. Therefore, if it is possible, it is best that those who are united in fornication be separated. But if they are completely happy living together, let them submit to the penalty for fornication but without separation, so that nothing worse may happen.

(27) Regarding a priest who out of ignorance is involved in an illegitimate marriage, I have formulated the appropriate regulation: he may retain his seat, but he must refrain from all other activities. For such a person pardon is enough. It would not make sense for someone who ought to be treating his own wounds to be blessing another. For to bless is to impart holiness. How can someone impart holiness to another, when he does not possess it himself because of the fault of ignorance? He should not bless, either in public or in private, nor should he distribute the body of Christ to others, nor perform any liturgical function. But he should be content with his position and entreat the Lord with tears to forgive the sin he committed in ignorance.

***

(31) If a woman's husband has gone away and disappeared, and if she remarries before she has evidence of his death, she commits adultery.

***

(34) Our fathers did not order women to be publicly exposed if they had committed adultery and dutifully confessed their fault or were convicted by other means, so that we might not become the cause of their death after their conviction. But they ordered that these women should be excluded from communion until they had fulfilled their period of penance.

(35) In the case of a man deserted by his wife, the cause of

the desertion must be investigated. If it is clear that she left without reason, he is deserving of pardon, and she is deserving of punishment. Pardon will be given to him, so that he may receive communion with the church.

(36) Soldiers' wives, who remarried after their husbands disappeared, are subject to the same principle as wives who have not waited for the return of their husbands from a journey. There should be some concession in this case, however, because there is greater reason to suppose that the husband has died.

(37) A man who marries after having abducted another man's wife is guilty of adultery in the case of the first woman he abducted, but he is without blame in the case of the second woman.

(38) Young women who have followed [a man] against their fathers' will commit fornication. But if they are reconciled to their parents, it appears that there may be some remedy for the deed. They should not be restored to communion immediately, however, but only after three years of penance.

(39) A woman who lives with an adulterer is herself an adulteress for the whole time.

(40) A [slave] woman who gives herself to a man against the will of her master commits fornication. But if at a later time she takes the opportunity to enter into a marriage as a free woman, it is a true marriage. The former case is fornication, the latter is marriage. For the contracts of those who are under the authority of others have no validity.

(41) A widowed woman who has authority over herself may live with a husband without blame, if there is no one to prevent their cohabitation. As the apostle says: *If the husband has died, she is free to marry whomever she wishes, but only in the Lord.*[12]

(42) Marriages contracted without the consent of those in authority are fornications. If neither the father nor the master is alive, they are free to live together; the marriage is valid,

---

12. 1 Cor 7:39.

just as if the authoritative parties had given their consent to the union.

***

(46) If a woman has unknowingly married a man who is temporarily deserted by his wife, and if she is then put away because his first wife has returned to him, she has committed fornication, but only out of ignorance. Therefore, she is not forbidden to marry, but it is better if she remains as she is.

***

(48) The woman who has been abandoned by her husband ought, in my opinion, to remain as she is. For the Lord has said: *If anyone puts away his wife, except because of fornication, he causes her to commit adultery.*[13] By calling her an adulteress, he forbade her to have intercourse with another man. For how can the man be regarded as guilty because of the adultery, but the woman not be guilty, when she has been called an adulteress by the Lord because of her intercourse with another man?

(49) Women who have been forcibly violated are free from blame. Therefore, if a slave girl has been forced by her master, she is not to be held guilty.

(50) There is no law regarding trigamy. We do, however, regard such unions as a defilement to the church. But we do not cast any public condemnation on them, since they are preferable to unrestrained fornication.

BASIL OF CAESAREA, LETTER 217 TO AMPHILOCHIUS

(53) The widowed slave perhaps has not committed a serious fault, if she chooses a second marriage under the pretext of rape. Thus there is no room for an accusation in this case. It is her choice that is judged, not her pretext. But it is clear that she remains guilty of digamy.

---

13. Matt 5:32.

***

(58) The man who commits adultery will be excluded from participation in the sacred rites for fifteen years. During the first four years, he will weep; for the next five he will be a hearer; for the next four he will kneel; and for the next two he will stand [with the congregation] without communion.

(59) The fornicator will be excluded from participation in the sacred rites for seven years. For two years he will weep; for two he will be a hearer; for two he will kneel; and for one he will stand. In the eighth year he will be received into communion.

***

(68) Those who enter into marriage within the prohibited degrees of kinship, if it is discovered that the union resulted in sinful acts, shall receive the penalty of adulterers.

(69) If a lector has intercourse with his betrothed before they are married, he will be allowed to read after a suspension of one year, remaining without promotion. If he has secret relations without betrothal, he will be removed from the ministry. The same rule applies to the minister.

***

(77) The man who abandons his wife to whom he has been legitimately united and takes another is liable to the penalty of adultery, according to the statement of the Lord.[14] But it has been decided by the canons of the fathers that such men shall weep for the first year, be hearers for the next two years, kneel for the next three years, stand with the faithful for the seventh year, and in the eighth year be deemed worthy of the offering, if they have repented with tears.

(78) Let the same rule be observed in the case of those who marry two sisters, although at different times.

(79) Men who have a mad passion for their stepmothers are

---

14. Cf. Matt 5:32; Mark 10:11; Luke 16:18.

subject to the same canon as those who have a mad passion for their own sisters.

(80) The fathers have nothing to say about polygamy, since it is beastly and utterly foreign to the human race. I regard it as a worse sin than fornication. Therefore, it is reasonable that such persons be subject to the canons, namely one year of weeping, three years of kneeling, and then reception.

18.

Two Nuptial Blessings

The final two texts in this anthology represent yet another genre of early Christian literature: the nuptial blessing. Included here are two sets of prayers for the blessing and veiling of a couple at a Christian marriage ceremony. It is not known when the practice of a distinctive Christian ritual for marriage originated. The earliest Christians may have followed some practices of Judaism, which celebrated weddings with a procession, the wearing of a crown or wreath by the bride and groom, a feast, and the pronouncement of a blessing by the groom. In the treatise *To His Wife,* Tertullian referred to "that marriage which the church unites, the offering strengthens, the blessing seals, the angels proclaim, and the Father declares valid" (2.8). Some scholars regard this as evidence of a Christian marriage ceremony in the early third century, although this seems unlikely.[1]

The earliest undisputed references to a nuptial blessing are found only at the end of the fourth century. Ambrosiaster (ca. 380) referred at several points to a nuptial blessing that was

1. For the view that Tertullian's statement represents a specifically Christian marriage ritual in the early third century, see Kenneth Stevenson, *Nuptial Blessing: A Study of Christian Marriage Rites* (Oxford: Oxford University Press, 1983), 16–19. For a different view, see Korbinian Ritzer, *Le mariage dans les églises chrétiennes du Ier au XIe siècles* (Paris: Cerf, 1970), 110–20.

bestowed only on first marriages. Later bishops of Rome, such as Siricius (384–399) and Innocent I (401–417), also mentioned the practice of veiling and referred to liturgical formulas of blessing. The marriage poem of Paulinus of Nola assumes that some Christian marriages were celebrated in church, that both spouses were veiled, and that the bishop pronounced a blessing, so this practice may have started to become more common by the early fifth century, although the case of Julian may have been exceptional since the spouses were the children of bishops.

The two liturgical texts translated here are the earliest surviving examples of the Roman nuptial blessing. The *Verona Sacramentary* is extant in an early seventh-century manuscript (Verona 85), but it may reflect liturgical practices of the church of Rome that are much earlier. The *Hadrianum,* a sacramentary of the Gregorian type, was sent by Pope Hadrian (784/785) to Charlemagne in response to the emperor's request for a pure specimen of Roman liturgical practice. The prayers contained in this document are clearly dependent on the *Verona Sacramentary,* which is altered at several points.

Both liturgical blessings reflect traditional Christian theological themes. Marriage is acknowledged to be part of God's plan, established at the beginning of creation for the purpose of procreation. The indissolubility of marriage is affirmed, as well as its role in the bonding of human society. Both texts cite married women of the Old Testament (Rachel, Rebekah, and Sarah) as examples to be emulated. The Gregorian text adds the mystery of Christ and the church signified in the bond of married persons.

VERONA SACRAMENTARY

HERE BEGINS THE NUPTIAL VEILING

(1) Hear us, almighty and merciful God, so that your blessing may bring to completion what is done through our ministry. Through . . .

(2) We ask you, O Lord, to receive the gift we offer you on behalf of the sacred law of marriage. May you, who have created this work, also continue to order it properly. Through . . .

3) We ask you, O Lord, to look with favor on this offering of your maidservant. We humbly beseech your majesty on her behalf that just as you have granted her to reach the proper age for marriage, once she has been joined in the marital union through your gift, you may enable her to rejoice in the offspring she desires and may graciously bring to her and to her husband the length of years that they desire. Through . . .

(4) We ask you, almighty God, to support with your holy favor that which your providence has established and to keep in lasting peace these persons whom you will unite in lawful union. Through . . .

(5) Give aid to our prayers, O Lord, and graciously assist the institutions that you have established for the propagation of the human race. May that which is joined by your authority be preserved by your help. Through . . .

(6a) Father, Creator of the world, you gave birth to all living creatures and established the origins of procreation. By your own hands you gave Adam a companion, whose bones, growing from his bones, signified an equal nature by means of a marvelous diversity. From this time forward the unions of the marriage bed, which were decreed for the increase of an entire multitude, have bound together the alliances of the human race, so that they might gather together the whole world. Thus it was pleasing to you, thus it was necessary—since what you made similar to the man was much weaker than what you made similar to yourself—that the weaker sex should be joined to the stronger one, so as to make one out of the two and so that offspring of both sexes might flow from their mutual pledge. In due succession, then, posterity was to follow, past generations to be succeeded by future ones, so that the human race, though destined for death, might have no end, despite the brevity of life. So then, Father, sanctify the first efforts of your handmaid who is to marry, so that, joined in a good and prosperous marriage, she may keep the commandments of the eternal law. May she remember, O Lord, that she has entered this covenant not so much to enjoy what spouses are permitted as to observe and keep the holy pledges of God.

(6b) May she marry in Christ, as one who is faithful and chaste, and may she always imitate the examples of the holy women. May she be loving to her husband, like Rachel; wise, like Rebekah; faithful and long-lived, like Sarah. May the author of duplicity find nothing to take from her; may she remain ever reliant on faith and the commandments. May she fortify her weakness with the strength of discipline. United to a single bed, may she flee all illicit relations. May she be dignified in her modesty, respected in her purity, learned in the wisdom of heaven. May she be fruitful in offspring, trustworthy and innocent. And may she come at last to the repose of the blessed and to the kingdom of heaven. Through . . .

HADRIANUM

PRAYER AT THE VEILING OF SPOUSES

(1) Hear us, almighty and merciful God, that your blessing may bring to completion what is done through our ministry. Through . . .

(2) *Over the gifts:* We ask you, O Lord, to receive the gift that is offered on behalf of the sacred law of marriage. May

you who granted this work also guide it properly. Through . . .

(3) *Preface:* It is truly right and just, proper and helpful for our salvation. You, who have joined the marriage compacts with the sweet yoke of concord and the indissoluble bond of peace, so that the chaste fruitfulness of holy spouses might be preserved to multiply children of adoption [by God]. For your providence, O Lord, and your grace arrange both of these: so that what generation adds to the splendor of the world, regeneration leads to the increase of the church. And, therefore, with the angels and archangels, with the thrones and dominations, and with the entire host of the heavenly army, we sing the hymn of your glory, saying forever: Holy, Holy, Holy . . .

(4) We ask you, O Lord, to accept this gift of your servants that they offer you on behalf of this your handmaid, whom you have deigned to bring to the state of maturity and to the day of marriage. On her behalf, we pour forth humble prayers to your majesty that you may graciously deign to unite her with her husband, we ask, Lord, that you be favorably inclined.

(5) *Before the Peace of the Lord this prayer is said:* Look with favor on our prayers, O Lord, and graciously assist the institutions that you have established for the propagation of the human race, so that what is joined by your authority may be preserved by your help. Through . . .

(6) *The blessing:* O God, you who made all things out of nothing by the power of your goodness, at the beginning of the creation of the universe you established for man, made in the image of God, the inseparable assistance of woman. Out of the man you gave to the woman the origin of her flesh, thereby teaching that what had been created out of one ought never to be separated.

(7) O God, you have consecrated the conjugal union with so excellent a mystery in order to signify the sacrament of Christ and the church in the bond of married persons: God, through whom woman is united to man and society, estab-

lished at the beginning, is given through that blessing, which is the only decree that was not removed either by the penalty of original sin or by the flood.

(8) Look with favor on this your handmaid who is to be joined in marital union, as she asks to be strengthened by your protection. May her yoke be one of love and peace; may she marry in Christ, as one who is faithful and chaste. May she always imitate the holy women. May she be loving to her husband like Rachel; wise, like Rebekah; faithful and long-lived, like Sarah.

(9) May the author of duplicity find nothing in her actions to take hold of. Relying on faith and the commandments, may she remain united to one bed and avoid all illicit relations. May she fortify her weakness with the strength of discipline. May she be dignified in modesty, respected in purity, learned in the wisdom of heaven.

(10) May she be fruitful in offspring, trustworthy, and innocent. May they come at last to the repose of the blessed and to the kingdom of heaven. And may they see their children's children, even to the third and fourth generations, and reach the old age they desire. Through our Lord . . . The Peace of the Lord be always with you.

(11) *At the conclusion:* We ask you, almighty God, to support with your holy love those things that your providence has established, so that you may keep in lasting peace these persons who have been united in a legitimate union. Through . . .

Select Bibliography

The following abbreviations are used in this bibliography and elsewhere in this book:

CSEL   *Corpus scriptorum ecclesiasticorum latinorum*

GCS   *Die griechischen christlichen Schriftsteller der ersten drei Jahrhunderte*

PG   *Patrologia Graeca*

PL   *Patrologia Latina*

SChr   *Sources Chrétiennes*

PRIMARY SOURCES (IN THE ORDER IN WHICH THEY APPEAR IN THIS BOOK)

Hermas. *The Shepherd*. Greek text in *The Apostolic Fathers: Greek Texts and English Translations*. Edited by Michael W. Holmes. 3rd edition. Grand Rapids: Baker Academic, 2007.

Tertullian. *To His Wife*. Latin text in *Tertullien: À son épouse*. Edited by Charles Munier. SChr 273. Paris: Cerf, 1980.

———. *Exhortation to Chastity*. Latin text in *Tertullien: Exhortation à la chasteté*. Edited by Claudio Moreschini. SChr 319. Paris: Cerf, 1985.

———. *On Monogamy*. Latin text in *Tertullien: Le mariage unique*. Edited by Paul Mattei. SChr 343. Paris: Cerf, 1988.

Clement of Alexandria. *The Educator.* Greek text in *Clément d'Alexandrie: Le Pédagogue.* Edited by Claude Mondésert. SChr 108. Paris: Cerf, 1965.

———. *Miscellanies.* Greek text in *Clemens Alexandrinus.* Vol. 2, *Stromata.* Buch I–VI. Edited by Otto Stählin. GCS 15. Leipzig: Hinrichs, 1906. 2nd ed. revised by Ludwig Früchtel. GCS 52. Berlin, 1985.

Acts of Thomas. Greek text in *Acta apostolorum apocrypha.* Edited by Max Bonnet and Richard Lipsius. Leipzig: Mendelssohn, 1903.

Methodius of Olympus. *Symposium.* Greek text in *Méthode d'Olympe: Le Banquet.* Edited by Herbert Musurillo. SChr 95. Paris: Cerf, 1963.

Lactantius. *Divine Institutes.* Latin text in *L. Caeli Firmiani Lactantii opera omnia.* Edited by Samuel Brandt. CSEL 19. Vienna: Tempsky, 1890.

John Chrysostom. *Homily 20 on Ephesians.* Greek text in *S. P. N. Johannis Chrysostomi archiepiscopi Constantinopolitani opera omnia quae exstant.* Edited by Jacques-Paul Migne. PG 62. Paris, 1862.

Ambrosiaster. *Commentary on 1 Corinthians.* Latin text in *Ambrosiastri qui dicitur Commentarius in epistulas Paulinas. Pars secunda: In epistulas ad Corinthios.* Edited by Heinrich Josef Vogels. CSEL 81.2. Vienna: Hoelder-Pichler-Tempsky, 1968.

Jerome. *Against Jovinian.* Latin text in *Sancti Eusebii Hieronymi Stridonensis presbyteri opera omnia.* Edited by Jacques-Paul Migne. PL 23. Paris, 1883.

Pelagius. *To the Matron Celantia.* Latin text in *Sancti Pontii Meropii Paulini Nolani opera.* Pars I: Epistulae: Appendix. Edited by Wilhelm Hartel. CSEL 29. Vienna: Tempsky, 1894.

Augustine. *The Good of Marriage.* Latin text in *Opera: De bono coniugali.* Edited by Josef Zycha. CSEL 41. Vienna: Tempsky, 1900.

———. *Sermon 354A.* Latin text in *Augustin d'Hippone: Vingt-*

six sermons au peuple d'Afrique. Edited by François Dolbeau. Paris: Institut d'Études Augustinienne, 1996.

———. *Letter 6* to Atticus.* Latin text in *Epistolae ex duobus codicibus nuper in lucem prolatae.* Edited by Johannes Divjak. CSEL 88. Vienna: Hoelder-Pichler-Tempsky, 1981.

Paulinus of Nola. *Carmen 25.* Latin text in *Sancti Pontii Meropii Paulini Nolani Opera.* II: *Carmina.* Edited by Wilhelm Hartel. CSEL 30. Vienna: Tempsky, 1894.

Canons of the Council of Elvira. Latin text in *I canoni dei concili della chiesa antica.* II: *I concili Latini.* 3: *I concili spagnoli.* Vol. 1. Edited by Franco Gori. Rome: Institutum Patristicum Augustinianum, 2013.

Basil of Caesarea, *Canonical Epistles.* Greek text in *Sainte Basile: Lettres.* Edited by Yves Courtonne. Paris: Les Belles Lettres, 1961.

Verona Sacramentary. Latin text in *Le mariage dans les églises chrétiennes du Ier au XIe siècles.* Edited by Korbinian Ritzer. Paris: Cerf, 1970.

Hadrianum. Latin text in *Le mariage dans les églises chrétiennes du Ier au XIe siècles.* Edited by Korbinian Ritzer. Paris: Cerf, 1970.

SECONDARY SOURCES

Balch, David, and Carolyn Osiek. *Early Christian Families in Context: An Interdisciplinary Dialogue.* Grand Rapids: Eerdmans, 2003.

Beatrice, Pier Franco. *The Transmission of Sin: Augustine and the Pre-Augustinian Sources.* Translated by Adam Kamesar. Oxford: Oxford University Press, 2013.

Broudéhoux, J. P. *Mariage et famille chez Clément d'Alexandrie.* Paris: Beauchesne, 1972.

Brown, P. *The Body and Society: Men, Women, and Sexual Renunciation in Early Christianity.* New York: Columbia University Press, 1988.

Clark, Elizabeth A. "'Adam's Only Companion': Augustine

and the Early Christian Debate on Marriage." *Recherches Augustiniennes* 21 (1986): 139–62.

Collins, Raymond F. *Accompanied by a Believing Wife: Ministry and Celibacy in the Earliest Christian Communities.* Collegeville, MN: Liturgical, 2013.

Cooper, Kate. *The Fall of the Roman Household.* Cambridge: Cambridge University Press, 2007.

Crouzel, H. *L'Église primitive face au divorce: Du premier au cinquième siècle.* Paris: Beauchesne, 1971.

Deming, Will. *Paul on Marriage and Celibacy: The Hellenistic Background of 1 Corinthians 7.* 2nd edition. Grand Rapids: Eerdmans, 2004.

Evans Grubbs, Judith. *Law and Family in Late Antiquity: The Emperor Constantine's Marriage Legislation.* Oxford: Oxford University Press, 1995.

———. *Women and Law in the Roman Empire: A Sourcebook on Marriage, Divorce, and Widowhood.* London: Routledge, 2002.

Harper, Kyle. *From Shame to Sin: The Christian Transformation of Sexual Morality in Late Antiquity.* Cambridge, MA: Harvard University Press, 2013.

Hersch, Karen. *The Roman Wedding: Ritual and Meaning in Antiquity.* Cambridge: Cambridge University Press, 2010.

Hunter, David G. *Marriage, Celibacy, and Heresy in Ancient Christianity: The Jovinianist Controversy.* Oxford: Oxford University Press, 2007.

Reynolds, Philip Lyndon. *Marriage in the Western Church: The Christianization of Marriage During the Patristic and Early Medieval Periods.* Supplements to *Vigiliae Christianae* 24. Leiden: Brill, 1994.

———. *How Marriage Became One of the Sacraments: The Sacramental Theology of Marriage from Its Medieval Origins to the Council of Trent.* Cambridge: Cambridge University Press, 2016.

Ritzer, Korbinian. *Le mariage dans les églises chrétiennes du Ier au XIe siècles.* Paris: Cerf, 1970.

Rouselle, Aline. *Porneia: On Desire and the Body in Antiquity*. Translated by Felicia Pheasant. Oxford: Blackwell, 1988.

Schmitt, Émile. *Le mariage chrétien dans l'oeuvre de saint Augustin: Une théologie baptismale de la vie conjugale*. Paris: Études Augustiniennes, 1983.

Searle, Mark and Kenneth W. Stevenson. *Documents of the Marriage Liturgy*. Collegeville, MN: Liturgical, 1992.

Stevenson, K. *Nuptial Blessing: A Study of Christian Marriage Rites*. New York: Oxford University Press, 1983.

Treggiari, Susan. *Roman Marriage: Iusti Coniuges From the Time of Cicero to the Time of Ulpian*. Oxford: Clarendon, 1991.

Veyne, Paul, ed. *A History of Private Life from Pagan Rome to Byzantium*. Translated by A. Goldhammer. Cambridge, MA: Belknap Press of Harvard University Press, 1987.

Wheeler-Reed, David. *Regulating Sex in the Roman Empire*. London: Yale University Press, 2017.

Index of Subjects

Index of Scripture

Index of Ancient Authors

Index of Modern Authors